Principles of Management

Dr. K. Natarajan

M.Com., M.Phil., Ph.D.,
Professor & Head,
P.G. Department of Commerce,
S.V.N. College,
Madurai.

Dr. K.P. Ganesan

M.Com., MBA., M.Phil., Ph.D., C.G.T.,
Associate Professor & Head,
Department of Business Administration,
Sourashtra College,
Madurai.

Himalaya Publishing House

ISO 9001:2015 CERTIFIED

First Edition : 1993
Second Edition : 1994
Third Edition : 1997
Fourth Edition : 2002
Fifth Revised Edition : 2004
Sixth Edition : 2006
Reprint : 2008, 2009, 2011
Seventh Revised Edition : 2012
Reprint : 2014, 2015, 2018, 2020
Reprint : 2021, 2022
Reprint : 2023

Published by : Mrs. Meena Pandey
for **HIMALAYA PUBLISHING HOUSE PVT. LTD.,**
"Ramdoot", Dr. Bhalerao Marg, Girgaon, **Mumbai - 400 004.**
Phone: 022-23860170/23863863, Fax: 022-23877178
E-mail: himpub@bharatmail.co.in; **Website:** www.himpub.com

Branch Offices :

New Delhi : "Pooja Apartments", 4-B, Murari Lal Street, Ansari Road, Darya Ganj, New Delhi - 110 002. Phones: 011-23270392, 23278631; Fax: 011-23256286

Nagpur : Kundanlal Chandak Industrial Estate, Ghat Road, Nagpur - 440 018. Phones: 0712-2738731, 2721215

Bengaluru : Plot No. 91-33, 2nd Main Road, Seshadripuram, Behind Nataraja Theatre, Bengaluru - 560020. Phones: 080-41138821, 09379847017, 09379847005

Hyderabad : No. 3-4-184, Lingampally, Besides Raghavendra Swamy Matham, Kachiguda, Hyderabad - 500 027. Phones: 040-27560041, 27550139

Chennai : No. 34/44, Motilal Street, T. Nagar, Chennai - 600 017. Mobile: 09380460419

Pune : First Floor, "Laksha" Apartment, No. 527, Mehunpura, Shaniwarpeth, (Near Prabhat Theatre), Pune - 411 030. Phones: 020-24496323/24496333; Mobile: 09370579333

Cuttack : Plot No. 5F-755/4, Sector-9, CDA Markat Nagar, Cuttack - 753 014, Odisha. Mobile: 09338746007

Kolkata : 3, S.M. Bose Road, Near Gate No. 5, Agarpara Railway Station, North 24 Parganas, West Bengal - 700 109. Mobile: 9674536325

DTP by : Sunita and Shilpa
Printed at : M/s Sri Sai Art Printer, Hyderabad. On behalf of HPH.

Preface to the Seventh Revised Edition

We thank the students and teachers for their continued patronage of this book. The seventh edition incorporates the suggestions and expectations of the students and teachers without altering the basic features that are valued by them.

Features of Seventh edition:

- A chapter on Modern Management Techniques in Functional Management has been added in this edition.
- A chapter on 'Case study' relating to variety of an addition management problems is in the present edition.
- To test the understanding and knowledge of the students, various types of questions have been given at the end of each chapter.

Dr. K. Natarajan

Dr. K.P. Ganesan

Preface to the Seventh Revised Edition

[illegible]

[illegible]

- [illegible]
- [illegible] in the present edition.
- [illegible] at the end of each chapter.

Dr. K. [illegible]

Dr. [illegible]

Preface to the First Edition

The subject **"Principles of Management"** occupies an important place in the course content of Commerce and Management education offered by various Universities. The present book is written in a simple and lucid style covering the various aspects of management. This book will enable the students to acquire basic knowledge of management.

The book is student-oriented and expected to serve their needs fully.

We acknowledge our indebtedness to M/s Himalaya Publishing House Pvt. Ltd. for publishing this book. We are grateful to Mr. Sivankutty Nair, area representative, Himalaya Publishing House Pvt. Ltd.

We shall look forward to suggestions and constructive criticisms for improving the subsequent editions of the book.

Dr. K. Natarajan

Dr. K.P. Ganesan

Acknowledgements

We are grateful to the teachers and well-wishers for their encouragement and suggestions to prepare the seventh edition.

We are indebted to all the members of the M/s Himalaya Publishing House Pvt. Ltd. for bringing out this edition in time.

We look forward to comments and suggestions from the readers.

Dr. K. Natarajan

Dr. K.P. Ganesan

Contents

Detailed Contents

Chapter 1

Management — An Introduction

Chapter Outline:

Definitions — Nature of Management — Management Skills — Management — Science or Art — Is Management a Profession? Why Management? — The Management Process — The Aim of Managers? — Administration vs. Management — Model Questions

The Industrial Revolution in Europe affected a great impetus to the growth and diversification of business enterprises. Replacement of human and animal power by machines, new inventions and increased demand for goods led to the expansion of commercial undertakings and the establishment of branches in foreign countries. The rapid developments achieved in the field of communication, transportation, automation and energy sources have immensely influenced modern industrial life.

All the major achievements of society have been made possible through organised effort. The need for organised work has been recognised by man when he realised that single-handedly he cannot achieve anything due to his inherent limitations — biological, mentrn, psychological and social.

Such organised effort is found in the production of goods and services by business enterprises. Management is an essential input in all organised endeavour. It involves harnessing of resources and integrating human effort. Thus, management is a dynamic life-giving element in every organisation. Management is not restricted to factory, shop or office.

It is necessary for business firms, government enterprises, educational and health services, military organisations, trade associations and so on.

Peter Drucker has observed in his book, *'Practice of Management'*: "The emergence of management as an essential, a distinct and leading social institution is a pivotal event in social history."

"Rarely in human history has a new institution proved indispensable so quickly; and even less often has a new institution arrived with so little opposition, so little disturbance, so little controversy."

The modern age is termed as the 'age of organisations'. 'Peter Drucker has also made similar observations: "Our society has become a pluralistic society in which every social task has been entrusted to large organisations — from producing economic goods and services to health care, from social security and welfare to education, from the search for new knowledge to the protection of the natural environment. The organisations by co-ordinating the efforts of different individuals enable us to reach goals that would otherwise be much more difficult or even impossible to achieve".

The emergence of giant corporations in large numbers has necessitated the growth of management as a discipline. As a discipline, it has drawn knowledge, tools and techniques from a number of disciplines and that is why it is known as interdisciplinary.

I. Definitions

The term 'management' yields to a number of interpretations and as such a precise definition of management is difficult to be arrived at. Different experts have defined management from different points of view.

Frederick W. Taylor emphasised its engineering aspects; Elton Mayo stressed the 'human relations'; Massie and Terry viewed management as a process; for Simon, it is decision-making.

Harbison and Myers have defined management as an 'economic resource, as a system of authority and as a class of elite'.

Thus, economists have viewed management as a factor of production in view of the ever-increasing industrialisation and innovation.

It is appropriate to point out a few of other important definitions of management.

1. **Mary Parker Follett:** "Management is the art of getting things done through people."
2. **Harold Koontz:** "Management is the art of getting things done through and with people in formally organised groups. It is the art of creating an environment in which people can perform and individuals could co-operate towards attaining of group goals."
3. **Joseph Massie:** "Management is defined as the process by which a co-operative group directs action towards common goals."
4. **American Society of Mechanical Engineers:** "Management is the art and science of preparing, organising and directing human efforts to control the forces and utilise the material of nature for the benefit of men."
5. **Michael H. Mescon:** "Management is the process of planning, organising, leading and controlling the efforts of organisational members and of using all other organisational resources to achieve the stated organisational goals."
6. **Frederick W. Taylor:** "Management is the art of knowing what you want to do... in the best and cheapest way."
7. **John F. Mee:** "Management may be defined as the art of securing maximum prosperity with a minimum of effort so as to secure maximum prosperity and happiness for both employer and employee and give the public the best possible service."
8. **Lawrence A. Appley:** "Management is the development of people and the direction of things. Management is personnel administration."
9. **Rose Moore:** "Management means decision-making."
10. **Stanley Vance:** "Management is simply the process of decision-making and control over the action of human beings for the express purpose of attaining predetermined goals."
11. **Donald J. Clough:** "Management is the art and science of decision-making and leadership."
12. **George R. Terry:** "Management is a distinct process, consisting of planning, organising, actuating and controlling, performed to determine and accomplish stated goals by the use of human beings and other resources."

13. **Delton E. Farland:** "Management is the process by which managers create, direct, maintain, and operate purposive organisations through systematic, co-ordinated, and co-operative human effort."

In short,

1. Management is concerned with getting things done through and with people.
2. Management is directing the efforts of people to achieve the goals of the organisation.
3. Integration of men, material and machine to achieve the goals/ the cornerstone of management.
4. Development of people is an essential aspect of management.

II. Nature of Management

The nature of management is based on the features of management. The following are identified as the nature and characteristics of management.

1. **Management is a Group Activity:** Management co-ordinates all resources, such as human, physical, finance and the like to attain the maximum level of productivity. So it is a joint effort but not individual effort.
2. **Management is a Factor of Production:** Recently, management is considered as another factor of production in addition to land, labour, capital and organisation. This is because managerial skills pave a way for bringing the resources together and putting them for the production of goods and services.
3. **Management is an Universal Process:** As a process, it includes managerial functions of planning, organising, staffing, directing, controlling and co-ordinating. So, it applies universally to all kinds of organisations. Besides, it is found in all institutions such as a family, a club, a business unit, a college, a local body or government.
4. **Management is Goal-oriented:** The aim of all business management is to accomplish the goals of an enterprise. To achieve these objectives, management employs all the resources scientifically. So, it is rightly said that management is goal-oriented.

5. **Management is a Social Science:** No rigid rules or principles could be laid down with regard to human behaviour. Besides, it is more an art of getting things done by others. So, it is now regarded as a soft social science.
6. **Management is a Dynamic Function:** As an organic entity, an enterprise is changing with an over-changing environment. The change in management concept leads to change in the environment of business through innovations.
7. **Management is a Profession:** It is a profession because managers need to possess specialised managerial knowledge, training and skills.
8. **Management is a Multi-disciplinary Subject:** Management concept draws upon many other disciplines such as economics, commerce, sociology, anthropology, psychology, mathematics, social science, computer, etc. Though it is a new discipline, it is old wine in the new bottle.
9. **Management is a System of Authority:** According to Harbison and Myers, management is a rule-making and rule-enforcing body and within itself it is bond together by a web of relationship between superiors and subordinates. It shows that the feature of management is identified through another feature of management. It means that the task of management deals with getting things done not only through the people but also with the help.
10. **Management is a Distinct Entity:** Management involves getting things done through people rather than doing itself. So, it is a distinct type of work.

III. Management Skills

Every manager needs three basic kinds of skills — technical, human and conceptual. Technical skill is the ability to use the procedures, techniques and knowledge of a specialised field. Medical practitioners, chartered accountants, musicians and engineers have technical skills in their respective fields. Human skill is the ability to work with, understand and motivate other people, as an individual or in groups. Conceptual skill is the ability to co-ordinate and integrate all of an organisation's interests and activities. It involves the manager's ability to see the organisation as a whole, to understand how its parts operate, to anticipate how a change in any of its parts affect the whole. Although all these skills are essential to a manager, their relative importance depends mainly on the manager's rank in the organisation. Technical skill is most important in the junior levels. Human skill is important for managers at every level. The importance of conceptual skill increases as one rises through the ranks of the management system.

Managers at every level plan, organise, lead and control. But they differ in the amount of time devoted to each of these activities depending upon the kind of organisation and type of job the manager holds.

IV. Management — Science or Art?

The question whether management is a science or an art is widely discussed in management literature. Science is a systematised body of knowledge based on certain principles capable of general application. Science is systematic in the sense that certain relationships between variables have been ascertained, tested and established. Natural events are observed first; facts are determined through the use of scientific methods; through continuous observations facts are verified. Hence, the knowledge obtained is verifiable. Science includes clear concepts, theories, and other accumulated knowledge developed from hypotheses, experimentation and analysis.

Art is bringing about a desired result through the application of skill. It is the application of knowledge and skills to accomplish results. Arts like painting, poetry and music require the artists' vision, knowledge of respective arts and successful communication.

Management — A Science: Management is scientific in the sense that the principles governing formulation of goals, hypotheses, collection of data, analysis and interpretation of facts, testing the conclusions and arriving at solutions are the same as that of science. However, the manager has to operate under certain limitations imposed by changing business conditions.

Management is not an exact science like natural sciences. Management can never be an exact science. It deals with human beings and it is a social science. However, the scientifical character of management is evident. The adoption of mathematical models, analytical tools, forecasting techniques and control systems for conducting time and motion studies, market research, morale, motivation, leadership and decision-making process are evidence of scientific character in management.

Management — An Art: Management is an art because it requires vision, knowledge and communication. Just as the artistic skills are developed, managerial skills can be developed. Management is an art in the sense that management principles are developed not for the sake of knowledge but for application for specific situations.

Management — Both Science and Art: A manager to be successful, requires the knowledge of management principles and also application of the principles. Hence, it can be concluded that management is a science and an art.

Theoretical knowledge must be supplemented and perfected by practical knowledge. Both theory and practice are equally important for management.

V. Is Management a Profession?

The term 'professional management' has acquired an unenviable position in the corporate sector these days. What is profession? Is Management a profession?

A profession has the following characteristics:

1. A systematic body of principles, techniques, skills and specialised knowledge;
2. A prescribed way of entering the profession through minimum training and competence;
3. A strict code of ethics or standard of conduct
4. A representative body or association that enforces standards and to control the entry to the field through licencing and so on; and
5. A commitment to service rather than financial rewards.

Management appears to be a profession in some respects if the above-mentioned guidelines are applied. It is true that management as a discipline contains a well-defined body of knowledge and a number of sophisticated tools and techniques meant to translate the theory into practice. Hence, a number of institutions offer management education. However, other guidelines such as licencing requirements, code of ethics and service motto are lacking in management. The entry into the profession is not regulated in any country. There is no universal code of conduct to be followed by managers in industries. In the absence of a code of ethics, the service motto is less adhered to. It can be concluded that management is not a profession in the strict sense of the term.

VI. Why Management?

The success or failure of a business unit depends on two main factors such as technology and human resources. Technology helps people to do more and work better. At the same time, employees who are the assets of a business unit can contribute greatly to achieve the goal.

This situation raises a question. How best the management is going to bring about co-ordination of internal environment with external environment?

The best answer is that it can be co-ordinated to a greater extent through an effective and efficient management. So, management is essential for success of a business unit in this context.

Management is needed to guide and direct people to allocate resources to the most profitable ways and ensure its maximum use. Besides, it is a must to ensure proper communication and to motivate people to contribute to achieve the goals of business unit. Therefore, it is concluded that management has become inevitable input of business enterprise.

VII. The Management Process

The whole process of management can be easily understood as a series of separate functions such as planning, organising, staffing, directing and controlling.

Planning: Planning involves selecting the courses of action that a company will follow. There are various types of plans ranging from goals and objectives to the detailed action plans. Plans become the guides by which: (1) the organisation obtains and commits the resources required to reach the objectives; (2) members of the organisation carry on activities consistent with the chosen objectives and procedures; and (3) progress towards the objectives is watched and measured so that corrective action can be taken if progress is unsatisfactory.

Planning involves the selection of goal for the entire organisation. Objectives are evolved for different departments and divisions. Once the objectives are finalised, programmes are designed for achieving them in a systematic manner.

Plans made by top management for the organisation as a whole may cover periods as long as five to ten years. Planning at the lower levels covers much shorter periods such as a week or a few days.

Organising: Organising involves establishing an intentional structure of roles for people in an enterprise to fill. Organising involves: (1) determination of activities required to achieve goals; (2) grouping of these activities into departments or sections; (3) assignment of such groups of activities to a manager; (4) delegation of authority to carry them out; (5) provision for co-ordination of activities; and (6) providing information horizontally and vertically in the organisation structure.

The managers must have the ability to determine what type of organisation will be needed to accomplish a given set of objectives and they must have the ability to develop that type of organisation.

Staffing: Staffing involves setting job requirements for the job to be done. It includes selection, appraisal, compensation, training and development of candidates so as to accomplish the tasks effectively. Staffing is concerned about filling and keeping filled the positions provided by the organisation structure.

Leading: The activity of leading involves working directly with people. It deals with predominantly interpersonal aspects of managing. It is the art of influencing people so that they will follow willingly and enthusiastically towards the achievement of organisational goals. Leading involves motivation, leadership styles and approaches and communication.

Controlling: The controlling function of management enables the manager to ensure that the actions of the organisation's members move the organisation towards its stated goals. It involves four main steps:

1. Establishing standards of performance.
2. Measuring current performance and comparing it against the established standards.
3. Detecting deviations from standard goals.
4. Taking action to correct performance that does not meet those standards.

A model of management process is presented so far. In practice, the management process does not involve five separate sets of activities, but a group of interactive functions. These five functions do not necessarily occur in the sequence presented. In fact, various combinations of these activities are going on simultaneously in every organisation. However, this model provides a useful approach to understand the management process.

VIII. The Aim of Managers

It is widely held that the aim of business managers is to earn profit. Profit is only a measure of a 'surplus' of sales over expenses in carrying out some type of business. In reality, in business and non-business organisations, the managers are expected to create profit, i.e., a 'surplus.' Apart from that, managers are primarily concerned with establishing an environment in which people can attain group goals with the least amount of time, money, materials and personal dissatisfaction. Thus, the aim of managers is basically the same in business and non-business organisations. It is also the same at every level: the Managing Director of a business unit, Inspector General of Police, Dean of a Hospital, Cricket Manager and Principal of a College and Vice-Chancellor of a University as managers have the same aim. The purpose of their operatiofls may differ but their managerial aim is the same.

IX. Administration vs. Management

The terminological conflict between administration and management has been examined by many modern writers.

Administration and management are separate functions: Writers like Ordway Tead, Oliver Shelden, William Spriegel, William Schultse hold the view that administration is broader than management. Administration is a policy-making function but management is concerned with carrying out the broad policies laid down by the administration. Administration is a top level activity and management is a lower-level function. Administrators think but managers act.

Writers such as E.F.L. Breach, Henry Fayol, Kimball and Kimball maintain that management is a wider concept than administration. Administration handles the current problems arising out of the policies laid down by the managemen Management is the rule-making and rule-enforcing activity. It is a comprehensive term which includes administration as a part of it.

Administration and management are synonymous: Another group of writers like William Newman, Harold Koontz, Dalton E. McFarland and Earnest Dale do not make any distinction between the two terms. A manager or an administrator has to perform both the 'thinking' and 'doing' functions. From a practical point of view, it is impossible to place administration and management in two separate compartments in an undertaking. Top management is chiefly concerned with performing administrative activities whereas managers at lower levels are predominantly concerned with executive function. This is shown in Fig.1.1

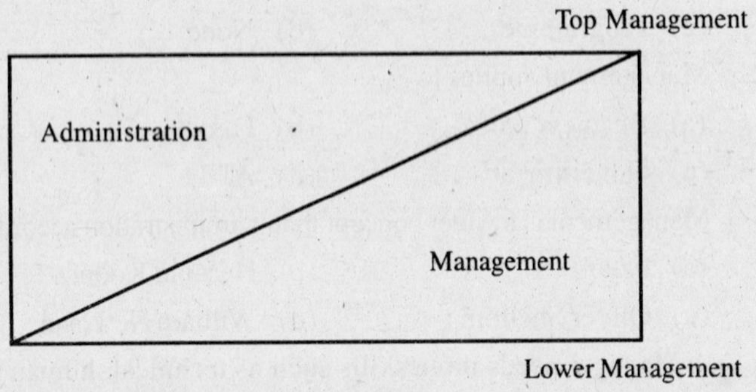

Fig. 1.1

Hence, it can be concluded that there are divergent views with regard to the terminological conflict between management and administration. However, these two terms are used interchangeably in this textbook.

Model Questions

Section A

1. Define management.
2. What are the characteristics of management?

Section B

3. Are management and administration different?
4. Is management a profession?
5. Is management a science or an art?

Section C

6. 'Management is getting things done through people.' Discuss.
7. Describe the functions of management.
8. Explain the different kinds of skills needed by a manager to perform the task of management.
9. Explain the nature of management.

I. Multiple Choice

1. Management is the art of getting things done through
   (a) People (b) Planning
   (c) Programme (d) None
2. Management applies to
   (a) Business unit (b) Family
   (c) Government (d) All
3. Management is a wider concept than administration according to
   (a) Fayol (b) Hernold Koontz
   (c) Oliver Sheltom (d) William Newman
4. A Manager needs three skills such as technical, human and
   (a) Conceptual (b) Process
   (c) Accuracy (d) None
5. Management is a
   (a) Profession (b) Principles
   (c) Performance (d) None

Answer:

1. (a) People, 2. (d) All, 3. (a) Fayol, 4. (a) Conceptual,
5. (a) Profession

II. Say, 'True or False'

6. Management means decision-making.
7. Management is a multi-disciplinary subject.
8. Management is both science and art.
9. There is universal code of conduct to be followed by managers in industries.
10. Planning is one of the activities involved in the management process.

Answer:

6. True, 7. True, 8. True, 9. False, 10. True

III. Fill in the blanks

11. ____________________ is the development of people and direction of things.
12. Management is a ____________________ activity.

13. _______________ skill is the ability to co-ordinate and integrate all of an organisation's interests and activities.
14. _______________ of people is an essential aspect of management.
15. A manager has to perform both 'thinking' and __________ function.

Answer:

11. Management, 12. Group, 13. Conceptual, 14. Development, 15. Doing

Chapter 2

Different Approaches to the Study of Management

Chapter Outline:

The Empirical or Case Approach — The Interpersonal Behaviour Approach — The Group Behaviour Approach — The Co-operative Social System Approach — The Socio-technical System Approach — The Decision Theory Approach — The Mathematical or Management Science Approach — The Managerial Roles Approach — The Contingency. Approach — The Systems Approach — Model Questions

Academic writers and practitioners have shown a keen interest in management. Consequently, a number of approaches have been developed to explain the nature, concepts, theories and techniques underlying managerial practice. The variety of approaches and the different views have resulted in confusion and Harold Koontz called this situation 'the management theory jungle'. Now the jungle sems to have changed and new approaches have emerged.

The various approaches to the study of management are categorised as follows:

1. The empirical or case approach.
2. The interpersonal behaviour approach.
3. The group behaviour approach.
4. The co-operative social system approach.
5. The socio-technical systems approach.
6. The decision theory approach.

7. The mathematical or management science approach
8. The managerial roles approach.
9. The situational or contingency approach
10. The systems approach.

I. The Empirical or Case Approach

The advocates of this school believe that management is a study of experiences of managers. This approach is based on the assumption that the experiences, methods and techniques of successful managers will provide a guideline to other practitioners. The following are the broad features of empirical school of management:

1. Management is the study of experiences.
2. The managerial experience can be passed over to the practitioners and students.
3. The techniques used by successful managers in the past can be used by future managers.
4. By studying the experience of large number of managers some sort of generalisations can be made.
5. Learning through experience is a conventional way of acquiring skills in management.

This approach has many limitations.

(i) Book

(ii) The contradictions in experiences have not helped in developing management as a discipline.

Koontz has cautioned that there is a positive danger in relying too much on past experience.

But a manager has to work under dynamic situations. The situations of the past may not be exactly the same in the present. The past experiences may not fit a situation of the future.

II. The Interpersonal Behaviour Approach

The exponents of this approach have viewed that managing depends upon the relationships among the people working in the organisation. In their opinion, good management rests on the ability of managers to develop interpersonal competence among members and to support collaborative effort at all levels of the organisation. This approach is based on the premise that the goals of the organisation are accomplished through and premise that the goals of the organisation are accomplished through and with people. Hence, the study of management should be confined to the human behaviour in organisation and related matters. Interpersonal and intrapersonal phenomena form the main body of human relations.

The exponents of this approach are heavily oriented towards individual psychology and and social psychology. Good managing involves the study of human interactions and human behaviour and motivation and leadership. However, the interpersonal behaviour approach does not cover the entire field of management. Apart from psychological training, managers need to know something about planning, forecasting techniques, control devices and organisation structure in order to ensure the accomplishment of managerial tasks.

III. The Group Behaviour Approach

The approach is mainly concerned with the behaviour of people in groups. It has its oriention in sociology and social psychology. The exponents of this approach have viewed management as a study of group behaviour patterns. This approach recognises any enterprise as a social arrangement which is made up of many social units within it. The social units comprise people with various cultural backgrounds and interacting attitudes and conflicts. Therefore, a manager should understand human relations. This approach emphasises interpersonal relations among people and draws its concepts from psychology, sociology and social psychology. However, group behaviour approach does not cover the entire field of management.

IV. The Co-operative Social System Approach

Chester I. Bernard is considered to be the founding father of this school. The exponents of this approach have looked upon organisation as a social system composed of people who work in co-operation. Bernard saw social system as the co-operative interaction of the ideas, forces, desires and thinking of two or more people.

The management should analyse social and group behaviour in the context of the social system. Efforts should be directed towards establishing harmony between the goals of the organisation and the goals of the groups.

However, the advocates of this approach have mistakenly treated management and sociology as synonymous. This approach neglects many concepts, principles and techniques which are important to managers.

V. The Socio-technical System Approach

E.L. Trist and his associates at the Tavistock Institute, England, developed the socio-technical system approach. This group found that social problems should not be studied in isolation. The social system is profoundly affected by the technical system. The personal attitudes and group behaviour are heavily influenced by the technical system in which people work. Hence, the social system and technical system should be made harmonious. If harmony is not found between both the systems, changes should be made in the technical system.

This approach has mainly focussed its attention on production office operations, automobile assembly line, chemical processing and transportation. However, a systematic analysis and co-ordination between social and technical systems are capable of producing much managerial benefits.

VI. The Decision Theory Approach

The exponents of this approach viewed decision-making as the core of management practice. This approach believes that decision-making is the central focus of management theory.

This approach is significant to practicing managers. The management, according to social system approach, should take decisions that will reflect the interest not only of one group but of all others concerned with the organisation.

This approach is suitable for managing problems at shop floor level rather than handling the total managerial problems.

Organisation can be treated as a combination of decision centres. The members of the organisation are decision-makers. All the factors that affect decision-making, i.e., the processes, the techniques, social and psychological aspects of decision-makers, the information system etc., are the subject matter of the study. The entire management theory can be built around decision-making.

Decision-making is the vital aspect of management. But management is more than decision-making. So, decision-making is a narrow focus on which to build a total theory of management is difficult.'

VII. The Mathematical or Management Science Approach

The exponents of this approach have viewed management as a system of logical processes which can be expressed in mathematical symbols and relationships. The problems of management can be solved through the application of appropriate simulation and analytical mathematical techniques.

This approach provides a powerful and logical tool for simplifying and solving complex problems. Linear Programming, Game Theory, Index Number, Time Series Analysis, Simulation, Waiting Line Theory and Sampling are some of the quantitative techniques widely used in management today. However, they can only be treated as tools in managerial practice. It is difficult to call it a separate school of management.

VIII. The Managerial Roles Approach

This approach has been popularised by Henry Mintzberg of the McGill University. He systematically studied the activities of five chief executives in various organisations and classified the managerial roles they played. From his research, he concluded that managers perform ten different roles such as:

1. Interpersonal Roles: (a) the figure-head role (performing ceremonial and social duties as the organisation's representative), (b) the leader role and (c) the liason role.

2. Informational Role: (a) the recipient role (receiving information about the operations of the unit), (b) the disseminator role (passing information to subordinates), and (c) the spokesperson role (transmitting information outside the organisation).

3. Decision Roles: (a) the entrepreneur role (b) the disturbance-handler role, (c) the resource allocator role, and (d) the negotiator role, (dealing with various groups of people).

The roles identified by Mintzberg are evidences of planning, organising, leading and controlling. However, Mintzberg's roles approach has overlooked activities such as structuring organisation, selection, appraisal of managers and formulation of strategies. The managerial roles approach is inadequate to evolve a practical theory of management.

IX. The Contingency Approach

The basic idea of contingency approach is that there is one best approach to management. There are many effective ways to perform various managerial functions.

This approach advocates that managerial actions and organisational design must be appropriate to the given situation. A particular action is valid only under certain conditions. There are no plans, organisation structures, leadership styles or controls that will fit all situation.

In other words, managerial action is contingent upon external environment applying a contingency approach requires that managers diagnose a given situation and adopt to meet conditions present.

Contingeny approach highlights the multivariate nature of organisations and explain how organisations operate under varying conditions. With its help, the managers can design actions which are appropriate to their respective conditions.

This approach advocates that the managers should develop situational sensitivity and practical selectivity. Adoption of this approach can be useful in formulation of strategies, design of organisations, planning information system, establishing communication and control system, shaping motivational and leadership approach, resolving conflicts and managing change etc.

The contingency approach is subject to the following limitations:

1 Literature on contingency approach is not adequate. It has no adequately spelt out various types of action that can be taken under different situations. Unless this is done, this approach cannot offer much assistance to the practice of management.

2. The contingency theory is complex. Even a simple problem involves analysing a number of components, each of which having innumerable dimensions. As a result, empirical testing becomes difficult.

3. It suggests a proactive stategy in coping with the environment, i.e., it merely suggests what managers can do in a given situation. A proactive strategy where managers would be able to steer the organisation through complex environment with their creative and innovative efforts is needed for an organisation.

X. The Systems Approach

A system is a set of inteconnected or interrelated parts. Each part may have sub-parts. The parts and sub-parts are mutually related to each other directly or indirectly. In a system, the separate but interrelated elements work for a common goal.

For example, the universe is a system which includes many systems of stars and galaxies. Human body is a system composed of many sub-systems such as nervous system, digestive system etc. A system is merely a sum of all parts but their arrangement must be orderly. The arrangement of parts make the system an organised whole. The whole becomes greater than the total of individual parts.

The systems approach views organisation as a whole rather than the totality of its parts.

It emphasises the interrelatedness and interdependence of all activities within the organisation. It provides a unified focus to organisational efforts.

The systems approach treats organisation as an open system. Contrary to the closed system, an open system has interaction with enviomment. In this interaction, they import energy and export output. It receives inputs such as raw material, labour, capital and information from the society. These resources are combined and transformed by business organisations into desirable output of goods and services. There are three aspects involved in this transformation process: input, mediator and output. The system works as a mediator in the process.

In this process, the system restores some of the inputs taken from the environment. Restoring inputs taken from the environment helps the system to grow. For example, a business organisation survives and grow over a period of time by earning profit in the process of transforming input into outputs. Further, an open system is subject to environmental changes and so they are flexible and dynamic.

Systems approach to management provides a conceptual basis as well as guidelines for establishing a more efficient system for planning, organising, directing and controlling. It considers management in its totality and provides an integrated approach of managing. It forces the managers to look upon his buisness as an open adaptive system. Management is viewed as a subsystem of a social system. As a subsystem, management is required to adapt and cope up with environmental changes.

Modern thinkers consider management as a system of integrating activities aimed at making best use of the resources. In its present state, systems theory provides management with concept from every movement including Operations Research, Organisational Behaviour, Management Information System, Industrial Dynamics and Socio-technical System.

Model Questions

1. Discuss the various approaches to the study of management.
2. Explain the significance of the following schools of thought
   (i) The decision theory approach.
   (ii) The systems approach.
   (iii) The empirical approach.

I. Multiple Choice

1. According to empirical approach, management is a
   (a) Study of experience of managers
   (b) Decision-making
   (c) A system of logical processes
   (d) Depends upon the relationship among people
2. There is no one best approach to management according to
   (a) Systems approach
   (b) Contingency approach
   (c) Socio-technical system approach
   (d) Group behaviour approach
3. Management depends upon the relationship among the people working in the organisation according to
   (a) Group behaviour approach
   (b) Co-opeartive social system approach
   (c) Socio-technical system approach
   (d) Interpersonal behaviour approach
4. Which approach emphasises the interrelatedness and interdependence of all activities within the organisation?
   (a) The Contingency approach
   (b) The Managerial role approach
   (c) The Systems approach
   (d) None

5. The problems of management can be solved through application of mathematical techniques according to
   (a) Management science approach
   (b) Management roles approach
   (c) Co-operative social system approach
   (d) Empirical approach

Answer:

1. (a) Study of experience of managers, 2. (b) Contingency approach, 3. (d) Interpersonal behaviour approach, 4. (a) The Contingency approach, 5. (a) Management science approach

II. Say, 'True or False'

6. A system is a set of interrelated parts.
7. Decision theory approach is suitable for managing problems at shop floor level.
8. The contingency theory is a complex one.
9. According to socio-technical system, there should be harmony between goals of the organisation and goals of the people.
10. Group behaviour approach covers the entire field of management.

Answer:

6. True, 7. True, 8. True, 9. False, 10. False

III. Fill in the blanks

11. The system approach treats organisations as an ______ system.
12. The social system and technical system should be made______.
13. _______ approach is concerned with the behaviour of people in group.
14. _______ is the founding father of the co-operative social system approach.
15. According to the Contingency approach, the managerial actions must be appropriate to the given ___________.

Answer:

11. Open, 12. Harmonious, 13. Group behaviour, 14. Chester Bernard, 15. Situation.

Chapter 3

Management Thinkers

Chapter Outline:

Early Management Thinkers — Forerunners of Modern Management — Modern Thinker — Management By Objectives (MBO) — Management By Exception (MBE) — Model Questions

I. Early Management Thinkers

The early management thinkers include Robert Owen, Charles Babbage, Metcalf and Henry Towne.

Robert Owen (1858-1971)

Robert Owen was the manager of many cotton mills at New Lonark, Scotland. In those days, the working and living conditions of workers were unbearable. So, Robert Owen paid attention towards labour welfare. He made efforts to improve the working conditions in the factory and provide facilities to workers. He introduced a system of open rating of worker's performance and a system of motivation for increasing productivity. He believed that the improvement in working and living conditions of workers would lead to higher production and profit.

Charles Babbage (1792-1871)

Charles Babbage was a mathematician and a teacher. He emphasised that good machines and efficient workers would not necessarily ensure the success of a business. But good management is the most important element in a successful business. He advocated division of labour, specialisation and assignment of labour on the basis of skill.

Henry Robinson Towne (1844-1924)

Towne was an innovator in the field of management. He motivated engineers to study management and recommended for a combination of management with engineering. He also pleaded for an association where persons connected with industries could exchange their experiences.

Henry Metcalfe (1847-1917)

Metcalfe was a reputed manager of an army. He viewed that the art of management should be founded on the accumulated observations which could be built up to check performance. These observations should be systematically presented. He believed in maintaining important records and discarding superfluous charts and reports.

II. Forerunners of Modern Management

Frederick Winslow Taylor (1856-1915)

Taylor was the first to insist on the introduction of scientific methods in management. He started his career as machine shop labourer in a small mill and rose up to the position of Chief Engineer in a steel mill. During his career, he observed that the attitude of workers was not enthusiastic towards work. They wasted time and energy. There was no standard of performance. The spirit of co-operation between the labourers and management was completely absent.

Taylor's ideas on scientific management are contained in his two books *'Shop Management'* and *'Principles of Scientific Management'*. Taylor emphasised the spirit of scientific enquiry to the problems of production and the entire area or management.

Taylor's scientific management is based on the following principles of management.

1. Determining one best method of performing each task.
2. Scientific selection and education of workers.
3. Spirit of friendly co-operation between management and workers.

1. Determining One Best Method of Performing Each Task: The management is responsible for determining the standard task for every worker through careful investigation. The standard task is the amount of work which an average worker will be able to do in a day in a day in an atmosphere of mutual trust and co-operation.

2. The Scientific Selection and Education of Workers: The procedure of selection of workers is to be systematised. The task of selection is to be entrusted to a central personnel department. The selection of workers is to be followed by proper placement and systematic training.

3. Spirit of Friendly Co-operation between Management and Workers: The success of scientific management rests on the fundamental change in the attitude of management and workers. Both must recognise that one cannot prosper at the expense of the other. There should be friendly co-operation between them.

The mechanisms of scientific management are as follows:

1. Time and Motion Study.
2. Functional Foremanship.
3. Standardisation of Tools and Equipments.
4. Differential Piece Rate System.
5. Establishing Planning Department.

1. Time and Motion Study: The basic purpose of time study is to determine the proper time for performing an operation.

Motion Study: It is the study of the movements of workers in performing operation. The purpose of motion study is to eliminate unnecessary motions.

2. Functional Foremanship: Under the plan, the supervision of the work is entrusted to specialists, each one of whom advises the worker in his own particular function. Taylor contemplated light functional foremen. They are: the route clerk, the instruction card clerk, the time and cost clerk, the shop disciplinarian, the gang boss, the speed boss, the repair boss and the inspector.

3. Standardisation of Tools and Equipments: Standardisation means the process of bringing uniformity. The tools should be of uniform type for the same job. Besides, the quality of materials and the method of handling materials should be standardised.

4. Differential Piece Rate System: Under this system, the workers who perform the standard task within the prescribed time are paid a much higher rate than those who are not able to come up to the standards set.

5. Establishing a Planning Department: Establishing a planning department is an important part of scientific management. The planning department will receive instructions with regard to the quantity and type of products to be produced and take steps towards planning and control of production.

Taylor is known as the father of industrial engineering and scientific management. However, his contributions invited opposition from both workers and management and he died broken-hearted.

Henry Laurance Gantt (1861-1919)

Gantt was a close associate of Taylor. He realised that the incentive wage plan of Taylor was too rigorous. The standard set for a worker was too high. He introduced the task and bonus system which provided both security and incentive to the workers. This system is superior to Taylor's differential piece rate system, as it is human in its operation.

He introduced a chart designed for scheduling production activities which is known as Gantt's Chart. It is considered to be a powerful chart in the hands of managers.

Frank B. Gilbreth (1868-1924) and Mrs. Lillian M. Gilbreth (1878-1972)

Frank Gilbreth was an admirer of Taylor. He had complete faith in the message of scientific management and he popularised scientific management when it was under clouds. Gilbreth devoted his entire life to 'motion study', and a search for doing a 'job in a better way'. His work in the area of motion study is considered to be a pioneering work, and it constitutes the basis of modern motion study techniques.

Gilbreth started his career as an apprentice brick layer in the firm of Whiddey and Company in 1895. Later, he started his own contracting business. In 1904, he married Lillian M. Gilbreth, a noted psychologist and a management consultant. Both worked as a team and devoted their life in the quest for one best way of doing the work.

The Gilbreths developed a microchronometer, a cycle graph, the chronocyclograph, the process chart and the flow diagram.

The method of study, techniques and methodology of Gilbreth are still being used, despite tremendous technological advancement. After the death of Gilbreth, his wife carried forward his message. She was a specialist in human relations. Her renowned work. *'The Psychology of Management'* laid the foundation of human relations. The professional team of the Gilbreths proved to be a strong combination of complementary talents.

Henry Fayol (1841-1925)

Fayol's contribution to management theory is unique and valuable. Henry Fayol was a French mining engineer who rose to the position of chief executive in a French mining and metallurgical company. He was the first man to advocate the view that management should and can be taught. From his 50 years of managerial experience and experiments, he came to the conclusion that the principles of administrative science could be universally acceptable.

He published his outstanding work *'General and Industrial Management'* in 1961 in French. It was widely read and published in 1949 in English. He was concerned with management at the levels of organisation. His major attention was on general management and overall control.

According to Fayol, management was a process composed of five elements, namely, planning, organisation, command, co-ordination and control. Fayol's classification has been universally accepted. Out of his vast administrative experiences, he laid down fourteen principles.

1. **Division of Work:** The objective of division of labour is to derive the benefits of specialisation — it helps a person to acquire an ability and accuracy with which he can do more and better work. The principle of division of labour can be applied to all levels of organisation.
2. **Authority and Resposibility:** Authority is the right to give order and the power to exact obedience. Responsibility is the obligation to perform the work in the manner desired and directed by the superior. Authority and responsibility go together. Authority should match responsibility.
3. **Discipline:** Discipline is obedience, application, energy and outward mark of respect. Discipline is what leaders make it. Experience and tact on the part of a manager enable him to choose the degree of sanctions to be used such as warnings, fines, suspensions, dismissals etc.
4. **Unity of Command:** This principle implies that the employee should receive orders from only one superior for any activity. If it is violated, there will be undermining of authority. Unity of command will make authority responsibility clear to everybody. It would be easy to fix responsibility in case of default. There will be harmonious relationship between superior and subordinates.

5. **Unity of Direction:** Unity of direction means 'one unit-one plan' for a group of activities having the same objective. Unity of direction is concerned about the body corporate whereas unity of command is concerned about the functioning of personnel. For the accomplishment of a group of activities having the same objectives, there should be one head and one plan.

6. **Scalar Chain:** It is the line of authority from the chief executive to the lowest level in the organisation. Each communication, either upwards or downwards, must flow through each position in the line of authority.

   There are two disadvantages in the scalar chain:

   (i) Communication takes too much of time.

   (ii) There is possibility of distortion of message as superior may add or delete something to actual message.

   Therefore, scalar chain should be rigid. Fayol suggested that 'gang blank' or 'direct contact' could be thrown without weakening the chain of command.

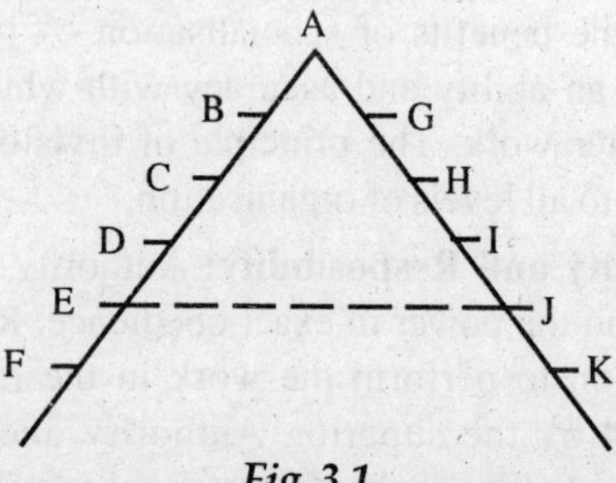

Fig. 3.1

In figure 3.1, there are two ladders of authority, one from A to F and the other A to K. If E wants to communicate with J in the scalar chain, information must flow upwards from E to A through D, C, B and then downwards from A to J through G, H, Q and I. In order to allow swift action, according to Fayol, E and J should be allowed to exchange information directly.

7. **Subordination of Individual Interest to the General Interest:** The interest of one employee or a group of employees should not prevail over that of the concern. The superiors should set an example in firmness and goodness. Common interest must prevail over individual interest.

8. **Remuneration:** Fayol insisted that wages and salaries should be neither low nor high. It should be *fair* and satisfactory for the services rendered.
9. **Centralisation:** Everything which goes to increase the importance of the subordinates' role is decentralisation and everything which goes to reduce it is centralisation. According to Fayol, centralisation and decentralisation are questions of proportion, a matter of finding optimum degree for a particular concern.
10. **Order:** Fayol believed that there *should be a place for everything and everyone.* At the same time, everything and everyone should be in their places. This is a principle of organisation relating to things and persons.
11. **Equity:** Equity is the combination of *kindness and justice.* The principle of equity suggests that the managers should be fair and impartial in dealing with their subordinates. The application of equity ensures devotion and loyalty from workers.
12. **Stability of Tenure of Personnel:** Stability of tenure is essential to get an employee accustomed to a new work and succeed in doing well. There should be reasonable security of job. Instability of tenure is the cause and consequence of lack of success. Efficiency is always promoted by a stable labour force.
13. **Initiative:** It develops an atmosphere of mutual trust and understanding. Team spirit inspires the workers to work harder and improve quality of work. The freedom to propose a plan and to execute it is known as initiative. This increases zeal and energy on the part of human beings (within the limits of authority and discipline, employees with initiative should be encouraged).
14. **Esprit de Corps:** This principle advocates *team spirit.* The manager should encourage *esprit de corps* among his subordinates.

In addition to the fourteen principles of management, he mentioned six activities that are going on in any organisation. These activities are as follows:

1. Technical (production, manufacture, adaptation);
2. Commertial (buying, selling, exchange);

3. Financial (search for an optimum use of capital);
4. Security (protection of property and persons);
5. Accounting (stock-taking, balance sheets, cost statistics); and
6. Managerial (planning, organising, commanding, co-ordinating, controlling).

According to Fayol, the managerial activity was the most important and universal in all organisations. Thus, Fayol viewed that six separate activities of an enterprise, five functions of management and fourteen principles constitute a complete theory of management.

Max Weber

Max Weber was a German social scientist who had an academic background and teaching experience. He propounded the principles of ideal bureaucracy. Under a bureaucracy, the organisation structure has the following features:

1. Tasks are divided into very specialised jobs.
2. A rigorous set of rules must be followed.
3. A stable and well-defined hierarchy of authority should exist.
4. Superiors adopt an impersonal attitude in dealing with subordinates.
5. Written rules, decisions and keeping of extensive files.
6. Specified qualifications for individuals holding office.
7. Employment and promotions based on merit, technical competence.
8. Lifelong employment and adequate protection of individuals against arbitrary dismissal.

An organisation can be considered bureaucratic, depending on the extent to which the above features are present.

Elton Mayo (1880-1949)

Eiton Mayo emphasised the importance of human factor in a work situation. He and his associates conducted the famous Hawthorne Studies during 1924-1932. There were four phases in the study.

1. **The Illumination Experiments:** The objective of these experiments was to observe the influence of illumination upon the levels of output. A test group and a control group were involved in these experiments. For the test group, variations

in the intensity of lighting were made and for the control group, it was kept constant. But output of both groups increased steadily. It was concluded that the cause for increased output was to be found elsewhere.

2. **Relay Assembly Test Group:** In this experiment, six women telephone relay assemblers were placed in two separate rooms. In one room, the working conditions were altered and in the other, they were not changed. It was found that output went up in both rooms, irrespective of changes in the working conditions. Mayo concluded that physical conditions had no impact on output. The sympathetic attitude of supervisors, freedom in work environrnent, treatment to the workers and a sense of belongingness were responsible for improved job performance.

3. **Mass Interviewing Programme:** In this programme, the workers were interviewed by indirect questioning by researchers. It was found that many problems of worker-management co-operation were the result of the emotionally-based attitudes rather than that of the objective difficulties in the situation. The workers were guided by a 'logic of sentiment', whereas the management was concerned with the 'logic of cost and efficiency.' Thus, a conflict becomes inevitable.

4. **The Bank Wiring Observation Group:** A group of 14 workers participated in the experiment. They were paid on group basis. An individual's pay was dependent on the output of the entire group and his own individual output. It was assumed that highly efficient workers would exert pressure on less efficient workers to increase output and thus take advantage of group effort. It was found that the group imposed standard for output. The cohesive group was indifferent to the financial incentives.

Findings of Hawthrone Experiments:

1. The buisness organisation is a social system. It is not merely a formal structure of functions in which production is determined by the official prescription but by the production norms set up by social norms. People are social beings and their social characteristics determine the output and efficiency in the organisation. Thus, the human factor is the most important in organisations.

2. At the workplace, workers create groups which is different from official group. This group determines the norms of behaviour of members. The group norms affect individual behaviour in a significant way.
3. There is emergence of informal leadership as against formal leadership. The informal leader is more important in directing group behaviour.
4. Money is less a factor in determining output than group standards, group sentiments and sensitivity.

A.F. Stoner summarises the contribution of Elton Mayo:

1. Productivity is not an engineering function.
2. A true concern for people buys rich dividends.
3. People's management skills as opposed to technical skills are necessary for a successful leader.
4. Good interpersonal and intergroup relationship among the people are to be maintained to obtain productivity and gains.

Mary Parkett Follett (1868-1933)

Follett applied psychological and sociological methods for solving managerial problems. Contributions of Follett are as follows:

1. There should be co-ordination between human efforts and the goals of the organisation.
2. A person should not take or order another person. Both should agree to take order from the situation.
3. Conflict may be constructive. The integration of ideas of both parties is the best way to solve the conflict.
4. Leaders are not only born but through proper behaviour they can be made also.
5. Authority belongs to the job and stays with the job.
6. The way in which the members of the group act towards each other and the overall impact of the group on individual member is an important phase of the study of human relations.

Chester I. Bernard (1886.1961)

Chester Bernard in his book, *'The Functions of the Executive'*, has observed that the executives carry on the entire process of management through three essential executing functions:

1. Providing a system of communication.
2. Promoting the acquisition of essential effort; and
3. Evolving and defining the purposes and objectives of the organisation.

According to him, authority is the character of communication (order) in a formal organisation by virtue of which it is accepted by members of the organisation. The organisations fail whenever they are not able to maintain authority.

III. Modern Thinker

Peter F. Drucker

Peter F. Drucker is a professor, management consultant and a great management thinker. He has become a legendary figure in the world of management.

Drucker has viewed: "Managing a business cannot be a bureaucratic, an administrative or even a policy-making job...must be a creative rather than adaptive task. Hence, introducing innovation is an important task of a manager".

Here, innovation is used in a broader sense. The development of new ideas, combining old ideas and new ones, adaptation of ideas from other fields and to encourage others to carry out innovations constitute innovations.

To Drucker, management is a practice rather than a science. As a discipline, it has its own tools, skills, techniques and approaches.

Drucker has observed that the modern society is a society of institutions. All major tasks are performed by organisations. Knowledge is the foundation of modern organisations.

Drucker has advocated decentralisation of functions. It helps the management to devote itself to its functions. Decentralisation defines the functions and responsibilities of the employees. It creates yardsticks to measure the effectiveness in jobs.

Competence is the essential requisite for a manager. In an organisation, he performs three tasks:

(i) Setting specific purposes and mission for the institution;
(ii) Making work productive and the worker achieving;
(iii) Managing social impacts and social responsibilities.

Drucker is concerned with 'futurity'. He points out that mankind should take change as a challenge and try to cope with it.

The concept of management by objectives (MBO) is regarded as the major contribution of Drucker.

IV. Management By Objectives (MBO)

MBO calls for setting of specific and verifiable objectives at the different levels of the organisation. These objectives are set toward expected results for all units in quantitative terms. In this process, superiors and subordinates jointly identify the objectives and define each individual's area of responsibility. This makes everyone to know what is expected of them and motivate for higher performance.

Process of MBO

1. **Goal Setting:** MBO starts with the establishment of clear and concise goals of performance which are understood and accepted by superiors and subordinates alike.
2. **Action Plan:** An action plan provides the means by which an objective is realised. The superior should sit with each subordinate and review the action plan once it is developed. It helps in finding out the efficient methods of accomplishing goals.
3. **Final Review:** In this phase, the actual results are compared with the predetermined standards. An appraisal is made in an atmosphere of mutual trust and confidence. The emphasis is for improving performance and not for criticising the subordinate for failure.

MBO is believed to be an innovation in modern times and it is said to make the organisation performance-oriented and socially useful.

Benefits of MBO

1. **Clear Goals:** MBO insists upon precise, clear-cut and measurable goals. The goals arrived at after the meeting of various levels of members of the organisation results in team spirit and commitment.
2. **Control Easier:** A clear set of verifiable goals serve as a basis for better control.
3. **Objective Appraisal:** MBO offers the basis for assessing the performance. Objectives are impartial as employee's performance is evaluated against verifiable goals.

4. **Motivational Force:** MBO offers a feeling of true participation in the task from its inception. It enables the superior and subordinates committed to the same goals.
5. **Morale:** Participative decision-making and two-way communication psychologically influence the subordinates and result in better morale among the employees.

Limitations of MBO

Some of the limitations of MBO which prevent it from achieving good results are as follows:

1. **Time-consuming:** Initial goal-setting requires a lot of time at all levels of the organisation. The periodic progress and final review sessions also consume time.
2. **Increases Paperwork:** MBO process requires a lot of reports, instructions, manuals and newsletters. To be aware of what is going on, regular reports and performance data are sent to the top management. Therefore, MBO increases paperwork.
3. **Goal-setting Problems:** Sometimes, overemphasis on quantifiable and measurable goals result in losing sight of qualitative goals like job satisfaction and employee attitudes.
4. **Organisational Problems:** The MBO philosophy needs to be taught to all participants in the organisation. Too many objectives also tilt the priorities and confuse the subordinates. Proper care should be taken to monitor whether the objectives are consistent with the management philosophy.

V. Management by Exception (MBE)

According to James A.F. Stoner, Management by exception is defined as "the controlling superior should be informed about an operation's progress only if there is a significant deviation from the plan or standard. It means that the problems involving unusual or non-recurring matters should be referred to superiors, whereas recurring matters should be handled by subordinates. The principle of management by exception is to relieve top level executives from routine matters. Besides, it is a vital concept dealing with the delegation of authority and control."

Process of Management by Exception

1. **Measurement:** It assigns values to performance, past and present. Without measurements, it is hardly possible to adopt management by exception concept.

2. **Projection:** The result obtained from the measurements analysis are projected to future expectations.
3. **Selection:** It involves the factor which could be used to follow progress towards business unit's goals.
4. **Observation:** It deals with the measurement of current performance.
5. **Comparison:** It means comparison between budgeted performance and actual performance. Exceptions that require attention are identified.
6. **Decision-making:** In the final stage, appropriate action should be taken to correct deviations and set right variations.
7. **Benefits of Management by Exception:**
   (a) It deals with major and most urgent problems. As a result, managerial talents are utilised effectively.
   (b) It ensures better delegation of authority which in turn results in better opportunities for self-motivated employees.
   (c) It provided qualitative and quantitative measuring rods for appraising performance.
   (d) It saves executive's time. Because routine and reoccurring matters are taken care of by subordinates.
   (e) It helps managers to take three-dimensional view of organisational accomplishments, i.e., making most of the data on past performance, current condition of work and future projection.
8. **Management is a Multi-disciplinary Subject:** Management concept draws upon many other disciplines such as economics, commerce, sociology, anthropology, psychology, mathematics, social science, computer, etc. Though it is a new discipline, it is old wine in the new bottle.
9. **Management is a System of Authority:** According to Harbison and Myers, management is a rule-making and rule-enforcing body and within itself it is bound together by a web of relationship between superiors and subordinates. It shows that the feature of management is identified through another feature of management. It means that the task of management deals with getting things done not only through the people but also with the help.

Model Questions

Section A

1. What is unity of command?
2. What is unity of direction?
3. What is scalar chain?
4. State the concept of MBO.
5. What is time study?

Section B

6. Explain the process of MBO.
7. Discuss the advantages and disadvantages of MBO.
8. What is functional foremanship?

Section C

9. Explain Fayol's principles of management.
10. Discuss the contributions of Taylor to management thought.
11. Explain Hawthorne Experiments and their significance.
12. Explain the findings of Hawthorne experiments.

I. Multiple Choice

1. Observing the influence of illumination upon the levels of output was the objective of
   (a) Relay assembly test group
   (b) Mass interviewing programme
   (c) The bank wiring observation group
   (d) The illumination experiments
2. The principles of ideal bureaucracy was propounded by
   (a) Elton Mayo (b) Max Weber
   (c) Fayol (d) Taylor
3. The line of authority from the chief executive to the lowest level of organisation is called
   (a) Unity of command (b) Unity of direction
   (c) Scalar chain (d) Order

4. During 1924-1932, Hawthorne Experiment was conducted by
   (a) Elton Mayo (b) Follet
   (c) F.W. Taylor (d) None
5. Management by Objectives (MBO) concept was developed by
   (a) Peter F.Drucker (b) Chester Bernard
   (c) Fayol (d) None

Answer:

1. (d) Illumination experiments, 2. (b) Max Weber, 3. (b) Scalar chain, 4. (a) Elton Mayo, 5. (a) Peter F. Drucker

II. Say, 'True or False'

6. Follet applied phychological and sociological methods for solving managerial problems.
7. Scientific selection and education of workers is one of principles of management advocated by F.W. Taylor.
8. MBO starts with the establishment of clear and concise goals.
9. Management by exception (MBE) is advocated by Elton Mayo.
10. The combination of kindness and justice is equality.

Answer:

6. True, 7. True, 8. True, 9. False, 10. False

III. Fill in the blanks

11. ____________ introduced a chart designed for scheduling production activities which is known as Gantt's chart.
12. Under a ______________, rigorous set of rules must be followed.
13. ___________ study is the study of the movement of workers in performing operations.
14. MBO offers the basis for assessing the ______________.

15. The principle of management by exception is to relieve top level executive from ______.

Answer:

11.Henry Laurance Gantt, 12. Bureaucracy, 13. Motion, 14. Performance, 15. Routine matters.

Chapter 4

Planning

Chapter Outline:

Definitions — Characteristics — Elements of Good Planning — Planning Process — Benefits of Planning — Limitations of Planning — Requisites for Making Effective Planning — Final Addition — Model Questions

The term 'planning' has been used by human beings since times immemorial. What else can explain the buildings of the Pyramids and other great wonders of the ancient world. In fact, we cannot conceive of human civilisation without some elements of planning. Hence, a person should plan today in order to flourish tomorrow. Planning enables individuals to bridge the gap between present and future. The necessity of planning also arises because of the fact that business units have to operate, survive and progress in a highly dynamic economy where changes may be sudden and extensive, i.e., changes in technology, consumer's preference, fiscal policies and the like. The managers have to deal with the problems that arise out of these changes. As pointed out by Terry, "Successful managers deal with foreseen problems and unsuccessful managers struggle with unforeseen problems. The difference lies in planning". Hence, planning at the organisational level is a must.

Planning is the fundamental function of management. It is concerned with the future activity. Future is uncertain and its prediction is always difficult. Instead of leaving the future events to chance, they are made to happen in a certain recognised manner through planning.

Planning is the determination of a future course of action to achieve the desired result. It is deciding in advance what to do, how to do it, when to do it and who is to do it. Thus, planning sketches a complete picture of things to happen in the enterprise.

Planning is the beginning of all other processes of management. Planning is basic to all the functions. No organising, staffing or control can be decided without planning. It flows through all the functions, viz., organising, staffing, directing, communication and control as their life-blood.

I. Definitions

1. **Koontz and O'Donnell:** "Planning is an intellectual process, the conscious determination of courses of action, the basing of decision on purpose, acts and considered estimates."
2. **Theo Haimann:** "Planning is deciding in advance what is to be done. When a manager plans, he projects a course of action, for the future, attempting to achieve a consistent, co-ordinated structure of operations aimed at the desired results."
3. **Louis A. Alien:** "Management planning involves the development of forecasts, objectives, policies, programmes, procedures, schedules and budgets."
4. **Joseph Massie:** "Planning is the process by which a manager looks to the future and discovers an alternative course of action open to him."
5. **Alford and Beatty:** "Planning is the thinking process, the organised foresight, the vision based on fact and experience that is required for intelligent action."

II. Characteristics

The following are the characteristics of planning:

(a) Primacy: Planning precedes other functions in the management process. It is the primary requisite before other managerial functions step in. The other managerial functions, viz., organisation, staffing, directing and control, can be performed only after the necessary planning has been done so it gets primary everywhere.

(b) Intellectual Process: Planning is an intellectual process of taking decisions based on the estimated future events. Managers take the necessary steps to fight against future events. So, it is a process of looking ahead.

(c) Pervasive: Planning is a pervasive activity covering the entire enterprise with all its segments and every level of management. It is equally important for large and small firms.

(d) Continuity: Planning is a never-ending activity. One plan makes another plan to be followed by a series of other plans. Again constant changes make planning a continuous activity.

(e) Precision: The meaning, scope and nature of planning must be precise. It must pinpoint the expected results exactly. Any error in planning may lead to serious mistakes in the other functions.

(f) Goal-oriented: Planning involves setting the objectives of an organisation for achieving the business target well in time. Objectives can easily be achieved by a sound planning process.

III. Elements of Good Planning

The planning function which is the basis for other managerial functions has to be performed at all the levels of management. Top management deals with strategic plans which are long-range plans. Middle management is concerned with the tactical administrative plans which are mostly medium-range plans. Lower management is concerned with operational plans which are short-range plans. These can be arranged in a hierarchy, because a higher level plan gives/generates lower level plan as presented below:

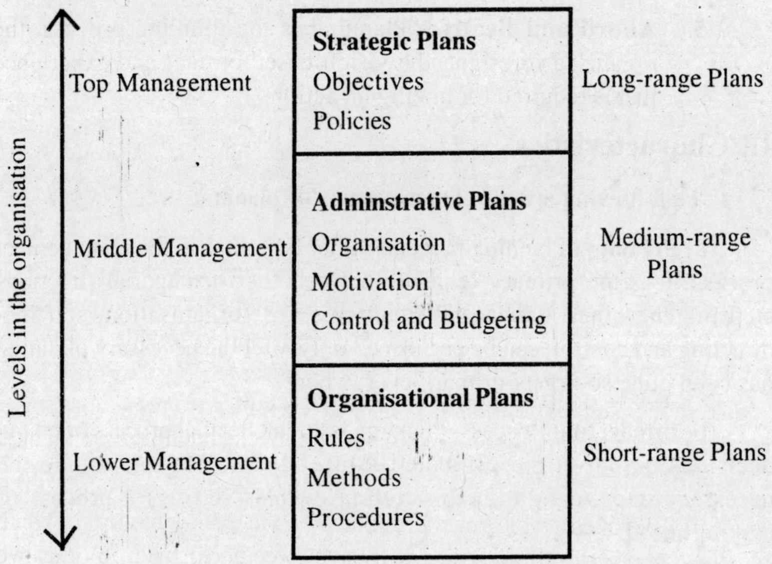

Fig. 4.1 Hierarchy of Plans

The planning has the following elements:

1. Objectives: Organisations are artificially created for achieving some common objectives. Objectives give meaning and purpose to a business enterprise. According to Koontz and O'Donnell, "Objective is a term commonly used to indicate the endpoint of a management programme." From this definition, one can understand that objectives decide where we want to go, what we want to achieve and what is our destination. In other words, objectives are goals established to guide the efforts of the company and to achieve the end result of the business.

Organisational objectives may be classified into two categories, viz.: (i) internal objectives, and (ii) external objectives. Internal objectives relate to the maximum profitability, high liquidity, best services to employees, high return to shareholders and the like. External objectives relate to the services to the customers and their satisfaction. It is rightly pointed out that the management process begins with setting the organisational objectives. Peter Drucker has identified eight key areas in which organisation would set up its objectives. In other words, while establishing the organisational objectives, the following eight areas should be taken into account without fail:

(i) Market standing,
(ii) Productivity,
(iii) Physical and financial resources,
(iv) Profitability,
(v) Innovation,
(vi) Manager performance and development,
(vii) Work performance and attitude, and
(viii) Public and social responsibility

2. Policies: Policies are guideposts for managerial action. Policies are guides to thinking and action of subordinates in any enterprise. It is the general rule, which may be a written statement or oral understanding, to be followed in repetitive situation. For example, promotion of employees within the organisation is a policy to be observed by all. Policies help to attain the objectives of the organisation. Policies are also sub-plans since they also determine some course of action to be followed in order to attain the objectives.

3. Procedures: Procedure indicates the exact manner in which the integrated series of activities will have to be performed. In other words, procedure charts out the specific manner in which actions are taken and accomplished. In other words of George R. Terry, "A procedure is a series of related tasks that make up the chronological sequence and the established way of performing the work to be accomplished." For example, the selection of employees may take the following procedure:

(i) Application form,

(ii) Written test,

(iii) Group discussion,

(iv) Preliminary interview at lower level,

(v) Final interview at top level,

(vi) Medical check up,

(vii) Appointment, and

(viii) Orientation.

Distinctions between Policy and Procedure:

(i) A policy is a guide to thinking whereas a procedure is a guide to action.

(ii) Policies are flexible whereas procedures are rigid.

(iii) A policy lays down the broad area of action whereas a procedure determines the sequence of definite acts.

(iv) Procedures are framed within the jurisdiction of policy.

4. Rules: A rule is a specific and detailed guide to action. Rules are also standing plans, as they prescribe in advance what is to be done or not to be done in a specific situation. Rules are like procedures but rules do not lay down any sequence of action. Rules must be strictly followed. Rules are definite and they do not leave any scope for discretion on the part of subordinates. 'No smoking', 'Stop when the red light is on', 'No entry' are some examples of rules.

5. Strategies: Strategy is described as interpretative planning. In the words of Haimann, "Strategy is an interpretation of policy." The strategy concept is borrowed from military science. In the military, plans are changed and modified very often for the purpose of meeting the movement of the enemy. Similarly, in business enterprise, managers bring changes in corporate plans and policies in accordance with the tactics adopted by competitors. The nature and form of stratgy is not static. It is an action to meet the specific demand of the situation.

6. Programmes: Programme is a sequence of activity to implement the policies. It specifies as step-by-step approach to guide, the action necessary to reach a predetermined goal. It assembles the individual plans in the form of policies and procedures and put them in a workable form to achieve the objectives.

7. Project: A project is a small programme. Each project has a definite goal concerning task assignment and time. It is actually a proposal of investment which can be separately evaluated and appraised through the cost benefit analysis.

8. Schedules: Schedule is a process of establishing a time sequence for the work to be done. It prescribes the exact time when each step would begin and when it would terminate.

9. Budgets: A budget is a plan containing a statement of expected results expressed in numerical terms. Budgets may be prepared in terms of rupee, man-hours or unit.

10. Standards: A standard is a guide for performance evaluation. In other words, it is a norm set by the management in order to evaluate the performance of business activities.

11. Forecasting: The primary purpose of business forecasting is to predict trends in economic conditions. Forecasting reduces uncertainty about the business unit. According to Glueck, "Forecasting is the formal process of predicting future events that will significantly affect the functioning of the enterprise."

IV. Planning Process

The planning process may differ from plan to plan or from one organisation to another. So, it is impossible to prescribe a particular planning process for all organisations and for all types of plans. However, the major steps involved in planning process are given below.

Steps in planning process:

Table 4.1

Sl. No.	Items	Policy	Procedure	Method	Rule
1.	Definition	Guides to decision making.	Guides to action.	One best way of doing things.	Guide to action.
2.	Nature	Indicates the broad area of action	Specifies the broad area of policy	It is one step of procedure	Define what should and should not be done.
3.	Formulation	Formulated at top level of Management	Formulated relatively at the low level of Management.	Formulated after careful research, experimentation and analysis.	Formulated by managers after finding out what is good or what is bad for an employee/organisation.
4.	Discretion	Requires judgement and interpretation	Tells the subordinate exactly what to do in particular situation; used only when discretion is not needed.	Tells the subordinate how one step of a procedure should be formulated.	There is no room for discretion.
5.	Example	Promotion policy Transfer policy Recruitment policy	Promotion procedure indicate the basis for promotion, qualification, experience, specialisation etc.	What is the best way to measure the employee's skills or competence?	'Do not smoke' is a rule.

(i) Determination of objectives.

(ii) Establishment of planning premises.

(iii) Identification of alternative courses of action.

(iv) Evaluation of alternative courses of action.

(v) Selecting the best course of action from the alternatives.

(vi) Formulating action plan.

(vii) Follow-up action.

1. Determination of Objectives: The first step in the planning process is the determination of objectives. The organisational objectives should be segmented into the key areas of operation and then should be divided according to the various departments and sections. The objectives so decided should be specific and clear. Objectives determine what is to be done and what is to be accomplished with the help of other components of planning.

2. Establishment of Planning Premises: Planning is based upon assumptions and predictions. Such assumptions and predictions about the future shape of things are known as planning premises which are classified into the following five categories:

(i) Internal and External Premises: The factors which are available within the business organisation are said to be internal premises. The important internal factors which influence the level of internal planning premises are organisational objectives, policies, programmes, marketing condition, men, materials, money, machines, methods and the like. According to Henry Fayol, the entire plan of an enterprise is made up of many plans called forecasts which very often become basic internal premises. For instance, sales forecasting, capital forecasting, human resources planning, etc., are very crucial for plan formulation. Generally, the following questions may be asked while analysing the internal premises:

(i) Do we have enough resources of men, money, methods, machines, etc.?

(ii) Do we have up-to-date plant and machinery?

(iii) Do we have effective communication system and work environment?

(iv) Is the employee morale high?

(v) Is our profitability and liquidity O.K.?

(vi) Is our managerial leadership effective and so on?

For effective planning, the above-mentioned questions should be considered while taking the planning exercise.

The factors which are external to business organisation are said to be external premises. The important external premises to business enterprise are of a social, economic, political and technological nature. Some of the examples of the external premises are as follows:

(i) Government policies, viz., import and export policy, industrial policy, licence policy, and the like,

(ii) Population growth and structure,

(iii) Employment structure,

(iv) National income,

(v) Price levels,

(vi) Capital market situation,

(vi) Tax structure,

(vii) Regulations of the Reserve Bank of India,

(viii) Guidelines issued by the Registrar of Companies,

(ix) Directives of the Company Law Board.

(ii) Tangible and Intangible Premises: Tangible premises are those which can be seen and touched. It can be quantified one way or the other, such as men, methods, money, time, production and the like. On the other hand, intangible premises are those which are qualitative in nature. Tough intangible premises cannot be quantified, they cannot be ignored while planning. The following are the examples of intangible premises: human relations, company's goodwill, motivation and morale of employees and the attitude of management.

(iii) Constant and Variable Premises: Constant premises are those which behave in the same manner and fashion, irrespective of the course of action taken. Constant premises are definite and well-known. Examples of constant premises are: methods, men, machines, etc. Variable premises are those which are related to the course of action taken, such as the union-management relations, the Government management relations, Registrar of Companies management relations, etc.

(iv) Controllable, Semi-controllable and Uncontrollable: Controllable premises are those which are subject to the decisions of management and they are within the jurisdiction of the management. The examples of controllable premises are policies, procedures, rules and regulations, code of discipline, etc. followed in the organisation. These premises are controllable since they are formulated by the management.

Semi-controllable premises are those which can be controlled partially by the management. The examples of such premises are: labour-management relations, the demand of industry on the firm's share in the market, etc.

Uncontrollable premises are those which cannot be controlled completely by the management. The examples of such premises are: war, natural hazards, cyclones, earthquakes, emergency legislations, new discoveries and invention of new substitutes, etc.

(v) Foreseeable and Unforeseeable Premises: Foreseeable premises are those which are definite and well-known. They can be foreseen with certainty. Examples of foreseeable premises are: requirements of human resources, finance, materials, machines, etc. On the other hand, unforeseeable premises are those which may or may not have arisen in the course of action taken. Examples of such premises are strikes, lay-offs, lock-outs, wars, natural calamities, non-availability of materials, etc.

3. Identification of Alternative Courses of Action: Based on the objectives and planning premises, various alternatives are identified. Then the manager has to examine the various identified alternatives carefully in the light of planning premises.

4. Evaluation of Alternative Courses of Action: It is the real point of decision making. The manager is expected to compare the relative importance of the alternative courses of action by weighing the complex factors, both tangible and intangible, involved in each case. Examples of tangible factors are profit, cost, funds, return on capital and break-even point. The intangible factors are goodwill, public relations, morale of workers and the like. After a careful consideration of all the factors, the alternatives are evaluated through the operation methods. Then one of them is recommendated for selection.

5. Selecting the Best Course of Action from Alternatives: After evaluating the various alternatives, the best alternative is selected and decision is taken according to the choice made. The business enterprise then follows the suggested course of action.

6. Formulating Action Plan: After the best course of action is selected, the next task is to formulate derivative plans for the actual implementation of the basic plan. Therefore, derivative plans are made for each segment of the business enterprise like personnel, materials, production, marketing, finance and accounting. Derivative plans set the targets for the period ranging from one year to two years. Derivative plans integrate the objectives, policies, procedures, programmes, schedules and budgets of an organisation.

7. Follow-up Action: The basic plan and sub-plans so prepared are to be carried out. Then the actual performance is compared with the predicated performance. For this purpose, follow-up action is needed for taking actions. Hence, a regular follow-up action is needed for the effective implementation and accomplishment of the tasks assigned.

V. Benefits of Planning

There are many points in favour of planning. Some of the important benefits are summarised below:

1. Economy: Effective plans co-ordinate the organisational work and eliminate unproductive effort. Though planning involves a lot of time, energy and money for its formulation and implementation, it tends to minimise the costs of performance.

2. Enhances the Organisational Behaviour Climate: Planning provides scientific guidelines to its human resources to contribute positively and achieve the overall objectives of the organisation. When objectives are perfectly defined, job assignment can be fixed and everyone can begin to contribute the achievement of these objectives. This tends to improve the morale of the employees.

3. Reduces Random Activity: Planning involves an intelligent thinking. Every manager puts his thoughts in writing before acting. This allows manager to identify early problems as well as remedial measures. By thinking, a manager can minimise the chances of making hasty decisions and taking haphazard action. Moreover, planning minimises the chance of mistakes and unpleasant surprises. It helps in avoiding crisis management.

4. Leads to Overall Efficiency in the Organisation: Planning is a key to managerial success. By proper planning, the management can utilise the available resources effectively in order to achieve the goals of the organisation.

5. Provides Direction: Planning provides direction and a sense of purpose to the organisation. Once the organisation is able to find out what it cannot do over the next one year to five years, it can begin setting meaningful objectives.

6. Provides Basis for Control: Planning and control are said to be like the Siamese twins, i.e., inseparable. The control function depends on planning. Without planning, there is nothing to control but without control, planning is a wasteful and unproductive exercise. A manager can check the performance of the various departments, viz., production, marketing, finance and the like only by proper planning. A manager can compare the performance with the standard of targets laid down by the process of planning. Thus, it provides the basis for control.

VI. Limitations of Planning

It is rightly said that planning is not always on the credit side of the ledger. Planning will not give remedies to all types of management problems. Hence, it is not free from limitations. Some of the important limitations are discussed below.

1. Planning is Costly: Planning involves a lot of time, labour and money in collecting information, evaluating alternatives and selecting the best course of action. Planning cost increases when planning becomes more elaborate and formalised. Due to elaborate planning, additional personnel is to be recruited in order to carry out the planning activities. This tends to increase labour cost also. It is rightly pointed out that planning consumes much but contributes less. Since planning involves huge finance, it cannot be undertaken beyond a certain level. Before implementing a plan, the manager should be very careful about the cost proposition of such plan. Hence, it is a costly exercise.

2. Mental Attitude of Management Makes Planning a Wasteful Effort: Planning depends heavily on the values and mental attitude of management at various levels of the organisation. When the attitude of the management is not up to the mark, planning becomes a wasteful effort. Sometimes, managers are reluctant and they are psychologically opposed to planning as they think that the present is more important than the future. This kind of attitude seriously affects the planning activities which finally give room for the failure of business.

3. Dynamic Conditions Affect Planning Exercise: It is true that changes in the environment reduce the effectiveness of planning efforts. It is difficult for planners to forecast economic conditions. Besides, the assumptions on which planning is based may not hold good and the conditions under which plans are being implemented may differ from the assumed conditions. Hence, dynamic conditions makes the planners modify or revise the plans in accordance with the prevailing situation. Hence, planners should be careful about the business environment.

4. Premises May not be Fully Reliable: A plan depends upon reliable facts and information. If reliable informations are not available, planning will lose much of its value.

5. Planning is Time-consuming: Availability of time is also a limiting factor of planning. It is expensive in terms of time spent to formulate plans. Sometimes, it causes delay in taking action. An emergency situation in business requires prompt action and allow little time for thinking and planning. Therefore, at the time of an emergency, planning becomes upset completely and decisions made hand-to-mouth. Excessive time spent on completing the planning process directly affects the smooth functioning of the organisation.

VII. Requisites for Making Effective Planning

One should not believe that planning is wasteful work due to the various limitations. It is accepted that planning is an essential managerial function. Hence, managers should take precautions to make the planning exercise effective. The following factors help the manager to overcome the limitations and make the planning exercise effective.

1. Setting up an Effective Planning Department: Every business organisation should set up a separate department for carrying out the planning activites. This planning department tries to remove obstacles of planning by using the services of superior manager.

2. Participation in Planning Process: Plans are implemented by people. So, it is necessary to secure acceptance and commitment from them. One way to make plans effective is to solicit subordinate-manager's participation in the planning process.

3. The Plan Must be a Sound One: It is the top management which is responsible for the success or failure of any organisational process and planning is no exception. Therefore, while making the planning exercise, the top management should set the goals and objectives of the organisation clearly. Moreover, the top management should introduce an open system approach in order to make plans effective. This system suggests that managers must take into account interactions within their total environment in every aspect of planning to develop a sound plan.

4. Revise the Basic Plan Whenever Necessary: In a dynamic environment, planning is a situational process. To cope with the changing environment, situational plans must be developed. For this purpose, management should review its plans annually so as to match external opportunities with organisational resources in a proper way.

5. Integration of Long-term and Short-term Plans: It is advisable that both the long-term and short-term plans are integrated in order to make them effective.

6. Fit the Plan to the Situation: Planning, especially strategic planning, is a situational process. The problems of change require a situational approach to planning. For instance, in an attempt to capture the ever increasing demand for video sets, Philips India Limited obtained licence for manufacturing video sets. Now, the company has a wide product structure such as, audio sets, bulbs, video sets, assembling television etc. So, to cope with changing environment, situational plans must be developed.

VIII. Final Addition

Corporate Planning in Indian Organisation: When planning activity is undertaken at various levels of the organisation, it is called corporate planning. In management science, corporate planning, strategic planning and long-range planning are used interchangeably. Corporate planning covers many management functions not necessarily related to planning aspect only.

Corporate Planning in Indian organisations has received importance during the last 20 years. The importance is primarily due to the complexity of the problems on which the managers have to make decisions. Many companies in private and public sector have set up a separate corporate planning wing and they have formalised the planning process. The planning process at Associated Cement Company Limited is explained below.

Planning at Associated Cement Company Limited: Planning process at A.C.C. Limited includes both long-term and short-term. Long-term planning consists of policy decisions and it is generally based on the basis of a five-year plan. The decisions are finalised at the level of Board of Directors with regard to programmes, such as rehabilitation, expansion and diversification. These programmes require thorough analysis of the situation since they involve high cost of investment and longer gestation period.

Short-term plans are prepared in three areas such as, production, despatches and costs. Minute details are worked out in each of these areas. Steps involved in each of these areas start with the preparation of targets by various production units located at different places. These targets are submitted to the Head Office located at Mumbai for scrutiny, which scrutinises the targets in the light of those achievable under optimum conditions. Targets fixed under this process may be slightly higher than the targets submitted by each unit. These targets work as motivating factor to the various production units. The targets so envisaged by the Head Office are then discussed by the Head of the units. Thereafter, the agreed targets are fixed. These targets are put before the Executive Committee of Directors which analyse the information and makes suitable changes, if necessary, and places it before the Board of Directors which finally lays down the plans. Besides, capital and revenue budgets are prepared by the Head Office in the, form of consolidation of budgets prepared by various production units.

Model Questions

Section A

1. Define the term "Planning."
2. What is meant by planning premises?
3. What is strategy?
4. Distinguish between planning and forecasting.
5. Are policies a guidepost for managerial action?
6. What is policy?
7. What is objective?

Section B

8. "Planning is looking ahead and control is looking back." Discuss.
9. What are the limitations of planning?

10. Explain the need of planning in a modern complex organisation.
11. "Planning is the essence of management." Elucidate.
12. What are the benefits of planning?
13. Distinguish between policy and procedure.

Section C

14. Describe the elements of planning.
15. Elaborately explain the steps involved in the planning process in a modern organisation.
16. Bring out clearly the nature, scope and characteristics of planning in a business organisation.
17. What are the major planning premises for plan formulation?
18. Briefly explain the requisites for making planning effective.

I. Multiple Choice

1. Code of conduct is an example of
   (a) Controllable premise (b) Semi-controllable
   (c) Uncontrollable (d) Intangible controllable
2. A small programme is called
   (a) Schedule (b) Project
   (c) Budget (d) None
3. Guidepost for managerial action is
   (a) Rule (b) Policy
   (c) Programme (d) Strategy
4. A sequence of activities to implement the policy is
   (a) Programme (b) Budget
   (c) Plan (d) Procedure
5. Policies are
   (a) Short-range plan (b) Medium-term plan
   (c) Long-range plan (d) All

Answer:

1. (a) Controllable premise, 2. (b) Project, 3. (a) Rule, 4. (a) programme, 5. (d) All

II. Say, 'True or False'

6. Planning is the fundamental function of management.
7. Middle management is concerned with the tactical administrative plans.
8. A rule is a specific and detailed guide to action.
9. Planning is looking ahead and control is looking back.
10. Programme is not a sequence of activity to implement the policies.

Answer:

6. True. 7. True. 8. True, 9. True, 10. False

III. Fill in the blanks

11. Planning is the ____________ process.
12. Lower level management is concerned with the tactical administrative plans which are ____________.
13. ____________ indicates the exact manner in which the integrated serious of activities will have to be performed.
14. Policies are flexible whereas procedure are ____________.
15. ____________ is described as interpretative planning.

Answer:

11. Thinking, 12. Short – range plans, 13. Procedures 14. Rigid, 15. Strategy

Chapter 5

Decision-making

Chapter Outline:

Definitions — Characteristics of Decision-making — Nature and Importance — Types of Decisions — Theories of Decision-making — The Decision-making Process — Guidelines for Effective Decision-making — Model Questions

A decision is an act of choice wherein an executive forms a conclusion about what must be done in a given situation. In other words, a decision is the selection of the best course of action from among a set of alternatives. The word 'decision' is derived from the Latin word, 'Deciso' meaning ‘cutting away or cutting off’ or ‘in practical content,’ 'to come to a conclusion.'

A decision represents judgement. It implies freedom to the decision-maker regarding the final choice. In fact, decision-making is a universal requirement for all human beings. Each of us make decisions every day in our lives. For example, surgeons make life-and-death decisions, engineers make decisions on constructing projects, etc.

Executive ability is very often judged by the decision he makes. According to Peter Drucker, “Whatever a manager does, he does through decision-making.” So, decision-making is a central part of the management process. For any management, decision-making is the foremost function. A manager taking action against his subordinates is a kind of decision. While manager aims at profit maximisation he takes another kind of decision. Therefore, the manager right from the beginning takes decision after decision in order to achieve the desired results. That is why decision-making is sometimes described as 'the total task of a manager' or 'the heart of managing'.

I. Definitions

Various management thinkers have defined decision-making as follows:

1. **George R. Terry:** "Decision-making is the selection based on some criteria from two or more possible alternatives."
2. **Haynes and Massie:** "A decision is a course of action which is consciously chosen for achieving a desired result."
3. **Ray A. Killian:** "A decision in its simplest form is a selection of alternatives."
4. **Franklin G. Moore:** "Decision-making is a blend of thinking, deciding and acting."
5. **R.S. Davar:** "Decision-making may be defined as the selection based on some criteria of one behaviour alternative from two or more possible alternatives."

From the above definitions, it is clear that decisions are made to arrive at a solution for a given problem.

II. Characteristics of Decision-making

The following are the characteristics of decision-making:

(i) Decision-making is a choice between different available alternatives.

(ii) Decision-making is an intellectual process.

(iii) Decision-making is a continuous process that pervades all business activities.

(iv) Decision-making permeates all levels of management and covers every part of enterprise.

(v) Decision-making aims at achieving the organisational objectives.

III. Nature and Importance

Decision-making should be distinguished from problem-solving and choice-making. According to George P. Huber, choke-making is narrow in scope and refers to selecting the best one from among many alternatives. Problem-solving, on the other hand, is a broad term and refers to the broad set of activities necessary to find and implement a course of action.

1. **Goal-oriented:** Decision-making is goal-oriented process. Decisions are usually made to achieve the desired results.
2. **Dynamic Process:** It is characterised as a process. It is a process of using inputs effectively in finding out the solution of selected problems and the creation of outputs that have utility.
3. **Alternatives:** A decision problem implies a choice, choosing the best from among two or more alternative courses of action.

IV. Types of Decisions

Decisions may be of different types. Some of the important types of decisions are given below:

1. Basic and Routine Decisions: Basic decisions are concerned with the unique problems and one-time decisions demanding huge investment, such as a decision regarding new plant, computerisation, diversification of product line etc. Basic decisions require creativity, intuition and good judgement on the part of managers. On the other hand, routine decisions are repetitive in nature. It is concerned with short-term investment. For example, a manager can decide whether an employee's absence from work is excused or not based on the personnel policy.

2. Personal and Organisational Decisions: Personal decisions are made by a single individual. Decision to retire early, to resign the post are examples of personal decision which affect the organisation in an indirect way. For instance, the sudden decision of a popular cricketer to seek premature retirement may affect the cricket team badly. On the other hand, organisational decisions are made by managers in their formal capacity as managers. Such decisions reflect the basic policy of the company. Decisions relating to payment of dividend, alteration of authorised capital, capacity utilisation, adoption of new production technology, purchasing practice, and the like are examples of organisational decisions.

3. Programmed and Unprogrammed Decisions: Programmed decisions are repetitive in nature. Such decisions are made by lower level personnel. Such decisions are taken with a broad policy structure. Rules and policies are established well in advance to solve such recurring problems quickly. For example, granting leave to employees, purchase of raw materials, disciplinary action against late-comers etc., are programmed decisions. On the other hand, unprogrammed decisions are of a non-repetitive nature. Such decisions deal with unusual problems. Deciding where to locate a new branch office, when to propose to the branch manager, whether to wind up a sick unit or not are examples of unprogrammed decisions.

4. Major and Minor Decisions: Decisions may be classified as major and minor. For example, the decision relating to the purchase of a big generator worth of ₹ 10 lakh is a major decision. On the other hand, purchase of spare parts for the generator is a minor matter and may be decided by the factory supervisor.

V. Theories of Decision-making

The success or failure of an organisation depends upon managerial decisions. So, managers are supposed to be aware of the various theories of decision-making which help to solve problems by taking suitable actions. The following are the important theories of decision-making developed management thinkers:

1. The intuition or the traditional theory;
2. The classical theory; and
3. The administrative man or the behavioural theory.

1. The Traditional Theory: According to this theory, managerial decisions are taken by intuition. Intuition means taking a decision without really considering all the alternatives. So, it is otherwise known as intuition theory of decision-making. Here, a manager simply decides upon a course of action because he feels that the particular course of action is the best one. The major demerit of this theory is that rational thinking is ignored.

2. The Classical Theory: This theory implies that decisions are made rationally cent per cent perfect after considering the pros and cons of all the alternatives carefully. It overcomes the limitation of the traditional theory.

3. The Administrative Man or The Behavioural Theory: According to this theory, decisions are made on the basis of a limited model of the real situation. This theory implies that a manager makes decisions not only on the basis of facts and figures but also on the basis of his intuition, thinking capacity, habit and value system. So, it is called the behavioural theory.

The administrative model developed by Herbert A. Simon is associated with the decision-making behaviour of individuals and organisations. According to him, decision-makers are not able to make perfectly rational decisions due to lack of sufficient knowledge and ability to evaluate the alternatives. Besides, they work under conditions of bounded rationality. That is why Simon described his model as the "principle of bounded rationality." It means that the decision-maker rarely tries to find out the optimum solution to a problem. Moreover, instead of searching for and choosing the best alternatives, many decision-makers accept decisions that are only good enough rather than ideal. Such decisions are said to be "satisficing decisions." Fair price and reasonable profit are examples of satisficing decisions.

In recent times, quantitative techniques have been developed by modern thinkers. It consists of the game theory, linear programming, transportation, PERT CPM. etc., through which managerial problems can be solved scientifically.

VI. The Decision-making Process

In making decisions, the manager should observe certain steps and follow them in the proper sequence. The following are the six steps in decision-making process:

1. Identifying managerial problems.
2. Formulating managerial problems.
3. Developing alternative courses of action.
4. Evaluating the alternatives.
5. Selecting the best alternative.
6. Implementing and following up.

1. Identifying Managerial Problems: The first step in the decision-making process is recognising and identifying a managerial problem. An executive should be aware of the problem which requires immediate action. For example, sales of the organisation might be falling down during the last two years due to changes in competitive situation, higher operating costs, government regulations and the like. In order to perceive the problem, the executive is expected to monitor the environment of decision-making, knowing the possible causes and tries to define the real problem with the help of reports and statements. Therefore, executives should use their knowledge and experience in order to identify the exact nature of the problem.

2. Formulating Managerial Problems: Once the manager is aware of the problem, he must state the real problem. A problem well-defined is half-solved. So, problems identified should be formulated and stated in understandable manner. In order to state the real problem, the following questions should be considered:

(i) What is the problem?
(ii) Which problems to solve? and
(iii) What is the real course of the problem?

The manager is expected to find out the answer to the above questions while defining the problem.

3. Developing Alternative Courses of Action: After the problem is identified and formulated, the manager has to determine the available alternative courses of action that could be used to solve the problem. While developing the alternatives, the following points may be taken into account:

(i) Only realistic alternatives must be included in the list;
(ii) Factors like various laws and regulations, corporate policies, timing, cost, psychological aspects, etc., should be kept in mind;
(iii) Managers should apply creativity;
(iv) While developing alternatives, techniques like brainstorming and group participation may be effectively used; and
(v) While listing alternatives, the negative aspects should be ignored.

So, the development of alternatives is an innovative activity. It calls for divergent thinking of the decision-makers. For example, in an organisation, productivity has been declining due to the low morale of employees. To improve the morale of employees, the personnel manager of the organisation has developed the following alternatives:

(i) Adequate compensation package;
(ii) Incentive schemes for improved performance;
(iii) Restructuring the workload;
(iv) Offering internal promotion; and
(v) Providing children education scheme.

4. Evaluating the Alternatives: After developing the alternatives, the manager should try to compare the merits and demerits of each alternative through some criteria, such as the element of risk involved, economy of effort, resources available for implementation, results expected and the like. For example, while making the decision on purchasing a two-wheeler, a decision-maker might decide the four factors and decide to assign the following weights for them: External appearance (10), Price (6), Fuel (5), After-sales service (4). Table 5.1 indicates the evaluation of alternatives.

Table 5.1

Evaluation of Alternatives

Criteria	Rating-Alternatives				
	Weights	Moped	Hero-Honda	Bajaj Scooter	Bullet
External Appearence	10	5	8	7	10
Price	6	10	6	8	6
Fuel Savings	5	8	10	9	6
After-sales Service	4	6	6	10	8
Total		174	190	203	198

* Total expressed after multiplying the criteria with weights.

(Adapted from S.P. Robins, *Management*, Englewood Cliffs, N.J., Prentice-Hall, 1984, pp. 75-76).

The above rating is based on the assessment made by the decision-maker himself.

5. Selecting the Best Alternative: In this step, the manager selects the alternative that will maximise the results in terms of existing objectives. In other words, a manager should select the best alternative that solves the problem. In the above example, the decision-maker may select Bajaj Scooter as it indicates the highest point (203). Once the final choice is made, the next stage is to implement the decision.

6. Implementation and Follow-up: After selecting the best alternative, the manager is supposed to communicate to those members of organisation who are concerned with the problems. Effectiveness of decision in achieving the desired goals depends on its implementation. Further follow-up systems is essential to modify decision. It would be better to establish follow-up procedures to evaluate the implemented decision. Such follow-up systems ensures the achievement of organisational objectives.

VII. Guidelines for Effective Decision-making

The following guidelines are suggested for effective decision-making:

1. **Define the Goals:** Decision-making is goal-oriented. So, the goals achieved should be defined clearly and definitely.
2. **Ensure that the Decision Contributes to the Goal:** While making decision, the manager should select the best alternative that solves the managerial problem. In other words, the decision made should maximise the desired results.
3. **Adopt a Diagnostic Approach to Decision-making:** While making decision, the manager should find out the causes for the problems and try to give remedial measures from among alternatives.
4. **Ensure Successful Implementation of the Decision through Follow-up Procedures.**
5. **Evaluate the Result.**
6. **Be Flexible and Revise the Decision:** If the decision does not yield desired result, it should be revised.

Model Questions

Section A

1. Define decision-making.
2. What is rational decision?
3. Distinguish between decision-making and problem-solving.
4. "A problem well-defined is half-solved." Do you agree?
5. What is bounded rationality?

Section B

6. "Decision-making is the primary task of management," Discuss.
7. What are the basic elements of decision-making?
8. What are the characteristics of a good decision?
9. Explain the importance of decision-making.
10. "Good decision-making must be evaluated against future events." Comment.

Section C

11. Describe the process involved in making a decision.
12. Briefly explain the various theories of decision-making.
13. Enumerate the various types of decisions an executive is expected to take while running a business unit.

I. Multiple Choice

1. Decision to retire early by an employee is an example for
   (a) Organisational decision (b) Routine decision
   (c) Programmed decision (d) Personal decision
2. Managerial decisions are taken by intuition according to
   (a) The traditional theory (b) The classical theory
   (c) The behavioural theory (d) None
3. Effective decision-making should
   (a) Define the goals (b) Evaluate the result
   (c) Contribute to the goals (d) All
4. Purchase of spare parts for motor is an example for
   (a) Major decision (b) Minor decision
   (c) Personal decision (d) Basic decision
5. Programmed decisions are made at
   (a) Lower level (b) Middle level
   (c) Top level (d) All

Answer:

1. (d) Personal decision, 2. (a) The traditional theory, 3. (d) All, 4. (b) Minor decision, 5. (d) All.

II. Say, 'True or False'

6. Decision-making is a blend of thinking, deciding and activity.
7. Basic decisions are concerned with the unique problem.
8. The administrative model developed by Herbert A. Simon is associated with the decision-making behaviour of individuals.
9. Decision-making is goal-oriented process.

10. The development of alternatives does not call for divergent thinking of the decision-making.

Answer:

6. True, 7. True, 8. True, 9. True, 10, False.

III. Fill in the blanks

11. Decision-making is an ____________ process.
12. Development of alternative is an __________ activity.
13. A problem well-defined is __________ solved.
14. Organisational decisions are made by ____________.
15. In decision-making process, a manager should select the best alternative that solves the ____________.

Answer:

11. Intellectual, 12. Innovative, 13. Half, 14. Managers, 15. Problem.

Chapter 6

Organisation — Nature and Purpose

Chapter Outline:

Definitions — Elements of Organisation — Steps in Organisation — Importance — Types — Organisational Charts and Manuals — Model Questions

A sound organisation is the prerequisite for the success of any business enterprise. Organisation is the foundation upon which the entire structure of management is constructed.

The term 'organisation' is viewed in two ways: (i) Organisation as a structure; and (ii) Organisation as a process.

(i) Organisation as a structure means a network of specific relationships between individuals in an organisation, e.g., superior-subordinate relationship.

(ii) Organisation as a process means identifying, classifying, grouping and assigning various activities required to achieve the objectives.

After determining the objectives and deciding the plan, the next step in the management process is organising the activities to achieve the objectives.

I. Definitions

1. Louis A. Alien: "Organisation is the process of identifying and grouping the work to be performed, defining and delegating responsibility and authority and establishing relationships for the purpose of enabling people to work most effectively together in accomplishing objectives."

2. Oliver Sheldon: "Organisation is the process of combining the work which individuals and groups have to perform with the faculties necessary for its execution that the duties so formed provide the best channels for efficient, systematic, positive and co-ordinated application of available efforts."

3. Theo Haimann: "Organising is the process of defining and grouping the activities of the enterprise and establishing the authority relationships among them."

4. Mooney and Reiley: "Organisation is the form of every human association for the attainment of a common purpose. It is a process of relating specific duties or functions in a co-ordinated whole."

5. Harold Koontz: "Organisation means a formalised intentional structure of roles."

II. Elements of Organisation

The above definitions point out the following elements to organising:

1. Identification and classification of activities necessary to accomplish objectives.
2. Grouping these activities in the light of material and human resources.
3. Defining of responsibility.
4. Delegation of authority necessary to perform the activities.
5. Tying these groups vertically and horizontally through authority relationship and information flows.

III. Steps in Organisation

The following are the steps involved in organisation:

1. Identification of Activities: The entire work is broken down into component activities that are to be performed by all the employees.

2. Grouping of Activities: The closely-related and similar activities are grouped into departments or divisions. The departmental activities are further divided into sections. Grouping is done primarily on the basis of functions like production, sales etc. Then they are grouped on the basis of customers or process or geographical area.

3. Assigning Activities: The grouped activities are assigned to various positions such as the production manager, sales manager etc. The process of assignment of activities is carried down to the operative level of management.

4. Delegation of Authority: To discharge the responsibility, the employees must be given required authority.

5. Establishing Structural Relationship: The last step in the organisation process is defining the relationship among the people in the organisation in clear terms. Only then a person will know from whom he has to receive orders and to whom he is answerable. It enables people to work harmoniously together under all possible circumstances.

IV. Importance of Organisation

1. **Ensures Success of the Business:** A sound organisation contributes to the continuity and success of the organisation. If it is logical, clear-cut and streamlined to meet the present-day requirements, then the first requisite of sound management is achieved.
2. **Foster Co-ordination:** Different departments and sections, positions and jobs, functions and activities are welded together by structural relationship. This facilitates co-ordination.
3. **Avoid Duplication:** A proper organisation avoids duplication of activities. Poor organisation leads to the actual duplication of functions by managers as well as duplication of records.
4. **Facilitates Growth:** An organisation grows within the organisation structure which serves as the framework. Unless the organisation permits, expansion and diversification cannot proceed any further.
5. **Effective Delegation:** By proper division of labour, consistent delegation and clear job definition, the organisation structure relieves the managers of routine work. They devote most of their energy to planning for the future.
6. **Optimum Use of Human Resources:** Detailed job specification, right persons in the right job and matching of job with individuals enable the optimum use of human resources.
7. **Initiative:** A sound organisation induces independent creative thinking and initiative by providing well-defined areas of work and developing new and improved ways of doing things.

8. **Optimum Use of Technological Improvements:** A proper organisation structure responds to new technological developments. The high cost of installing, operating and maintaining data processing equipments necessitates a proper organisation structure.

V. Types of Organisations

Organisation may be classified as formal and informal organisation.

Formal Organisation: A formal organisation is deliberately designed to achieve the objectives of the enterprise. It is a system of well-defined jobs, each having a definite autority, responsibility and accountability. It is designed in advance and depicted in an organisation chart. A formal organisation is more or less an arbitrary structure. The individuals should adjust to the structure.

Informal Organisation: Within the formal organisation, informal groups develop spontaneously on the basis of friendship or common interest. Such an association of people is called an informal organisation. It represents a group or a number of groups to meet the needs and aspirations of members. An informal organisation refers to people's action in terms of needs and emotions and attitudes, not in terms of procedures and regulations. It has an unwritten constitution and conventions. The informal organisation is a necessary part of every company. The formal organisation which fails to recognise and provide for the operation of informal groups, loses its effectiveness.

VI. Organisation Charts and Manuals

An Organisation Chart is a diagrammatical representation of an organisation. It indicates the major functions and their relationship. The main line of communication, the downward flow of authority and upward flow of responsibility through all levels of management hierarchy are depicted in the chart.

Types of Charts

The Organisation Charts may be classified as: (i) Vertical; (ii) Horizontal; and (iii) Concentric or circular.

A vertical chart show the organisational structure in the form of a pyramid. The line of command proceeds from the top to the bottom in vertical lines.

A horizontal chart shows the organisational structure in the form of a pyramid which lies horizontally. The line of command moves from left to right. The highest position is shown at the left and the lower positions move toward the right.

A circular or concentric chart shows the top executive in the centre of the circle and the successive positions extend in all directions outward from the centre.

Organisational Manual

An organisational manual is prepared to show in detail the job descriptions as well as each position's relationship with other parts of the organisation. It serves as a useful supplement to organisation charts. It is usually in the form of book or booklet. A manual is an authoritative guide to the company's overall organisation.

Model Questions

Section A

1. Define organisation.
2. What are the elements of organisation?
3. What is organisational manual?

Section B

4. Describe the steps involved in organisation.
5. What are the advantages of organisation?
6. Distinguish between a formal and an informal organisation.
7. What is an organisation chart? Explain its types.

I. Multiple Choice

1. Organisation means a formalised intentional structure of
   (a) Roles (b) Rooms
   (c) Route (d) None
2. A proper organisation avoids duplication of
   (a) Action (b) Activities
   (c) Assets (d) None
3. An informal organisation represents a group to meet the needs of members
   (a) Not Officially (b) Officially
   (c) Legally (d) None

4. An organisation manual is prepared to show in detail the
   (a) Job description (b) Culture
   (c) Satisfaction (d) None
5. A circular chart shows the top executive in the centre of the
   (a) Control (b) Coverage
   (c) Circle (d) None

Answer:

1. (a) Roles, 2. (b) Activities, 3. (a) Not Officially, 4. (a) Job description, 5. (c) Circle

II. Say, 'True or False'

6. Organisation means a network of specific relationships between individuals.
7. Informal organisation is a system of well-defined jobs, each having a definite authority and responsibility.
8. An organisation chart is a diagrammatical representation of an organisation.
9. An organisation manual is an authoritative guide to the company's overall organisation.
10. Defining of responsibility is not one of the elements of organisation.

Answer:

6. True, 7. False, 8. True, 9. True, 10. False.

III. Fill in the blanks

11. Assigning activities is one of the steps in ______________.
12. A vertical chart shows the organisational structure in the form of a ______________.
13. A horizontal chart shows organisational structure in the form of a pyramid which lies ______________.
14. Defining the relationship among the people in clear terms is the ______________ step in the process of organisation.
15. Organisation is the form of every human association for the attainment of a common ______________.

Answer:

11. Organisation, 12. Pyramid, 13. Horizontally, 14. Last, 15. Purpose

Chapter 7

Departmentation

Chapter Outline:

Basis of Departmentation — By Number — By Time — By Function — By Product — By Territory — By Customer — By Process or Equipment — Matrix Organisation — By Mixing Types — Model Questions

The process of organisation involves identifying activities necessary to attain the objectives of the enterprise and the grouping of similar activities on some logical basis. The process of dividing and grouping related activities into units and smaller units for purposes of administration is called departmentation. The units are designated as divisions, units, branches, sections, jobs etc. Such units are managed as relatively independent administrative units and are accountable for their own objectives.

Koontz and O' Donnell define a department as "a distinct area, division or branch of an enterprise over which a manager has authority for the performance of specified activities."

I. Basis of Departmentation

There is no single best way of departmentation applicable to all organisations.

A brief description of the important bases of departmentation are discussed below.

II. Departmentation by Number

Departmentation by number was widely prevalent in the army and it was used among people who were performing similar duties. With advanced technology and specialisation, the usefulness of this departmentation has declined over the decades. Moreover, it is only useful at the lowest level of the organisation structure.

III. Departmentation by Time

At the lower levels of organisation, activities are grouped on the basis of time. When the normal workday is not adequate for economic and technological reasons, using of shifts is commonly adopted. In organisations, like hospitals railways etc. that work round the clock departmentation is based on time. The basic advantage of departmentation by time is that it makes manpower utilisation efficient.

IV. Departmentation by Function

In this method, all similar activities of the enterprise are grouped into major departments on the basis of basic functions such as production, marketing, personnel and finance. Within the major functional department, a manager may create secondary functions. For example, marketing department may be divided into sales, sales administration, advertising and sales promotion, marketing research etc. Fig. 7.1 shows departmentation by functions.

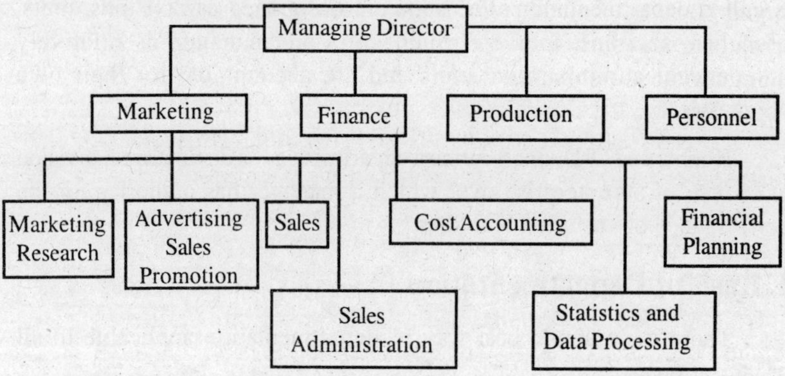

Fig. 7.1 Departmentation by Functions

This type of departmentation is suitable for small and medium-sized organisations.

Merits

The advantages of departmentation by functions are:

1. Creates efficiency through specialisation.
2. Easy to understand the structure as it is a logical reflection of functions.
3. Interdepartmental co-ordination is made easy.
4. Permit tight control at the top.
5. Effective utilisation of manpower and other resources.

Demerits

1. It is non-responsive to environmental changes.
2. Every manager supervises a narrow function. So, the responsibility for total performance rests with top management.
3. Co-ordination between functions is difficult.
4. Unsuitable when the operations cover a wider area.
5. Delay in decision-making due to overspecialisation.

V. Departmentation by Product

In large-scale enterprises, activities are grouped on the basis of product or product line. Product departmentation involves establishing each product as a relatively autonomous, integrated unit within the framework of the company as a whole. Departmentation by product should be resorted to when the maximum emphasis is to be placed on product expansion and diversification. The product and market characteristics also should be favourable for this dapartmentation. Fig. 7.2 shows the departmentation by product.

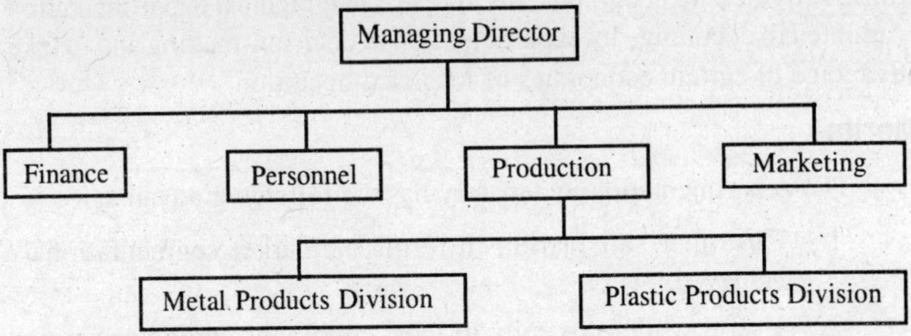

Fig. 7.2 Departmentation by Product

Merits

1. It simplifies the determination of profitability of each product line.
2. Top management secures more detailed information regardingthe markets with respect to specific products.
3. Often, it results in good customer relationship.
4. It furnishes measurable training ground for general managers.
5. A new division can be added without interrupting the existing structure. It permits growth and diversity of products and services.

Demerits

1. It Involves maintaining separate sales personnel for each product and results in duplication of money and resources.
2. Top management is forced to share the greater burden of establishing greater co-ordination and control.

Du Pont Company has different product groups such as electrochemical products, paints, varnishes, pigments, inorganic chemicals, nitro-cellulose plastics, rubber coated fabrics, textile, paper, dyes, ammonia, rayon and cellophane.

VI. Departmentation by Territory

Geographic departmentation means grouping of the primary activities of the business in terms of the geographic region or area to be served. The geographic division becomes a relatively complete administrative unit in itself, capable of catering to the needs of the region which constitutes its boundaries. Territorial departmentation is suitable for large-scale firms whose activities are geographically spread. Geographical departmentation is adopted to encourage local participation in decision-making and to take advantage of certain economies of localised operation.

Merits

The departmentation by territory has the following advantages:

1. Customer satisfaction in terms of market segmentation is achieved.
2. Useful while proximity to local conditions and opportunities result in low cost of operation such as lower freight charges, lower labour costs and lower rent.

3. Provides a good training ground for the salesmen to become sales supervisors.
4. Saves a substantial amount of transport costs.
5. Meets the demands of various regions effectively.

Demerits

1. More persons with managerial abilities are required.
2. Increases the problems of headquarters control.
3. High costs of co-ordination and control.
4. Multiplication of physical facilities leads to uneconomical operations.

Geographic departmentation should be selected when the special characteristics of the market and product indicate regional emphasis. Fig. 7.3 presents the departmentation by territory.

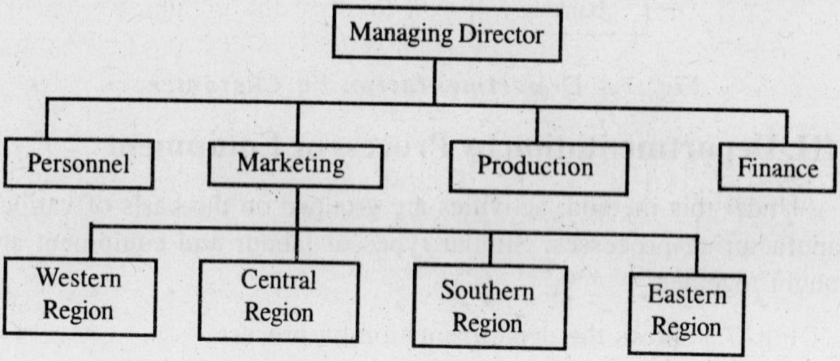

Fig. 7.3 Departmentation by Territory

VII. Departmentation by Customer

In this method, the activities are grouped into a number of departments on the basis of customers they serve. It is found in a variety of enterprises. A marketing department usually subdivided on the basis of customer. Such departmentation is useful in the case of companies which render specialised services.

Merits

1. It concentrates on customer needs.
2. It develops expertise in customer areas.
3. Useful to customer-oriented organisations.

Demerits

1. Sometimes it is difficult to meet the competing demands of the customers.
2. It requires managers and staff well-versed in customer needs.
3. Some customer groups may disappear during times of recession and the sales force may have to remain idle.

Fig. 7.4 shows the departmentation by customer in a bank.

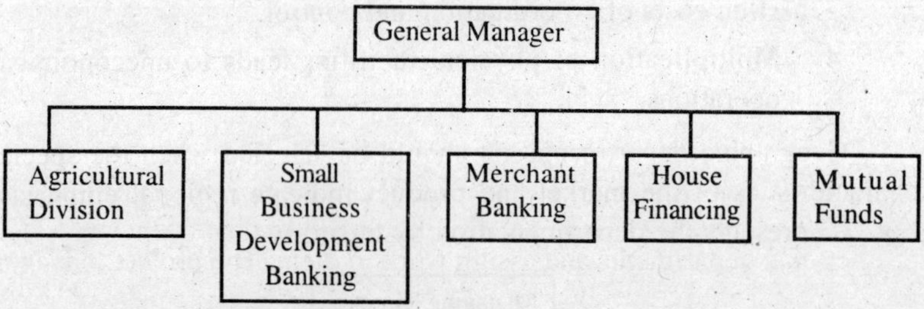

Fig. 7.4 Departmentation by Customer

VIII. Departmentation by Process or Equipment

Under this method, activities are grouped on the basis of various manufacturing processes. Similar types of labour and equipment are brought together.

Fig. 7.5 shows the departmentation by process.

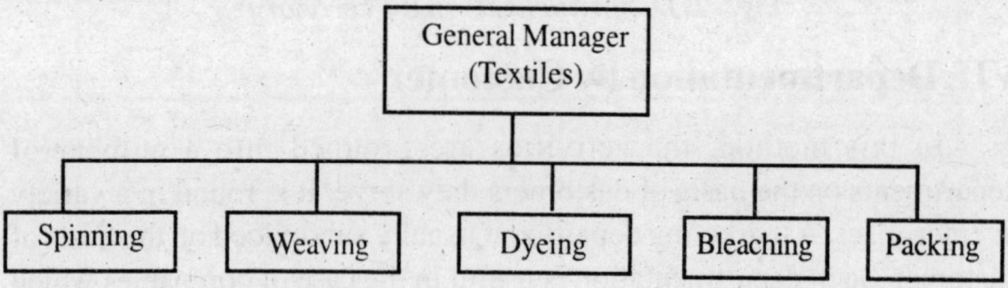

Fig 7.4 Process Departmentation

Merits

1. It provides for effective utilisation of equipment and special skill.
2. Facilitates co-ordination by grouping production facilities needed for completion of each distinct phase of work.

Demerits

1. There may be difficulty in co-ordination of the departments based on different processes.
2. There are chances of conflict between managers at different levels.

IX. Matrix Organisation

Matrix organisation is created by merging two complimentary organisations — the project and the functional. The project teams are composed of people from the functional departments who are assigned to the project for a specific period or for the duration of the project. When the assignment is over, they return to the functional departments.

Matrix organisation is built around a project. The project manager is put in charge to complete the project. He draws personnel from various functional departments and assign work to them. The project manager is given the authority and responsibility for the achievement of project objectives. Fig. 7.6 shows the model of matrix organisation.

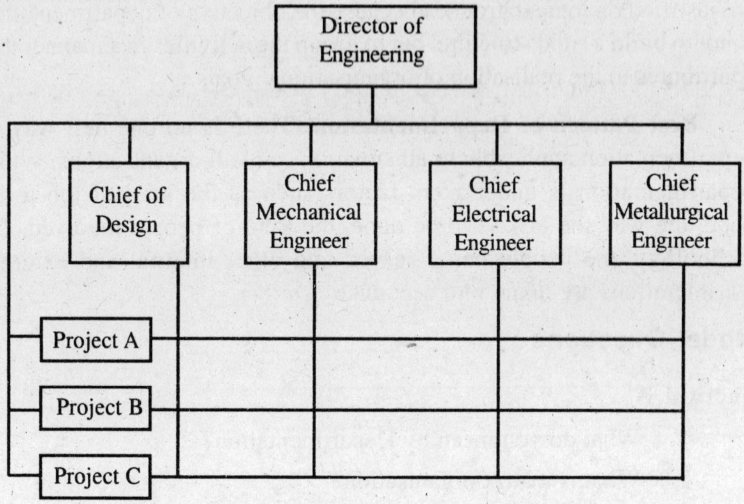

Fig. 7.6 Model of a Matrix Organisation

The following are the advantages of a matrix organisation.

Merits

1. Matrix organisation is useful when an organisation has a variety of projects.
2. It provides flexibility to the organisation.

3. Stimulates interdisciplinary co-operation.
4. Creates involvement among the employees.
5. Allows experts to move to crucial areas as and when needed.
6. Helps in completion of the project in time.

Demerits

1. The success of the matrix organisation requires a high level of interpersonal skills.
2. The administrative costs are high.
3. It leads to more discussion and conflicts than action.

X. Departmentation by Mixing Types

Many business concerns combine the advantages of functional product departmentation. For example, a bulk drug manufacturer may have centralised production, finance and personnel functions. The marketing department is functioning on the basis of territory. It takes the advantage of both financial and territorial departmentations. Such practices are justified on logical grounds because the objective of departmentation is not to build a rigid structure, but to group the activities in a manner that contributes to the realisation of organisational goals.

Best Pattern of Departmentation: There is no one best way of departmentation applicable to all situations and all organisations. While departmentation is undertaken, factors such as the kind of job to be done, the way the task is to be done, the kind of people involved, the technology, the people being served and other internal and external considerations are taken into account.

Model Questions

Section A

1. What do you mean by Departmentation?
2. What is matrix organisation?

Section B

3. Discuss the various bases for departmentation in an enterprise.
4. Explain the advantages and disadvantages of:
   (i) Departmentation by function
   (ii) Departmentation by product
   (iii) Departmentation by territory

5. Suggest a scheme of departmentation for a large business house with a network of sales all over India.

I. Multiple Choice

1. Departmentation by number is widely prevalent in
   (a) Army (b) Airport
   (c) Departmental store (d) none
2. Matrix organisation is built around
   (a) Function (b) Project
   (c) Area (d) None
3. Which form of departmentation action is unsuitable when operations cover a wide area?
   (a) Departmentation by time (b) By function
   (c) By Product (d) By process
4. Geographic departmentation means grouping of activities in terms of
   (a) Region (b) Customer
   (c) Time (d) Process
5. Departmentation by process is followed in
   (a) Supermarkets (b) Banks
   (c) Textiles (d) Retail stores

Answer:

1. (a) Army, 2. (b) Project, 3. (a) By function, 4. (c) Region, 5. (a) Textiles

II. Say, 'True or False'

6. Product departmentation involves establishing each product as a relatively autonomous, integrated unit within the framework of the company as a whole.
7. All similar activities of the enterprise are grouped into major department under departmentation by time.
8. Project manager is put incharge to complete the project under matrix organisation.
9. The success of the matrix organisation requires a high level of interpersonal skills.
10. Departmentation by customer creates efficiency through specialisation.

Answer:

6. True, 7. True, 8. False, 9. True, 10. False

III. Fill in the blanks

11. The process of dividing and grouping related activities into units is called __________.
12. Territorial departmentation is suitable for __________ firms.
13. Under the departmentation by process, activities are grouped on the basis of various ____________ process.
14. Matrix organisation is useful when an organisation has a variety of ______.
15. Customer satisfaction in terms of market segmentation is achieved under departmentation by ___________.

Answer:

11. Departmentation, 12. Large scale, 13. Manufacturing, 14. Projects, 15. Territory.

Chapter 8

Delegation of Authority

Chapter Outline

Authority — Responsibility — Delegation of Authority — The Process of Delegation — Principles of Delegation — Benefits of Delegation — Decisions in Delegation — Probems of Delegation — Making Delegation Effective — Model Questions

The function of organising deals with dividing the organisation into smaller units. The various units are to be knitted together to attain the organisational objectives. This is made possible through delegation and decentralisation of authority.

I. Authority

Authority is the right to act or direct the action of others towards the attainment of organisational goals.

Definitions

Fayol: "Authority is the right to give orders and power to exact obedience."

Koontz and O'Donnell: "Authority is the power to command others to act or not to act in a manner deemed by the possessor of the authority to further enterprise or departmental purposes."

The above definitions point out the following characteristics:

1. Authority is the right to perform certain tasks.

2. It confers the right on superiors to make decisions affecting the behaviour of subordinates.
3. Authority is the right of managers to direct the activities of subordinates that are appropriate in relation to organisational goals.

Power and Authority: Authority is the discretionary right to do certain acts whereas power is the ability to do something. A manager may have the authority but he may lack the power to do it. Manager's power is his ability to make subordinates do what he wishes them to do.

Types of Authority: According to Newman, authority is of four types such as legal, technical, ultimate and generational authority. Legal authority means an individual is legally permitted to take an action. Technical authority deals with the recognition of a person as an expert in a particular field. Ultimate authority indicates the original source from which one derives the right to take certain action. Finally, operational authority means to carry out the work. Newman states the executive making the delegation is himself authorised to take such action, he merely extends this permission to people working for him.

Sources of Authority: Authority is the sum of the powers and rights entrusted to make possible the performance of the work delegated. But there is divergence of opinion on whether the flow of authority is from the top to bottom or from bottom to top. There are various theories to explain the sources of authority, such as:

1. Formal or Traditional or Top-down Theory,
2. Acceptance Theory,
3. Competence Theory.

Formal authority theory deals with the authority flows from top to downward through the process of delegation in a business unit. Such formal authority is based on constitution, laws, social, religion, economic institution, etc. For example, corporate shareholders possess the ultimate authority to manage the affairs of the company. This rights or authority may be delegated to board of directors by such shareholders, in which task, may be delegated to the chief executive and so on. In this way, the rights of private property are transmitted through the business enterprise.

The Acceptance authority theory which is just opposite to the formal theory was developed by Chester Bernard. According to this theory, authority depends on the consent of the subordinates who accept the command of their superior.

According to competence authority theory, authority is generated by personal qualities of technical competence rather than formal authority. For example, accountant, engineers, etc., furnishes sound advice. These people may have no actual authority, yet this advice is sought and followed.

II. Responsibility

Responsibility is an obligation to carry out certain tasks. In an organisation, responsibility is the obligation of a subordinate to perform his duty as required by his superior. Responsibility is closely related to authority. Responsibility is exacted upwards whereas authority flows downwards. A manager is responsible ultimately for the performance of his duties even though he has delegated it to his subordinates. Therefore, responsibility cannot be delegated.

III. Delegation of Authority

Delegation takes place when one person gives another the right to perform work on his behalf and in his name. Effective managers usually delegate as many routine tasks as possible to subordinates and concentrate on exceptional tasks.

Delegation is the process of entrusting part of the work by the superior to his subordinates. A manager, single-handed, can achieve only a few tasks. There is a limit to what he can perform individually. There is also a limit to the number of subordinates for whom a manager can make decision. So, if a manager wants to achieve more, he can do so by delegation of authority.

IV. The Process of Delegation

The process of delegation consists of the following aspects:

(i) Assignment of Duties: The process of delegation starts with dividing the work into suitable parts. The manager has to decide what part of the work he will perform and what part will be transferred to his subordinates. Then he assigns the duties to subordinates indicating what he wants the subordinates to do.

(ii) Granting of Authority: Duties cannot be performed without granting of the necessary authority. So, the subordinates are given the requisite authority such as the use of resources, take necessary action etc., to perform the given job.

(iii) Creation of Accountability: Accountability is the obligation to carry out the responsibility with the help of authority in relation to the job entrusted. The subordinate to whom authority is delegated is also made accountable for the proper performance of the job entrusted to him.

V. Principles of Delegation

The following principles are considered to be guidelines for delegation of authority.

(i) Principles of Delegation by Results Expected: This principle implies that when authority is delegated, the superior should express clearly what he expects from the subordinates. The superior should also make the subordinates know what is expected of him.

(ii) Parity of Authority and Responsibility: Authority delegated should correspond to the responsibility of the subordinates. The responsibility for actions should neither be greater nor less than the authority granted. Both should be equal and co-extensive.

(iii) Principles of Absoluteness of Responsibility: In the process of delegation, the superior is not relieved of his responsibility and accountability. The superior is responsible for all acts of his subordinates.

(iv) Unity of Command: This principle requires that an order or guidance should always come from one superior. The subordinates should be made accountable to one superior for any given activity.

(v) Authority Level Principle: This principle requires that once a subordinate is assigned work and given authority to carry out the work he must be allowed to use his decision-making ability. It relieves managers of detailed supervision and enables them to concentrate on important decisions.

VI. Benefits of Delegation

(i) Reduces Managers' Burden: Delegation relieves the managers from performing duties of a routine nature. They are able to concentrate on important responsibilities. Thus, delegation reduces a manager's burden.

(ii) Develops Subordinates: Delegation develops subordinates by broadening their understanding and capacity. Subordinates assume responsibilities, make important decisions and perform varied tasks. Thus, subordinates develop their executive talents.

(iii) Provides Motivation: Delegation increases the job satisfaction of employees and encourages them to look forward to promotions in the future. So, it serves as a motivational device.

(iv) Improves Behavioural Climate: The granting of freedom to subordinates is an indication of confidence in them. Naturally, the subordinates also respond by developing a positive sense of responsibility. This improves the behavioural climate in the organisation and paves way for improved productivity.

(v) Provides Continuity: Delegation enables managers at lower levels to acquire experience in decision-making and gain competence to fill higher positions in the organisation. Thus, delegation ensures continuity in business.

VII. Decision in Delegation

Delegation does not appear to be simple in practice. To delegate prudentially, a manager must decide the following two questions:

1. What to delegate and what not to delegate?
2. To whom should authority be delegated?

L.A. Alien has given certain guidelines in this regard:

1. Most technical work can be delegated.
2. Routine and repetitive aspects of planning such as organising, leading and controlling can also be delegated provided the subordinates are endowed with the requisite abilities.
3. It is not necessary that delegation should consist of procedural details only. Delegation is a matter of judgment and personal assessment. Hence, experience is the best guide.
4. Final management decisions should not be delegated.
5. Overall technical problems affecting the lives of many people in the organisations should not be delegated.
6. Specific work or special work that subordinates cannot perform effectively should not be delegated.

Moreover, delegation should be directed towards those who have the capacity for accomplishment, the talents and abilities needed, necessary experience and courage to tackle the challenges. Managers should delegate to those whom they trust and respect and about whose performance they have some first-hand information.

VIII. Problems of Delegation

Most failures in effective delegation occur because managers are unable to apply the principles of delegation in practice. The following aspects are identified as 'trouble spots' as far as delegation is concerned:

(i) Receptiveness: A manager who knows how to delegate must be able to welcome others' ideas and compliment the ingenuity of his subordinates.

(ii) Willingness to Let Go: A manager who effectively delegates authority should relieve the right to make decisions to subordinates. It is quite common among managers to make decisions for posts which they have already left.

(iii) Willingness to Let Others Make Mistakes: True delegation will not be possible without any mistakes being committed by the subordinates. However, serious mistakes can be avoided by patient counselling and discerning questions. On no account should subordinates be discouraged by intimidation or unhealthy criticism.

(iv) Willingness to Trust Subordinates: Delegation implies a truthful attitude on the part of superiors and subordinates. Quite often, the superiors do not wish to delegate wisely, because they distrust subordinates.

(v) Willingness to Establish and Use Broad Controls: Sometimes, superiors do not plan carefully. Due to poor planning, they will find it difficult to establish broad controls. As such, their reluctance to delegate and trust subordinates arises from the superior's fear of loss of control.

(vi) Reluctance on the Part of Subordinates: The subordinates may be reluctant to accept authority because of the following reasons:

1. Lack of confidence
2. Fear of criticism
3. Fear of failure
4. Inadequate communication facilities
5. No sufficient incentives for accepting additional responsibility
6. Delegation will increase burden on them.

IX. Making Delegation Effective

Following are guidelines suggested for making delegation effective.

1. In view of the expected results, tasks should be defined well and adequate authority need to be granted.
2. Delegation of tasks is bound to be successful if the persons are selected in the light of the job to be done.
3. There should be free flow of information between the superior and the subordinates. Moreover, subordinates must be furnished with the relevant information to make timely decisions and interpret the authority delegated.
4. Broad controls can be established so that deviations from plans will be noticed promptly. Delegation accompanied by broad controls will ensure that authority is properly used.
5. Some managers reward effective delegation by granting more discretion and promoting to higher positions which serve as an incentive.
6. There must be a climate of trust and confidence among employees at all levels.

Effective delegation helps an organisation to use its resources efficiently. It is closely related to decentralisation in the sense that greater the amount of delegation, the more decentralised the organisation will become.

Model Questions

Section A

1. What is authority?
2. What is responsibility?
3. What is meant by delegation of authority?
4. What is the distinction between authority and power?

Section B

5. Explain the process of delegation.
6. What are the elements of delegation?
7. "Authority and Responsibility should be equal." Discuss.
8. State the obstacles in the process of delegation of authority.

Section C

9. Outline the major benefits of delegation of authority.
10. How is delegation made effective?
11. Explain the principles of delegation.

I. Multiple Choice

1. Authority is the right to give
   (a) Powers (b) Order
   (c) Responsibility (d) None
2. Operational authority is to carrying out the
   (a) Wards (b) Work
   (c) Supervisor (d) None
3. Authority flowing from top to bottom is called
   (a) Formal authority (b) Informal authority
   (c) Both (d) None
4. Responsibility is an obligation to carry out certain
   (a) Tasks (b) Talks
   (c) Tastes (d) None
5. In the process of delegation, the superior is not relieved of his
   (a) Responsibility (b) Power
   (c) Duty (d) None

Answer:

1. (b) Order, 2. (b) Work, 3. (a) Formal authority, 4. (a) Tasks, 5. (a) Responsibility,

II. Say, 'True or False'

6. Authority is the power to command others.
7. The acceptance authority theory was developed by Chester Bernard.
8. The process of delegation starts with dividing the work into suitable parts.
9. Duties can be performed without granting of the necessary authority.

10. The subordinates may be reluctant to accept authority due to lack of confidence.

Answer:

6. True, 7. True, 8. True, 9. False, 10. True

III. Fill in the blanks

11. Power is the ability to do ___________.
12. According to competence authority theory, authority is generated by personal ______ of technical competence.
13. ___________ is the process of entrusting part of the work by the superior to his subordinates.
14. ___________ is the obligation to carry out the responsibility.
15. Authority and Responsibility should be ___________.

Answer:

11. something, 12. Qualities, 13. Delegation, 14. Accountability, 15. Equal

Chapter 9

Centralisation and Decentralisation

Chapter Outline

Centralisation — Decentralisation — Factors Determining the Degree of Decentralisation of Authority — Advantages of Decentralisation — Disadvantages of Decentralisation — Model Questions

I. Centralisation

Centralisation refers to the systematic and consistent reservation of authority at central points within the organisation. Power is concentrated at the top levels in the management. A majority of decisions having to do with the work being performed are not made by those doing the work but at a point higher in the organisation.

Many organisations at the initial stage prefer centralisation of authority for two reasons: (i) Manager can be in touch with all operations; (ii) It facilitates timely decisions. As the organisation grows in size, the need for decentralisation arises due to the complexity of work.

Centralisation has certain advantages:

1. Centralisation binds all parts of the organisation together to attain the common goal.
2. In some matters, all units have to act in the same way, e.g., advertising, personnel policy etc. In such matters, centralised authority ensures uniformity of action.

3. Quick decisions, imaginative action and flexibility are possible under centralisation.
4. Centralisation is ideal to meet emergencies such as change in government policy, declining sales, competition and the like.
5. Communication and control becomes easier in the organisation.

II. Decentralisation

Decentralisation refers to the systematic effort to delegate authority to the lowest levels. It implies that the decision-making authority is dispersed throughout the organisation. Decentralisation is associated with democratic management where an individual's worth is respected.

According to Fayol, "Everything that goes is ideal to increase the subodinate's role is decentralisation, everything which goes to reduce it is centralisation."

Koontz views that the degree of decentralisation is greater when:

1. more number of decisions are made at lower levels;
2. more important decisions are made at lower levels;
3. more functions are affected by the decisions made at lower levels; and
4. minimum checking on the decisions made at lower levels.

Therefore, decentralisation actually refers to the degree to which authority is delegated to the lower levels. Decentralisation is an extension of the concept of delegation of authority. Absolute centralisation or decentralisation is not possible in practice. Koontz is of the view that "Centralisation and decentralisation are qualities like hot and cold with varying degree in practice."

III. Factors Determining the Degree of Decentralisation of Authority

1. Costliness of the Decision: Costliness of decision usually determines the extent of decentralisation. The more costly the decision to be made, the more likely that the decisions will be made at the upper levels of management. Quality control and financial aspects are usually centralised. Managers do not like to delegate authority for crucial decisions as they are ultimately responsible for it.

2. Desire for Uniformity of Action: The desire to get uniform policy with respect to quality, price, credit, delivery and service favour centralisation of authority. Uniform policy with respect to standardised accounting, statistics and financial records help to compare efficiencies of departments and bring down costs. Uniformity of action in personnel matters is important and this can be made surc by a degree of centralisation.

3. Size of the Organisation: As the organisation grows in size, the complexities of organisation require more decisions to be made in many places. One cannot state arbitrarily what this size can be but one can prove that when the unit exceeds a certain size, the distance from the top to the bottom will affect quality and speed of decisions.

4. History of the Enterprise: The way a business has been built over the years, sometimes, determine the extent to which authority is decentralised. Companies which grow from within have a tendency to centralise authority. In companies that result from mergers and consolidations are likely to show a tendency to retain decentralised authority.

5. Management Philosophy: The philosophy of top management influences the degree of decentralisation. On many occasions, the top managers retain authority as they are not desirous of giving up activities which they enjoyed before the expansion of the business.

6. Geographical Dispersion: Decentralisaton is advantageous to organisations whose operations are dispersed over many distant places. The top management from headquarters cannot control the dispersed activities effectively as they are not aware of the local conditions and problems in general.

7. Availability of Managers: Availability of competent managers largely, determines the extent of decentralisation of authority. Adequate training of managers is the only solution to decentralisation.

8. Control Techniques: Development of control techniques a understanding of these control techniques on the part of managers will make managerial decentralisation a possibility. Improved statistical devices, accounting control and other control techniques are useful in this direction. In the absence of good control techniques, it is difficult for the top management to determine the effectiveness of decisions taken by subordinates.

9. The Pace of Change: The fast-changing nature of business with its complexity and expansion requires a large number of decisions. The dynamic conditions force the managers to delegate authority and thereby decentralise authority. In slow-moving businesses, which are well-established, the tendency to centralise authority is quite natural.

10. Environmental Influence: The important external forces that influence the extent of decentralisation are government control, national unionism and tax policies. Price control, wage regulations and various measures pertaining to labour adopted by government and the influence of national unions restrict decentralisation. In addition to it, the tax structure of the national and local governments have a regulatory effect on business. Such factors which are beyond the control of the business managers also determine the extent of decentralisation.

IV. Advantages of Decentralisation

1. Reduces the Burden of Executives: Decentralisation reduces the workload of executives by relieving them from routine operating problems.

2. Leads to Higher Performance: Decentralisation leads to quicker decision at the lower levels as such decisions need not be referred upwards. Moreover, people at the lower levels are motivated to take decisions that make maximum profit for the organisation.

3. Facilitates Diversification of Product Line: It facilitates product diversification in a multiproduct company by providing the requisite sales and market efforts and by treating each product line as separate and important.

4. Develops Competent Managers: Decentralisation offers opportunities for people to develop themselves. A decentralised unit becomes the testing and training ground for developing managers for higher level positions.

5. Improves Motivation: Decentralisation by giving authority and responsibility to subordinate managers makes work interesting and challenging and it increases motivation and satisfaction.

6. Ensures Control: Decentralisation often enhances performance and control by fixing responsibility.

V. Disadvantages of Decentralisation

1. Decentralisation puts much pressure on departmental heads which result in bitter interdepartmental rivalries. Such conflicts create problems of control and co-ordination.
2. Decentralisation has a marked tendency to increase cost by hiring staff specialised for each division.
3. If decentralisation is not followed properly, it will create chaos in the organisation in the absence of proper control.
4. There is more need for good managers in the decentralised structure.
5. High degree of self-motivation and self-control is required on the part of manager in order to make decentralisation effective.

Hence, decentralisation should not be applied blindly. The key to effective decentralisation is a proper balance between what is to be decentralised and what is to be centralised. However, a proper balance is not easy to achieve. Experience and common sense are the guides in this regard.

Model Questions

Section A

1. What is centralisation?
2. What do you mean by decentralisation of authority?
3. State the advantages of centralisation.

Section B

4. Distinguish between centralisation and decentralisation of authority.
5. Explain the advantages of decentralisation.
6. Discuss the nature of problems that arise from centralisation of authority.

Section C

7. Explain the factors that determine the degree of decentralisation in an organisation.
8. Dicuss the nature, benefits and limitations of decentralisation.

I. Multiple Choice

1. The systematic and consistent reservation of authority at central points with the organisation refers to

   (a) Centralisation (b) Decentralisation

   (c) Delegation (d) None

2. Everything that goes to increase subordinate's role is

   (a) Decentralisation (b) Centralisation

   (c) Declaration (d) None

3. Koontz views that the degree of decentralisation is greater when more number of decisions are made at

   (a) Lower level (b) Higher level

   (c) Middle level (d) None

4. As the organisation grows in size, the need for decentralisation arises due to the complexity of

   (a) Work (b) Words

   (c) Functions (d) None

5. Decentralisation is associated with democratic management where an individual's worth is

   (a) Respected (b) Returned

   (c) Reserved (d) None

Answer:

1. (a) Centralisation, 2. (b) Decentralisation, 3. (a) Lower level
4. (a) Work, 5. (b) Respected.

II. Say, 'True or False'

6. Centralisation binds all parts of the organisation together to attain the common coal.
7. Decentralisation often enhances performance and control by fixing responsibility.
8. Many organisations at the initial stage prefer centralisation of authority.
9. Decentralisation is not an extension of the concept of delegation of authority.
10. Quality control and financial aspects are usually centralised.

Answer:

6. True, 7. True, 8. True, 9. False, 10. True

III. Fill in the blanks

11. Decentralisation refers to the systematic effort to delegate authority to the ________.
12. Absolute centralisation or decentralisation is not ________ in practice.
13. ________ is of the view that "Centralisation and Decentralisation are qualities like hot and cold with varying degrees in practice".
14. Decentralisation offers opportunities for people to ________ themselves.
15. In slow-moving business, the tendency to ________ authority is quite natural.

Answer:

11. Lowest level, 12. Possible, 13. Koontz, 14. Develop, 15. Centralise.

Chapter 10

Span of Management

Chapter Outline

Meaning — Determining Proper Span — Factors Determining an Effective Span — Levels of Organisation — Advantages and Disadvantages of Narrow Span — Advantages and Disadvantages of Wide Span — Model Questions

I. Meaning

The concept of'span of management' refers to the number of subordinates that a manager can manage effectively. The term of management is also called span of control, span of responsibility or span of supervision. There is a limit to number of persons a manager can supervise effectively. So, the deciding of proper span of management is an important task of management while designing the organisation structure.

II. Determining Proper Span

Different persons at various times have attempted to find the proper span of management. According to Urwick, the ideal number of subordinates for all superior authorities is to be four. At the lowest level of organisation, it can be eight or twelve.

According to Hamilton, the average human brain can handle only three to six other brains. He studied the military organisations and concluded that the span should be smaller at the top level where complicated thought process is involved. The maximum span at the lowest level should not exceed six persons at any time.

V.A. Graicunas, in his theory, states that as the number of subordinates increases arithmetically, the number of potential relationship between the superior and the subordinates increases geometrically. He has given a mathematical formula for calculating the number of possible relationships.

$$N = n = \left(\frac{2^n}{2} + N - 1\right)$$

N = Number of relationship

n = Number of subordinates.

In actual practice, one finds a wide variety of practices among well-managed companies. Such a widely varying span indicates that spans cannot be stated in absolute terms. Modern approaches agree that there is no one correct span for all situations. It depends on various factors.

Graicunas has identified three types of superior-subordinate relationships such as:

(i) Direct Single Relationships,

(ii) Direct Group Relationships, and

(iii) Cross Relationship.

The above three types are briefly explained below:

(i) Direct Single Relationships: This type of relationship arises when many subordinates are placed under one superior. For example, if there are three subordinates namely A, B and C under one superior, i.e., 'Z', there will be three direct single relationships. It is shown in the following Fig. 10.1.

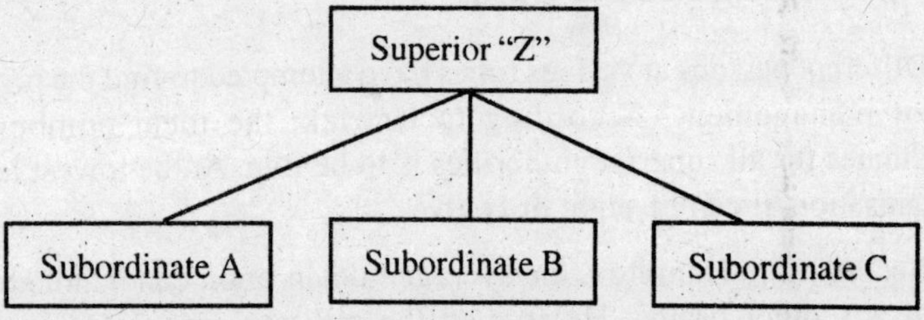

Fig. 10.1 Direct Single Relationships

(ii) Direct Group Relationships: It means relationship between the superior and his subordinates in all possible combinations. If there are three subordinates under one superior, there will be nine (9) such relationships. For example, A with B, A with C, C with A, C with B and so on with the superior.

(iii) Cross Relationships: Cross relationship arises due to mutual interaction of subordinates working under the same superior. A and B, A and C, B and A and so on are examples of cross relationships. This type of relationship paves way for six such relationships with three subordinates.

Graicunas has developed a formula to determine the various relationship with varying number of subordinates. If the number of subordinates is 'n', the number of various relationship will be as follows:

(i) Direct Single Relationships $= n$

(ii) Direct Group Relationships $= n(2n - 1 - 1)$

(iii) Cross Relationships $= n(n - 1)$

(iv) Total Relationships $= n\left(\frac{2^n}{2} + N - 1\right)$

This formula indicates that the number of subordinates go up in arithmetical progression whereas the number of relationships move up in geometrical progression as shown below:

Number of Subordinates	Number of Subordinates
1	1
2	6
3	18
4	44
5	100
6	222

Graicunas has stated that the most ideal span for a manager is six subordinates involving 222 relationships.

III. Factors Determining an Effective Span

An appropriate span of management for a manager depends upon seven general factors listed below:

1. Capacity of Supervisor: The capacity of a supervisor depends on such factors like his ability to understand the complicated problems, ability get along with people and ability to influence and induce loyalty. A better qualified supervisor will be able to supervise more employees effectively.

2. Capacity of Subordinates: Well-trained subordinates require less of the manager's time. If the subordinates are trained, developed, experienced competent, the superior can stop with occasional guidance. Capable competent subordinates facilitate a wider span of control.

3. Nature of Work: The span decreases if the subordinate's tasks complex and tough. Further, dissimilar jobs make a narrow span.

4. Clarity of Delegation of Authority: In an organisation where jobs are well-defined and authority is clearly defined, the subordinates require less of supervisor's time and attention. This makes the task of supervision easier and the span of management wider.

5. The Degree of Physical Dispersion: If the subordinates to be assigned to a manager are located in one area or within his direct supervision, the supervisor can supervise more number of people. If, however, subordinates are dispersed at different locations, a supervisor can manage only a few people effectively.

6. Information and Control System: An organisation in which sophisticated information and control system and objective standards are used to detect deviations from established plan, the superior can control a large number of subordinates.

7. Use of Staff Assistance: The availability of staff experts and their services enables managers to handle more number of subordinates easily. Use of staff assistance reduces the workload of managers, saves time, and so wider span of control is possible.

IV. Levels of Organisation

The span of management determines whether an organisation is flat or tall. A wider span of management is associated with a fewer organisational levels.This structure is called a flat structure. A narrow span results in many levels which is called a tall structure.

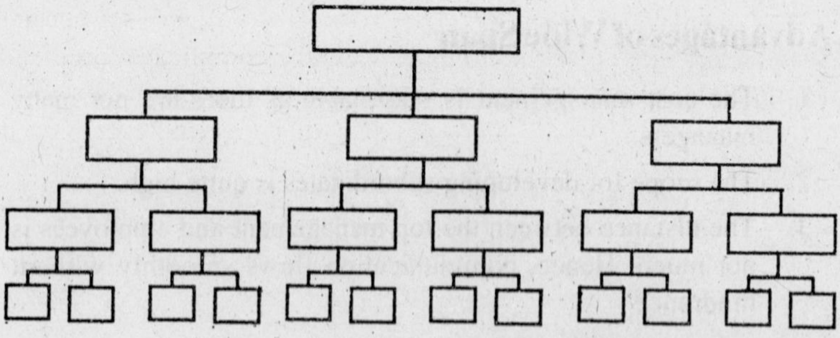

Fig. 10.2 Tall Structure — Narrow Span

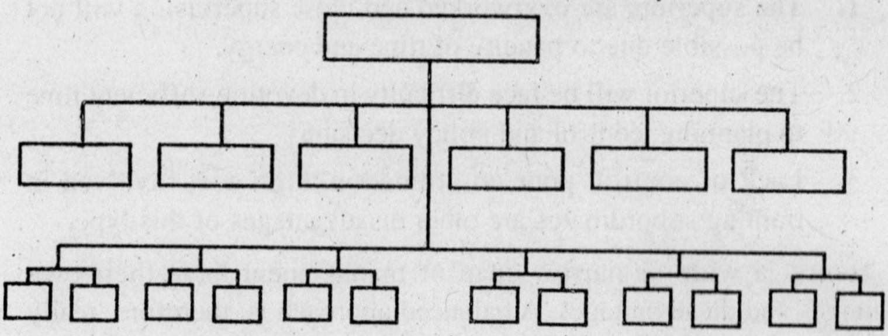

Fig. 10.3 Flat Structure — Wide Span

V. Advantages of Narrow Span

Narrow span results in effective supervision, control and co-ordination. The managers can devote their precious time to important organisational matter.

Disadvantages of Narrow Span

1. A large number of managers are required in a narrow span. Consequently, there is an overall increase in the cost of management.
2. Too many levels in the organisation widen the gap between the top management and the employees.
3. The process of control gets complicated.
4. Too many layers in the organisation lead to distortion of order, reports and instructions.

However, these disadvantages can be rectified by developing cross relationships among managers.

VI. Advantages of Wide Span

1. The cost management is reasonable as there are not many managers.
2. The scope for developing subordinates is quite high.
3. The distance between the top management and employees is not much. Hence, communication flows smoothly without hindrance.

Disadvantages of Wide Span

1. The superiors are overworked and close supervision will not be possible due to paucity of time and energy.
2. The superior will be face difficulty in devoting sufficient time to planning, control and policy decisions.
3. Lack of control, poor co-ordination, high cost involved in training subordinates are other disadvantages of this type.

Hence, a wide or narrow span of management have their own advantages and disadvantages. A balanced approach is, therefore, really needed.

VII. Limitations of Span of Control

According to Koontz and O'Donnell, the following factors affect the span of management:

(i) Time and Attention Spans: Time is precious and attention has its physiological limitations. So, the two favour a smaller span of control.

(ii) Personality and Energy Spans: The two factors are the qualities of individual manager. Manager with more of them can command a large number of subordinates, namely, personality and energy of managers have impact on span of control.

Koontz and O'Donnell have concluded that "the correct principle of span of management is that there is a limit in each managerial position to the number of persons an individual can effectively manage. But the exact number in each case will carry in accordance with the effect of underlying variables and their impact on the time requirements of effective managing."

The above factors determining the span of management indicates that there cannot be any fixed number of subordinates under one superior.

So, the span of management varies for different levels of management in the same business unit. To achieve efficiency, specialisation, proper control, and especially proper span, levels are to be created so that span of control is not unwieldy.

Model Questions

Section A

1. What is span of management?
2. What is tall structure?
3. Write a note on 'Graicunas' formula.

Section B

4. Discuss the modern concept of span of control.
5. What are the advantages of narrow span?

Section C

6. Explain the factors that determine the span of management.
7. Discuss the advantages and disadvantages of narrow and wide span.

I. Multiple Choice

1. Cross relationship arises when many subordinates are working under the same
   (a) Services (b) Superior
   (c) Special area (d) None
2. V.A. Graicunas states that as the number of subordinates increases the relationship increases
   (a) Arithmetically (b) Average
   (c) Geometrically (d) None
3. Which type of relationship arises when many subordinates are placed under one supevisor
   (a) Direct single relationship (b) Direct group
   (c) Cross relationship (d) None
4. There are many organisational levels in
   (a) Flat structure (b) Tall structure
   (c) Both (d) None

5. The number of subordinates that a manager can manage is called
   (a) Span of management (b) Delegation
   (c) Development (d) None

Answer:

1. (b) Superior, 2. (c) geometrically , 3. (b) Direct single relationship, 4. (b) Tall structure, 5. (a) Span of Management

II. Say, 'True or False'

6. According to Urwick, the ideal number of subordinates for superior authorities is to be four.
7. Graicunas has stated that the most ideal span for a manager is six subordinates involving 222 relationships.
8. According to V.A. Graicunas, the number of potential relationship between the superior and the subordinates increases arithmetically.
9. The better qualified supervisor will be able to supervise more employees effectively.
10. The span increases if the subordinate's tasks are complex and tough.

Answer:

6. True, 7. True, 8. False, 9. True, 10. False

III. Fill in the blanks

11. According to Hamilton, the average human brain can handle only three to ________ other brains.
12. Graicunas has identified _________ types of superior-subordinate relationships.
13. Cross relationships arises due to mutual interaction of subordinates working under the same _______.
14. A wider span of management is associated into a fewer _____________.
15. Narrow span results in effective supervisor control and ___________.

Answer:

11. Six, 12. Three, 13. Supervisor, 14. Organisational level, 15. Co-ordination.

Chapter 11

Forms of Authority Relationship

Chapter Outline

Line Organisation — The Staff — Line and Staff Organisation — Distinction between Line and Staff — Line-Staff Conflict — Improving Line-Staff Relationships — Functional Authority — Functional Foremanship — Committee Organisation — Model Questions

It is necessary to understand the authority relationship that exists among managers and between managers and their subordinates while designing an organisation structure. In this chapter, a brief description of the forms of authority relationship prevailing in the line, line and staff functional and committee forms of organisation, is given.

I. Line Organisation

Line is the oldest- type- of organisation. In this type of organisation, authority flows from the topmost executive to the bottom. The authority flows more or less in a straight line. So, it is called a line organisation. This kind of organisation is found in the military. It is otherwise known as a military organisation.

Advantages

The advantages of line organisation are:

1. It is easy to establish and operate.
2. It has clear demarcation of lines of authority, responsibility and accountability.

3. The direct line of command ensures unified control.
4. Unified control and fixed responsibility facilitate quick and prompt decisions.
5. It ensures flexibility to make suitable adjustments to realise the goals.

Disadvantages

The line organisation suffers from the following disadvantages:

1. Line officers are responsible for both planning and execution of the work. It is difficult for them to carry on all specialised functions simultaneously.
2. In this organisation, an executive is responsible for the performance of his unit. This places a great burden on him. Therefore, the efficiency of the department depends on the efficiency of the manager.
3. Upward communication is lacking in this type of organisation. The subordinates are not given an opportunity to express their opinion about the orders received or make suggestions for improvement.
4. As one executive controls the entire organisation, the scope for team spirit is little.

Suitability

The line organisation is suitable to the business enterprises where:

1. the method of operation is simple and work is of routine nature;
2. continuous processes are followed; and
3. automatic machines are used.

It is highly useful to small-sized business.

A simple chart of Line Organisation is given below:

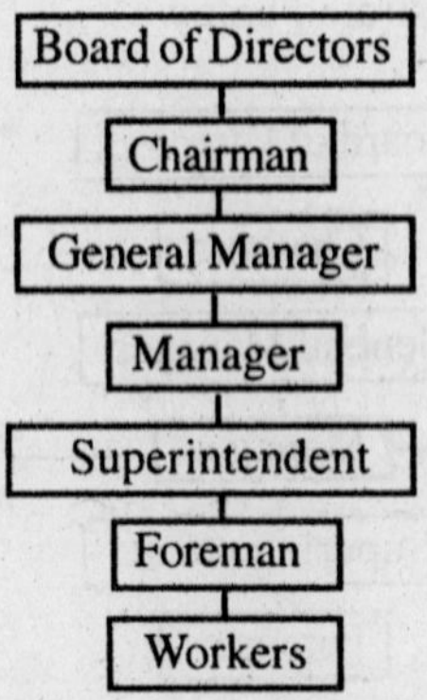

Fig. 11.1 Line Organisation

II. The Staff

The staff are experts who provide advice and service to the line officers. Their authority arises from their superior knowledge of a particular function. They do not have the power to command the line. But their advice is followed because of their higher status in the organisation.

In business organisations, two types of staff are found, namely, (1) Personal staff; and (2) Specialised staff.

1. Personal Staff: The burden of executives at higher level is reduced by personal staff. Personal staff comprises clerical and stenographic personnel. Personal staff answer routine letters, attend to phone calls, fix appointments and keep track of business agreements. They plan and supervise the routine clerical work of an executive's office.

2. Specialised Staff: Specialised staff provide advice and service to the company as a whole. Specialised staff provide services to personnel and maintenance, counseling and quality control.

III. Line and Staff Organisation

The combination of line with staff constitutes the line and staff organisation. The line managers are responsible for achieving the objectives. But they are not specialists. So they are provided with specialist advice and service. Legal consultants, economic analysts and public relations officers stand in the staff position.

Organisation structure with line and functional organisation combined together is illustrated below:

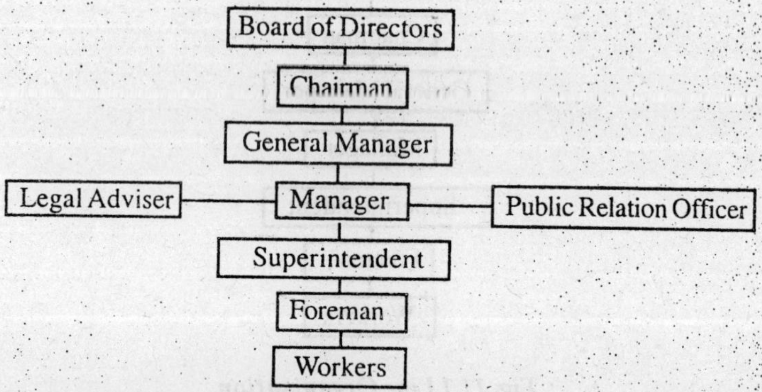

Fig. 11.2 Line and Staff Organisation

Advantages

The advantages of line and functional organisation are:

1. Expert advice becomes available to the line management.
2. Planned specialisation is possible.
3. It ensures greater efficiency since line managers get more time to devote to their line function.

Disadvantages

It also suffers from the following demerits:

1. It leads to conflict between line and staff since staff tends to assume line authority.
2. If the pattern of authority relationship between line and staff executives is not clearly indicated, there may be considerable confusion throughout the organisation.
3. As the staff officers take authority to put their recommendations into practice, their advice may be ignored by the line executives.
4. As the staff officer is not concerned with the execution of the plan, he may not take proper precautions and care before he advises the line officer.

IV. Distinction between Line and Staff

It is quite common to identify some departments as line departments and others as staff departments. Usually, production, finance and sales are treated as line departments and personnel and research as staff departments. This approach is inconclusive and ineffective since line and staff are characterised by relationships and not by departmental activities. Their departmental activities do not characterise the difference between line and staff.

Personnel is usually treated as a staff department. However, in a consultancy firm, the personnel department serves the line function by doing research studies, reports, and concerting conferences and seminars.

Public relations has a staff relationship but in a public relations consulting firm, it is a primary line function as the organisation provides service to clients.

In the E.I. Du Pont de Nemours Company, production, sales and research are line functions. In chemical industries, research and development is a line function together with production and manufacturing.

Hence, it is erroneous to classify line and staff as departmental activities. It should be classified by the authority relationship.

V. Line-Staff Conflict

In many organisations, the conflict between line and staff is a problem.

Line managers are usually viewed as important contributors to the organisation but the staff are not treated so. The line managers experience psychological problems, as in their view staff undermine their authority. The staff usually criticise the existing practices of the line which is not liked by the line managers. Many line managers consider that the counsel and advice provided by the staff is not well-balanced. They are considered to be theoretical and bookish. Hence, on many occasions, line managers are reluctant to accept the staff advice.

The staff often complain that they are not well-utilised by the line managers. They are informed after the decision have been made. In their view, the line managers often resist new ideas and are not open-minded.

According to Koontz and O'Donnell, there is probably no area of management which causes more difficulties, more friction and more loss of time and effectiveness, as the line and staff conflict.

VI. Improving Line-Staff Relationships

Solving the conflict between line and staff require high managerial skill, careful alteration to principles and guidance to personnel.

1. Understanding Authority Relationship: The duties and responsibilities of staff and line managers should be made clear. Also, the relationship of staff to line people and the limitations placed on the scope of staff activities should be made clear.

2. Acceptance of Staff Advice: Line managers must make proper use of staff whenever necessary. Staff in turn should help the line managers solve the organisational problems. Line managers should realise that competent staff assistants offer suggestions to aid and not to undermine or criticise.

3. Keeping the Staff Informed: It is expected on the part of line managers to inform the staff the decisions affecting their work and provide relevant information on concerned problems. Otherwise, the staff cannot function meaningfully.

VII. Functional Authority

Apart from the line and staff, a third form of authonty also exists in an organisation known as the functional authority. For the first time, F.W. Taylor proposed the idea of functional authority.

Functional authority permits a number of specialists to exercise authority within their area of competence. It is the right and power given to a specialist or a department to issue orders or instructions to other departments. It is binding on the line authority. But it does not carry the right to discipline for non-compliance. Functional authority is pursued for the sake of convenience and efficiency.

In other words, the management is divided into a number of functions like purchasing, selling, production, finance, personnel, research and development, etc. In order to introduce a functional organisation in a business unit, it is essential to take care of the following:

1. Only interrelated jobs are allotted to one department.
2. All activities must be divided into functions carefully and then allotted to functional departments.
3. There should be no duplication.

A simple chart of functional organisation is given below:

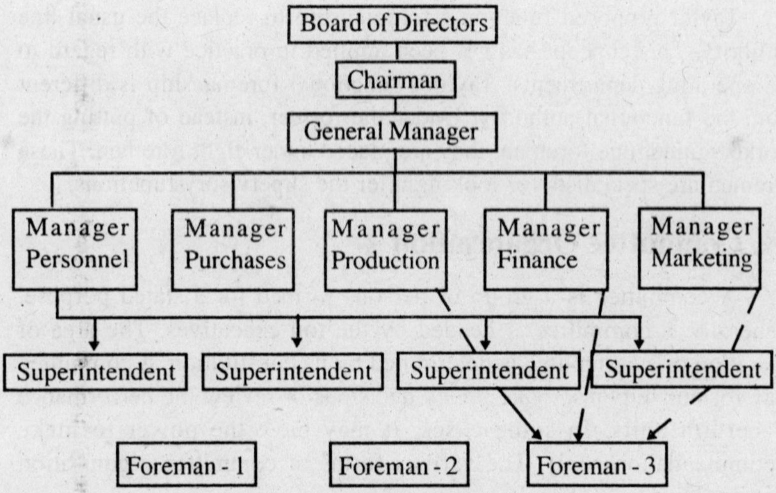

Fig. 11.3 Functional Organisations

Merits

The merits of functional organisation are:

1. Better division of labour takes place resulting in specialisation of functions and its consequent benefits.
2. It ensures greater efficiency since every person performs a limited number of functions.
3. It facilitates mass production since it covers both specialisation and standardisation.

Demerits

The following are the demerits of functional organisation:

1. Co-ordination becomes impossible in many cases. So, efficiency is affected to some extent.
2. It leads to conflict among foremen and superintendents or supervisors of equal status.
3. Disciplinary controls may become weak as a worker is commanded not by one person but a large number of persons.

VIII. Functional Foremanship

Taylor proposed functional foremanship to replace the usual line authority. This concept has not been applied in practice with regard to the operating departments. Taylor's functional foremanship is different from the functional authority. Under the former, instead of putting the workers under one foreman, they are placed under eight foremen. These foremen are specialists for looking after the supervisory functions.

IX. Committee Organisation

A committee is a group of persons formed for a stated purpose. Generally, a committee is headed by the top executives. The area of operation of a committee is determined by its constitution. A committee may formulate plans, make policy decisions or review the performance of certain units. In some cases, it may have the power to make recommendations only. The various forms of committee organisation are as follows:

(i) Finance Committee;

(ii) Production Committee;

(iii) Marketing Committee;

(iv) Personnel Committee;

(v) Directors' Committee.

The Board of Directors is one of the important forms of committee organisation.

Characteristics of a Committee

1. A committee is a group of person with a minimum of two persons. There is no prescribed limit as regards the maximum number of persons.
2. The committee is appointed to deal with one or more specific problems.
3. A committee can deliberate only on the matters that are brought before it.
4. A committee may be granted authority to make and carry out decisions. It may also serve merely in an advisory capacity.
5. A committee may be constituted at any level of the organisation. A person can be a member of more than one committee at the same time.

Benefits of Committee

Important advantages of the committee form of organisation are summarised below:

1. A committee brings together the abilities of a group of persons for finding solution to the problem. The group can make a thorough probing of the problem and its facts before arriving at a decision.

2. A committee enables managers to meet together in a session and discuss their problems or requirements for attaining the enterprise objectives. Thus, the committee facilitates co-ordination.

3. A committee is an excellent means of transmitting information and ideas to organisational members. All persons interested in the problem have simultaneous face-to-face communication through the proceedings of the committee meetings. Doubts and ambiquity can be removed in the meeting itself. This saves lot of time in communication.

4. The subordinates are allowed to participate in group decisions through committee forms. Participation in deliberations result in motivation for obtaining high performance.

5. A committee, through brainstorming and other creative activities, can produce valuable suggestions and advices. The exchange of information and ideas broadens the understanding of the business situation.

Defects of Committee

The committee suffers from the following defects:

1. The committee is an expensive device. The cost in terms of both time and money is high for preparation and conduct of meetings.

2. The functioning of the committee is slow and cannot take decision quickly. The meetings may be adjourned because of lack of time for thorough discussions so that decisions cannot be arrived at.

3. Committees have a tendency to compromise when a common agreement is not reached. Such compromised decisions are of mediocre quality.

4. In the absence of fixed responsibility for an individual member, the committee proves to be a breeding ground of inefficiency and evasion of responsibility.

5. A few members, by force of their strong personality, can dominate the committee. They force the members to come to a decision on the basis of their own thinking.

7. It acts as a check and safeguard against the abuse and misuse of powers. The Board of Directors is a plural executive which reviews and oversees the operations of the chief executive of the company.

A committee is a very popular form of organisation structure in a modern enterprise. So, there is a need to make it effective. The following are some of the measures suggested to make it effective:

1. The number of members in the committee should be limited and a reasonable one. The size of the committee should depend on the purpose of forming it and the need to get representation to different viewpoints.

2. The members of the committee should be carefully selected with due regard to their competence and commitment to the objectives.

3. The functions, scope and authority of the committee should be defined clearly. It should be put in black and white in unambiguous language. This will avoid confusion and wasteful efforts. The members of the committee must be clear about the functions, scope, responsibilities, and authority of the committee.

4. The success of the meeting largely depends on the chairman. He must meticulously plan the meeting, prepare agenda and arrange definite proposals for discussion. He must conduct the meeting efficiently. His job is to encourage other members to express themselves, to settle the differences and to maintain unity of the group and provide satisfaction to members.

5. It is necessary that the management should take adequate follow-up measures to implement the decisions of the committee.

Model Questions

Section A

1. What is line organisation?
2. Write a note on 'Functional authority.'
3. Distinguish between line and staff.
4. What is committee organisation?

Section B

5. Explain the advantages of line organisation.
6. State the features of line and staff organisation.
7. Explain the characteristics of committee organisation.
8. Discuss the line and staff conflict.
9. State the circumstances where line organisation can be used.

Section C

10. What are the advantages and disadvantages of committees?
11. State the conditions necessary for the success of committees.
12. Make suggestions to resolve line and staff conflict.
13. Compare line, functional and line and staff organisations. Which of these will be appropriate for a large manufacturing organisation?

I. Multiple Choice

1. The staff are experts who provide advice to
   (a) Workers (b) Line workers
   (c) Line officers (d) None
2. In line organisation authority flows from
   (a) Top to Bottom (b) Bottom to top
   (c) Horizontally (d) None
3. The number of foreman in functional foremanship is
   (a) 6 (b) 8
   (c) 10 (d) 6
4. Functional authority ensures
   (a) Co-ordination (b) Control
   (c) Better division of labour (d) None
5. The committee is appointed to deal one or more specific
   (a) Prices (b) Promotion
   (c) Problems (d) None

Answer:

1. (c) Line officer, 2. (a) Top to bottom, 3. (b) 8, 4. (c) Better division of labour, 5. (c) Problems

II. Say, 'True or False'

6. Line organisation is otherwise known as military organisation.
7. The line organisation is suitable where continuous processes are followed.
8. Specialised staff provide advice to the company as a whole.
9. A committee is a group of persons formed for a stated purpose.
10. The subordinates are not allowed to participate in group decisions through committee organisation.

Answer:

6. True, 7. True, 8. True, 9. True, 10. False

III. Fill in the blanks

11. __________ communication is lacking in line organisation.
12. The combination of line with staff constitutes the __________ organisation.
13. F.W. Taylor proposed the idea of functional __________.
14. The functioning of the committee is ________ and cannot take decision quickly.
15. __________ ensures greater efficiency since person performs a limited number of functions.

Answer:

11. Upward, 12. Line & Staff, 13. Authority, 14. Slow, 15. Functional organisation.

Chapter 12

Staffing

Chapter Outline

Meaning — Definition — Steps in Staffing Process — Job Analysis — Manpower Planning — Recruitment — Selection — Training — Performance Appraisal — Model Questions

I. Meaning

Staffing is an essential requisite for organisational success. Staffing involves the assessment of the manpower needed, selection, training and development and appraisal of personnel at periodic intervals. The objective of staffing is to obtain the best talented people for the organisation and to develop their skill and abilities.

II. Definition

Staffing is defined as "the process involved in identifying, assessing, placing, evaluating and developing individuals at work *(Schneider Benjamin)*.

III. Steps in Staffing Process

The following are the five steps in the staffing process:

(i) **Job Analysis:** Job analysis is a process through which the activities of work are analysed and the demand made by it on employees.

(ii) **Manpower Planning:** It involves an estimate of the present and future requirements of executive positions in the enterprise.

(iii) **Recruitment and Selection:** Recruitment means attracting applicants for the present or future jobs in an enterprise. Selection refers to evaluating applicants and choosing the best candidates to fill jobs.

(iv) **Training and Development:** Training and development refers to those activities that will increase the knowledge and skill of employees to perform their job.

(v) **Performance Appraisal:** It is the process of judging the effectiveness of executives and managers.

The above steps are elaborated here.

IV. Job Analysis

Job analysis deals with the detailed examination of the activities and the demand made by it on workers. Job analysis helps in determining the nature of a job and the major characteristics that are desirable in the job holder. Moreover, job analysis aids in analysing work process to find better methods of doing work in connection with work simplification. A complete analysis of the job can be built up by going through the following steps suggested by Prof. Bryan Livy.

(i) Identify and isolate the various tasks in a job.

(ii) Examine how tasks are performed.

(iii) Examine when and why tasks are performed.

(iv) Identify the main duties involved in the job.

(v) Identify the main areas of responsibility for various assignment of work.

(vi) Note the prevailing working conditions in respect of physical, social and financial aspects of the job.

(vii) Identify the personal demands which a job makes on an individual incumbent.

Job Description: The results of job analysis are expressed in job description. It is defined on the written statement of the main duties and responsibililies which a job entails. It includes the information, such as, name of job, summary of job, description of duties performed, equipment, materials used on job and so on.

Job Specification: Job specification refers to the summary of the personal characteristics required for the jobs. It describes the type of person required in terms of educational qualifications, experience, aptitudes and so on. In preparing job specifications, the minimum requirements for a job may be grouped as:

(i) Mental or educational requirements,

(ii) Technical or skill based upon previous training, experience and speed in operating mechanical devices.

(iii) Physical requirements such as height, strength, eyesight and age.

(iv) Responsibility for equipment, office records, materials and personal responsibilities.

Hence, job specification provides information for selecting right type of personnel for the job and for the development of a training programme.

V. Manpower Planning

Manpower planning is the application of the planning concept to the needs in number and kind. It includes — (i) taking stock of existing manpower; (ii) determining the status of the available personnel; (iii) discovering the untapped talent within the organisation; and (iv) assessing the future manpower requirements. The demand for managers has steadily grown in all expanding enterprises. Besides, retirement, resignation, death, etc., cause demand for managers. So, manpower planning should be made on a continuous basis.

VI. Recruitment

The recruitment process starts after the manpower requirement is ascertained. Recruitment is the process of searching for prospective candidates and stimulating them to apply for the vacant jobs.

Sources: There are basically two sources of recruitment: (i) Internal sources, and (ii) External sources.

(i) Internal Sources: 'Internal sources' refers to people currently working in an organisation. From this source, positions are filled through promotion or transfer.

Internal source has the following advantages:

1. It creates a sense of security among members.
2. It promotes a high morale among employees.
3. It ensures organisational stability.
4. It encourages employees in the lower ranks to aim for higher positions.

(ii) External Sources: The following are the external sources:

1. Advertisement.

2. Employment exchanges.
3. Educational institutions.
4. Consultants.
5. Campus interviews.
6. Recommendation of present employees.
7. Recommendations of Unions.
8. Deputation from other organisations.

The following are the advantages of recruiting people from outside:

1. It makes possible to choose from among a large number of applicants.
2. The organisation would get people with a varied and broader experience.
3. Sometimes, it helps to overcome internal rivalry.

VII. Selection

Selection of candidates starts after the completion of the recruitment process. Selection is the process of logically choosing individuals who possess the necessary skills and abilities to fill the job. Recruitment is often termed as positive, as its objective is to increase the number of applicants. Selection is termed as negative as it attempts to eliminate applicants.

The Selection Procedure: The selection procedure involves the following steps.

1. Application: Receiving application is the first step in the selection process. Application usually contains information regarding the personal background, educational qualifications, experience and references. Candidates who do not possess the required qualifications are eliminated and others are called for preliminary interview.

2. Preliminary Interview: The object of preliminary interview is to see whether the applicant is physically and mentally suitable for the job.

3. Tests: Candidates who pass the preliminary interview are asked to appear for the selection tests. Tests are conducted to measure the skills and abilities of prospective candidates in terms of specifications. Usually, the following tests are conducted:

(i) **Proficiency Tests:** It includes: (a) the achievement test to measure the knowledge and proficiency already achieved, and (b) dexterity test to test the efficiency in using hands to perform the job.

(ii) **Aptitude Tests:** Aptitude tests consist of:

(a) **Intelligence test:** to test the IQ of the candidate.

(b) **Attitude test:** to know the temperamental and emotional make-up handle the job.

(c) **Interest test:** to measure candidate's interest in the job.

(d) **Movement test:** to measure the speed and precision of movements of the candidate.

(iii) **Personality Tests:** These are also conducted with the assumption that personality is a key determinant to job success.

(iv) **Final Interview:** Final interview holds a central position in the selection procedure. It attempts to evaluate the candidate's qualifications for a particular job. The interview time may range from thirty to fifty minutes. It provides an opportunity to view, probe and judge the candidate's strengths and weaknesses for the positions.

4. Checking References: This procedure aims at ascertaining the correctness of the application. Many organisations do not pay attention to this aspect as it has little practical value.

5. Medical Examination: Certain jobs prescribe physical fitness standards as to height, weight etc. For such jobs, medical examination is conducted prior to placement of the candidate.

6. Placement: The final step in the selection process is to give the appointment order to the candidate specifying the place of work, gross emoluments, hours of work and other terms and conditions.

The selection procedure is shown in Fig. 12.1.

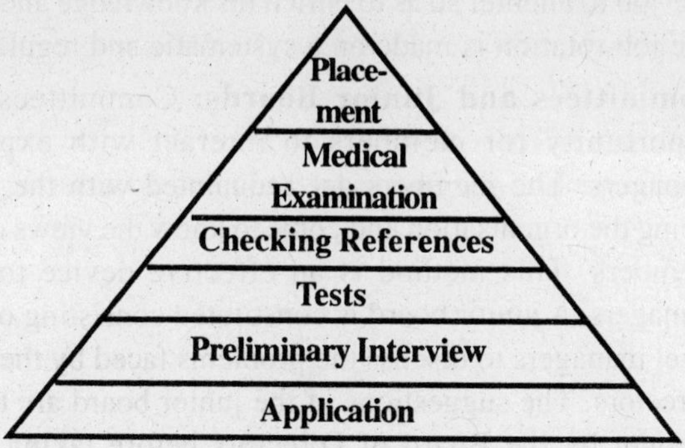

Fig. 12.1 Selection Procedure

VIII. Training

Training refers to the process of educating and developing selected employees so that they have the knowledge, skills, attitudes and understanding needed to manage the future position. Training begins on the very first day the employee starts work and it continues throughout his career.

Methods of Training: Training methods can be divided into two categories as follows: (1) On-the-job training; and (2) Off-the-job training.

1. On-the-job Training: On-the-job training is concerned with developing the employees in the present job. The following methods are employed in this direction:

(i) **Apprenticeship:** Under this method, a worker is appointed as an apprentice under a qualified senior worker. The apprentice learns the work by observing and asking the senior. This method is used in skilled trades such as carpentry, brick-laying, tailoring, etc.

(ii) **Coaching and Counselling:** Under this method, a senior executive is assigned the responsibility of imparting the skills needed for a management trainee to become an effective manager.

(iii) **Vestibule Training:** Under vestibule training, a new worker is trained in the specific skill in a special working area known as "vestibule school set up in the plant." The trainee is free to learn the job at his own rate.

(iv) **Job Rotation:** Under job rotation, a trainee is shifted from one job to another so as to enrich his knowledge and capacity. The job rotation is made on a systematic and regular basis.

(v) **Committees and Junior Boards:** Committees give an opportunity for members to interact with experienced managers. The members get acquainted with the problems facing the organisation and come to know the views of various members. This method is an effective device to develop managers. A junior board is constituted consisting of middle-level managers to discuss the problems faced by the Board of Directors. The suggestions of the junior board are taken into account by the Board of Directors before taking the final decisions.

2. Off-the-job Training: Off-the-job training is conducted away from the actual workplace. The following are some of the popular methods:

(i) **Lectures:** It is an effective means of imparting knowledge to a large number of members. Qualified persons conduct lectures suited to the needs of the employees. If lectures are delivered effectively and listeners are motivated properly, it is an effective method of training.

(ii) **Conferences and Seminars:** Conferences and seminars provide a platform for the exchange of ideas and experiences among employees of different organisations. They are excellent media for managerial development.

(iii) **Role Playing:** Under this method, employees are assigned certain roles to play. For example, a dispute between a superior and a worker is acted out. This method is based on the assumption that a person understands a situation if he is made to act the roles involved in it. The advantage of this method is that it helps to develop leadership skill and decision-making skill.

(iv) **Case Studies:** The trainees are given cases and asked to identify the problems, analyse the causes and suggest solutions. It serves as useful technique for developing the analytical ability of managers.

(v) **Training by Management Institutions:** Management associations and educational institutions conduct various programmes to develop managers. These programmes serve as a training ground for developing managers.

(vi) **Programmed Learning:** It consists of three functions, namely, (a) presenting questions, facts or information; (b) allowing the trainee to respond and (c) providing the necessary feedback on the accuracy of his answer. This practice makes the trainee learn while going through the materials supplied at his convenience. Compared to conventional methods, it is superior in three respects: (1) saving in learning time; (2) amount of immediate learning; and (3) long-term retention.

IX. Performance Appraisal

Performance appraisal is a process of evaluating the performance of an employee in terms of the requirements of the job. It is systematic and objective way of judging the relative worth or ability of an employee.

Performance appraisal makes-the employee know how well he is performing in his job. It also influences the employee's future level of effort and direction. Thus, it serves as a basis for improving the quality of performance of employees. It serves as a basis for improving the quality of the performance of the manager in his work. It also helps in building a sound personnel policy for an organisation.

Why Performance Appraisal?

Performance appraisal of employees serves several useful purposes:

1. It serves as a basis for promotion.
2. Identifies the strengths and weaknesses of an employee on his job and helps in selecting appropriate programmes of training and development.
3. Provides feedback to employees on job performance and thereby motivate him for better performance.
4. Provides useful information for making decision about employee compensation.
5. Make the superiors to observe their subordinates more closely which results in improved supervisors.

Methods of Performance Appraisal

The different methods of performance appraisal are explained here:

(i) Ranking Method: The employees, under this method, are ranked in the order of performance. This method is useful in small organisations. The best employee is placed in the first rank and the poorest in the last rank. The management normally selects some acceptable determinants on the basis of which ranks assigned.

(ii) Person-Person Comparison: This method compares the employee with some key people in the organisation for the purpose of analysis of certain factors as leadership, initiative and dependability.

(iii) Grading: In this method, the performance is defined in certain characterstics such as outstanding, excellent, good satisfactory and poor are defined in advance. The employees are put in particular category depending on their performance.

(iv) Graphic Scales: This method provides some kind of a scale for measuring differences between individuals in respect of job related factors such as quantity and quality of work, co-operation, initiative, dependability, attendance etc. The scale has several points, most commonly, five points. For example, the characteristic job knowledge may be divided into five categories: Exceptionally Good, Good, Average, Below Average and Poor. The rater can tick mark the category which feels best describes the person being rated. This is called discrete type.

Where just above the five category notations a continuous line is provided, the rater can tick at any point along its length.

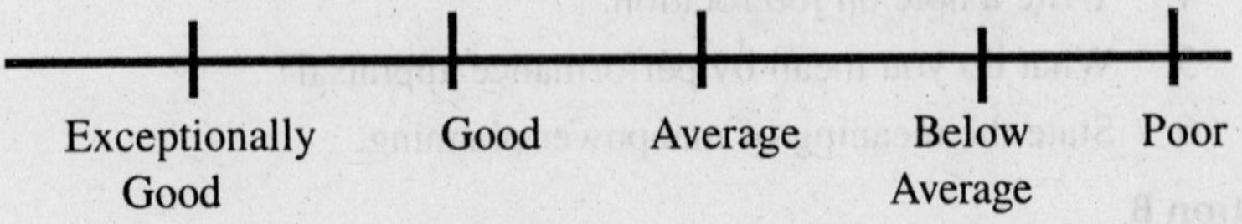

This is called continuous type.

The factors to be measured is selected on the basis of occupational category, e.g., sales, financial etc.

(v) Paired Comparison: According to this method, the supervisor compares each individual with all other individuals in the group. The number of comparisons to be made is $\frac{N(N-1)}{2}$.

(vi) Forced Choice Method: Under this method, rating elements are sets of four possible statements about the quality of a person such as — (a) industrious, (b) indifferent, (c) loyal, and (d) commands respect. The rater is asked to check two items, one of which is the most favourable and another unfavourable. This reduces rater bias in evaluation.

(vii) Critical Incidents: A critical incident is an incident which shows that an employee has succeeded or failed to do something. The superior continuously records these incidents under different columns provided in a specially designed notebook. Gradually, a record of debit and credit is built up. This evidence becomes the basis of evaluation.

(viii) Checklists: Checklist is list consisting of a number of statements about the worker and his behaviour. Each statement on this list is assigned a value depending upon its importance. The rater is asked to put plus sign, minus sign or a question mark against each statement. The worker's final rating is taken on an average of the scale values of all statements.

Model Questions

Section A

1. What is staffing?
2. What is recruitment?
3. What is on-the-job training?
4. Write a note on job rotation.
5. What do you mean by performance appraisal?
6. State the meaning of manpower planning.

Section B

7. State the various sources of recruitment.
8. Explain the various off-the-job training methods.
9. Explain the steps in staffing process.

Section C

10. Explain the various methods of training.
11. Briefly explain the methods of performance appraisal.
12. Discuss the important steps involved in the selection procedure.

I. Multiple Choice

1. Shifting a trainee from one job to another is known as Role playing
   (a) Job playing (b) Job rotation
   (c) Programmed learning (d) Vestibule training
2. Aptitude test consists of
   (a) Attitude test (b) Intelligent test
   (c) Interest test (d) All
3. The detailed examination of the activities involved in a job is called
   (a) Job description (b) Job analysis
   (c) Job satisfaction (d) None
4. The process of choosing individuals who possess necessary skills to fill the job is
   (a) Manpower planning (b) Recruitment
   (c) Selection (d) Interview
5. The method which compares each individual with all other individuals in the group is called

(a) Person-to-person comparison
(b) Graphic scale
(c) Ranking method
(d) Paired comparison

Answes:

1.(b) Job rotation, 2. (d) All, 3. (b) Job analysis, 4. (c) Selection, 5. (d) Paired comparison

II. Say True or False

6. In grading method, employees are ranked in the order of performance.
7. Performance appraisal is the process of judging the effectiveness of executives and managers.
8. Internal sources of recruitment involve people currently working in an organisation.
9. Aptitude test is conducted to increase the interest of candidate in the job.
10. On-the-job training is concerned with developing the employees in the present job.

Answer:

6. False, 7. True, 8. True, 9. False, 10. True

III. Fill in the blanks

11. ________ involves an estimate of the present and future requirements of job in the enterprise.
12. __________means a written statement of the main duties and responsibilities which a job entails.
13. ___________refers to the process of educating and developing selected employees.
14. Under grading method, the employees are ranked in the order of_________.
15. Performance appraisal serves as a basis for ___________

Answer:

11. Manpower planning, 12. Job description, 13. Training, 14. Performance, 15. Promotion

Chapter 13

Direction

Chapter Outline

Definitions — Characteristics of Direction — Importance of Direction — Nature and Scope of Direction — Principles of Direction — Types of Direction — Techniques of Direction — Model Questions

Henry Fayol has developed five functions of management, viz., planning, organising, command, co-ordination and control. The third function of management, i.e., 'Command' is known as 'Directing.' William Newman has viewed that direction is 'actuating.' So, the term 'Direction' stands for that managerial function which initiates organised action. Direction is the managerial function of guiding, motivating, leading and supervising the subordinates to accomplish the desired objectives. With proper direction, workers and staff become active and efficient and consequently, the physical assets like plant and machinery will be put to effective use.

Direction is concerned with mobilising and synthesising human resources and efforts to accomplish the goals of the organisation. It provides the necessary guidance and inspiration to people at work in order to carry out their assigned duties. So, it is rightly said that direction is a continuous process around which all performance resolves.

I. Definitions

1. Koontz and O'Donnell: "Direction is a complex function that includes all those activities which are designed to encourage subordinates to work effectively and efficiently in both the short- and long-run."

2. William Newman: "Directing (activating) deals with the steps a manager takes to get subordinates and others to carry out plans."

3. E. Dale: "Directing is telling people what to do and seeing that they do it to the best of their ability."

4. Theo Haimann: "Direction consists of the processes and techniques utilised in issuing instructions and making certain that the operations are carried out as originally planned."

5. S. S. Chatterjee: "Direction is the sum total of managerial efforts that is applied for guiding and inspiring the working teams to make better accomplishments in the organisation."

II. Characteristics of Direction

The above definitions point out the following characteristics of direction:

1. Direction is a managerial function.
2. It is a continuous process around which all managerial functions evolve.
3. The top level management in the organisation initiates direction and it is followed through the hierarchy.
4. The aim of direction is maintaining harmony among employees in the organisation.
5. Direction provides a link between the different functions in an organisation.

III. Importance of Direction

Direction is an indispensable managerial function since it is mainly concerned with human relations. Direction is important because in its absence, there may be incongruency between individual goals and organisational goals. As pointed out by Koontz and O'Donnell, "People are not primarily interested in the enterprise objectives but they have objectives of their own." Only by proper direction can the managers integrate the individual goals. So, Marshall has remarked that "direction is the heart of administration."

Direction is important because of the following reasons:

1. Direction integrates employees' efforts.
2. Direction bridges the gap between managerial decisions and its implementation.

3. Direction facilitates changes in the organisation.
4. Direction provides stability and balance in the organisation.
5. Direction attempts to get the maximum out of individuals.

IV. Nature and Scope of Direction

Direction plays a vital role in an organisation. Direction is a complex function that includes all those activities which are designed to encourage subordinates to work effectively. The scope of direction is wide. Keeping this view in mind, the modern management thinkers recognise 'direction' as an independent function of the management process. Direction has the following four elements, viz., (a) Supervision; (b) Motivation; (c) Leadership; and (d) Communication.

V. Principles of Direction

Direction deals with people whose behaviour and attitude are quite unpredictable. So, managers can follow some principles while directing their subordinates. The principles of direction can be broadly divided into two categories:

1. Principles relating to the purpose of directing; and
2. Principles relating to the process of directing.

(1) Principles Relating to the Purpose of Directing: The basic purpose of directing is getting the work done by people in order to attain the objectives of the organisation. In this context, the following principles are important:

(i) Principle of harmony of objectives; and

(ii) Principle of maximum individual efforts.

(i) Principle of Harmony of Objectives: The directing function must first of all resolve the conflict between individual goals (job security, incentives, promotion, etc.) and organisational objectives (both profit and wealth maximisation). A manager must try to bring about harmony between these two. When both the interests are harmonised through proper direction, the management will get better results from the work-force.

(ii) Principle of Maximum Individual Efforts: The success of an organisation depends on the contribution made by people working in it. The managers by adopting various techniques of direction can make the people contribute their maximum to the organisation.

(2) **Principles Relating to the Process of Direction:** Principles relating to the process of direction refer to those principles which make a particular direction technique effective and efficient. In this context, the following principles are important:

(i) Principle of unity of command;

(ii) Principle of direct supervision;

(iii) Principle of managerial leadership;

(iv) Principle of managerial communication;

(v) Principle of managerial control; and

(vi) Principle of follow-up.

(i) Principle of Unity of Command: Command must come from executive only. In other words, a person must get instructions and orders from only one superior and he must be responsible to that superior only. By this, the management can avoid 'dual command,' i.e., getting order from more than one supervisor. This situation leads to discipline, harmony etc. Hence, the principle of unity of command is essential.

(ii) Principle of Supervision: The principle of supervision refers to direct supervision of the activities by superiors. Since direct supervision involves face-to-face communication, it solves the problems of employees and boosts their morale.

(iii) Principle of Managerial Leadership: Leadership is the process of influencing individuals to achieve the goals of the organisation. Therefore, managers should be effective leaders.

(iv) Principle of Managerial Communication: The management should develop an effective communication system. A better communication system ensures efficiency of direction.

(v) Principle of Managerial Control: Without managerial control, direction becomes ineffective. So, effective and timely control make better direction.

(vi) Principle of Follow-up: Direction is a continuous process. Besides issuing directions, the management should get feedback from the workforce.

Feedback makes direction effective by adjusting the wheel of management in action.

VI. Types of Direction

Direction is of two types, viz., oral and written. According to Haimann, oral orders (oral directions) are almost invariably used when the action required is routine or relatively simple in character. Also, in time of an emergency, oral directions are used. On the other hand, written directions are comparatively more intelligible and so the chance of misunderstanding is less. Both types of directions are used in an organisation.

VII. Techniques of Direction

Effective direction can be achieved by adopting one or more of the following techniques:

1. Consultative direction;
2. Free rein direction; and
3. Autocratic direction.

1. Consultative Direction: Under this technique, executives consult their subordinates about the nature of the problem, its possibility and workability before taking a decision and issuing a directive. The success of this technique depends on the attitude of the subordinates.

2. Free Rein Direction: Under the free rein technique, the superiors motivate the subordinates to contribute their ideas, thoughts, etc., for solving a problem. This technique is being increasingly used by the organisation. This technique will show the best and quick results if the subordinates are highly educated.

3. Autocratic Direction: This technique is just the opposite to the free rein direction. Under this technique, the superiors give direct, clear and precise orders to their subordinates with detailed instructions as to how and what is to be done. The role of subordinates is neglected. In other words, there is no room for the initiative on the part of the subordinates. In a military organisation, this technique is used.

The choice of technique of direction depends on the size, nature, time and technicalities of the work in an organisation. A combination of one or more techniques may also be adopted.

Model Questions

Section A

1. Define direction.
2. Distinguish between direction and supervision.
3. "Direction is the heart of administration." Do you agree?
4. What are the three techniques of direction?
5. "Direction is telling people what to do." Do you agree?

Section B

6. What are the elements of direction?
7. Explain the different types of direction.
8. What are the principles of direction?
9. Explain the significance of direction.
10. "Direction is intimately concerned with getting things done." Discuss.

Section C

11. Discuss the nature, scope and characteristics of direction.
12. "Direction involves basically the understanding of human behaviour and guiding the behaviour in specific direction." Discuss.
13. "In the absence of direction, there may be incongruency between individual goals and organisational objectives." Comment.

I. Multiple Choice

1. Direction is known as
   (a) Command (b) Supervision
   (c) Communication (d) None
2. The supervisor motivate the subordinates in
   (a) Consultative direction (b) Free rein direction
   (c) Autocratic direction (d) All
3. Direction has the following functions
   (a) Supervision (b) Motivation
   (c) Communication (d) All

4. The direction is initiated by
   (a) Top level management (b) Middle level management
   (c) Low level management (d) All
5. Telling people what to do is
   (a) Directing (b) Motivating
   (c) Supervision (d) None

Answer:

1. (a) Command, 2. (b) Free rein direction, 3. (d) All, 4. (a) Top level management, 5. (a) Directing.

II. Say True or False

6. Direction is a managerial function.
7. Direction integrates employee's efforts.
8. Direction has three elements.
9. Under free rein direction, the supervisors do not motivate the subordinates to contribute their ideas, thoughts etc.
10. According to Haimann, oral directions are invariably used when the action required is routine and simple.

Answer:

6. True, 7. True, 8. False, 9. False, 10. True.

III. Fill in the blanks

11. _____ is the managerial function of guiding, motivating and supervising the subordinates.
12. The purpose of directing is harmony of objectives and maximum _________.
13. Direction bridges the gap between managerial decisions and _________.
14. In a __________ organisation, autocratic direction is used.
15. Direction is a __________ process.

Answer:

11. Direction, 12. Individual efforts, 13. Implementation, 14. Military, 15. Continuous.

Chapter 14

Supervision

Chapter Outline

Definition — The Role of Supervisor — Essential Qualities of a Supervisor — Functions of a Supervisor — Techniques of Supervision — Model Questions

Supervision is the first element of direction. "Super", refers to "from the above" and "vision" refers to "to see." So, supervision means overseeing the work of subordinates. It also refers to the guidance and instructions given to the employees.

I. Definition

Supervision is defined as "the direct and immediate guidance and control of subordinates in the performance to their task."

The above definition points out that supervision is guiding the subordinates and controlling of their activities so as to get their performance.

According to Dalton E. McFarland, supervision means the responsibilities of the first-line supervisor and general supervisors at the next higher level. So, supervision is done at all levels of management.

II. The Role of Supervisor

The position of a supervisor is a quasi-managerial one in an organisation. He is positioned between the management and the employees and serves as a Ink between them. So, he is described as "the man in the middle" or "whipping boy" or "buffer."

Supervisors are responsible for getting things done by issuing orders, laying down procedures and guiding the employees. They are differently designated as foremen, overseers, head-clerks, section officers superintendents and the like. S.S. Chatterjee views that "even the sincere effort and the splendid work of top management go unrewarded if supervision is faulty." He also points out that it is the supervisor who brings success or failure to the enterprise. So, the supervisor occupies a pivotal position in the organisation. Modern management thinkers say that supervision is "management to the workers".

III. Essential Qualities of a Supervisor

According to L.A. Alien, a supervisor is an authority who is responsible to get the work done. So, a supervisor should possess the following qualities:

(i) The supervisor should be well aware of the techniques of supervision.

(ii) He should possess all the qualities of leadership.

(iii) Since the position of the supervisor is quasi-managerial, he should possess managerial skills.

(iv) His acts should be unbiased and justifiable.

IV. Functions of a Supervisor

Peter F. Drucker has pointed out that "No organisation can functional well if the supervisors do not function effectively." In this context, the following are the important functions of a supervisor:

1. Managerial functions;
2. Assignment of task;
3. Human relations specialist;
4. Technician; and
5. Middleman function.

1. Managerial Functions: A supervisor does all the managerial functions of planning, organising, direction and control. As a planner, the supervisor determines what exactly is to be done by the employees. As an organiser, he brings workers, jobs, machines etc., together in a co-ordinated manner to achieve the objectives. As a leader, the supervisor leads the workforce to achieve the assigned tasks. So, a supervisor is said to be a key man in management.

2. Assignment of Tasks: The supervisor is responsible for setting performance goals in consultation with the management and allocating the work to the employees. Besides, he has to provide the necessary tools and equipments to the workers.

3. Human Relations Specialists: The supervisor acts as a counsellor, motivator and trainer to employees. As a counsellor, the supervisor solves the work-related problems of the group and represents the grievances to the management. As a motivator, the supervisor provides adequate facilities to workers for higher productivity. As a trainer, the supervisor educates workers. In other words, a supervisor does the function of an industrial psychologist. So, he is said to be a human relations specialist in an organisation.

4. Technician: A supervisor himself is a technician and he renders technical advice and imparts technical knowledge to workers.

5. Middleman Function: A supervisor acts as a middleman between the management and employees. Supervisors communicate the message of management to the workers and make known the grievances of workers to the management. So, he serves as a linking pin in the organisations.

V. Techniques of Supervision

The following are the three techniques of supervison:

(i) Autocratic technique;

(ii) Democratic technique; and

(iii) Free rein technique.

(i) Autocratic Technique: Under this technique, the supervisor dictates and issues orders to employees and the employees are bound to complete their job whether they are willing or not. The major defect of this technique is that the concept of human relations is completely ignored. However, this technique is used in the military organisation.

(ii) Democratic Technique: Under this technique, the workers are allowed to participate in the decision-making process. Here, the supervisor is not autocratic but he maintains good human relationship with workers which increases the overall profitability of the organisation. So, it is considered as a sound technique of supervision.

(iii) Free Rein Technique: Under this technique, workers are fully left free to work as satisfactorily as possible. So, the supervisors here only guide the workers. This technique ensures better supervision.

Model Questions

Section A

1. Define supervision.
2. "Supervisor is a key man in the organisation." Do you agree?
3. What is meant by the first-line supervisor?
4. Do you think that 'human relations' play a vital role in making supervision effective?
5. Who is a whipping boy in an organisation?

Section B

6. Explain the role of supervisor in the organisation.
7. Briefly explain the techniques of supervision.
8. "Supervision should be people-minded rather than production-minded." Discuss.

Section C

9. Discuss the functions of a supervisor in an organisation.
10. Explain the factors governing effective supervision.
11. "A good supervisor primarily deals with instructing, guiding and inspiring human beings towards greater level of performance." Discuss.

I. Multiple Choice

1. Supervisor means overseeing the work of

   (a) Superior (b) Subordinates
   (c) All (d) None

2. The workers are allowed to participate in the decision-making process in

   (a) Autocratic technique (b) Democratic technique
   (c) Free rein technique (d) None

3. A Supervisor educates the workers as a

   (a) Counsellor (b) Motivator
   (c) Trainer (d) All

4. As a motivator, the supervisor provides adequate facility

   (a) For higher productivity (b) Training
   (c) Technical advice (d) All

5. A supervisor should possess all the qualities of
   (a) Leadership (b) Leading
   (c) Listening (d) None

Answer:

1. (b) Subordinates, 2. (b) Democratic technique, 3. (d) All, 4. (a) For higher productivity, 5. (a) Leadership

II. Say True or False

6. Supervision deals with the responsibilities of the first line supervisor.
7. A supervisor acts as a counsellor.
8. A supervisor does all the managerial functions.
9. As a trainer, supervisor educates workers.
10. Under autocratic technique, the supervisor does not dictate and issue orders to employees.

Answer:

6. True, 7. True, 8. True, 9. True, 10. False

III. Fill in the blanks

11. ____________ is positioned between the management and the employees.
12. As a leader, the supervisor leads the workforce to achieve the assigned _______.
13. The action of supervisor should be unbiased and ______________.
14. The position of a supervisor is a ___________ managerial one.
15. Supervision should be people-minded rather than ____________ minded.

Answer:

11. Supervisor, 12. Tasks, 13. Justifiable, 14. Quasi, 15. Production

Chapter 15

Motivation

Chapter Outline

Definitions — Characteristics of Motivation — Motivation and Satisfaction — Importance of Motivation — Methods of Motivation — Theories of Motivation — Motivation and Morale — Morale and Productivity — Model Questions

The success or failure of a business organisation depends on the performance of people working in it. Generally, performance is determined by three factors, viz., ability, knowledge and motivation. [Performance = (ability + knowledge) × motivation]. Among the three, motivation is the most important factor since it deals with human behavior. The word 'motivation' is derived from the word 'motive' which means 'to move or to activate. 'Motivation is the task of making someone to act in the desired manner.

I. Definitions

1. **Koontz and O'Donnell:** "Motivation is a general term applying to the entire class of drives, desires, needs, wishes and similar forces that induce an individual or a group of people to work."
2. **J.E. Rosenz Weig and F.K. Kast:** "Motivation is an inspiration process which impels the members of the team to accomplish the desired goals."
3. **S. Zedeck and M. Blood:** "Motivation is a predisposition to act in a specified goal directed way."

4. **Edwin B. Flippo:** "Motivation is a process of attempting to influence others to do your will through the possibility of gain or reward".

5. **Scott:** "Motivation means a process of stimulating people to action to accomplish desired goals".

II. Characteristics of Motivation

The above definitions convey the following characteristics of motivation:

1. **Motivation is an Internal Feeling:** Motivation refers to a feeling within individuals that directs them to act in certain ways.

2. **Motivation Produces Goal-oriented Behaviour:** Motivation has a profound influence on human behaviour. It directs human behaviour towards the goals.

3. **Motivation can be Positive or Negative:** Positive motivation provides something to an employee in the form of additional pay, bonus, promotion, etc. for better performance. Negative motivation means penalties in the form of demotion, cut in salary, etc.

4. **Motivation is a Continuous Process:** Human needs are infinite. The feeling of needs is a continuous and unending process. So, motivation cannot be a time-bound process. It is a continuous process of satisfying the unending needs of the employees.

III. Motivation and Satisfaction

Motivation is a process of stimulating an individual to do an act which will bring satisfaction of a need and the accomplishment of a desired goal. Satisfaction refers to the contentment experienced by an employee when a want is satisfied. Motivation is the drive toward an outcome and satisfaction is the outcome already experienced. So, motivation and satisfaction are related but not synonymous concepts.

IV. Importance of Motivation

Motivation brings about the following advantages:

1. **High Level of Performance:** Performance is the result of ability and motivation. If the level of ability is equal to the demands of the job, the presence of motivation can improve the performance of work.
2. **Help Reducing Employee Turnover:** A proper system of motivation brings about satisfaction of employees which in turn increases their commitment to the organisation. They continue to stay in the organisation and the ultimate result is low labour turnover.
3. **Easy Availability of the Right Type of Personnel:** A proper system of motivation not only helps to retain the existing workers but also attracts people from outside to work for the organisation.
4. **Help Achieving Organisational Goals:** Motivation, by fulfilling the needs of the employees, causes a feeling of total involvement in the task of the organisation. They work wholeheartedly towards the accomplishment of organisational goals.
5. **Increase in Efficiency:** The motivated workforce ensures improved efficiency and higher output. Increasing labour efficiency benefits the employees and the organisation.
6. **Sense of Belonging:** A proper system of motivational scheme promotes closer identification between enterprise and workers. The workers will feel that the enterprises belongs to them and the interest of the enterprises is their own interest. This results in better relations between management and workers.

V. Methods of Motivation

A methods of motivation have been classified into two parts, viz., financial incentives and non-financial incentives.

1. Financial Incentives: Financial incentives represent monetary benefits to employees. Money has become a powerful motivator not only to satisfy the physical needs but also of obtaining social position and power. Financial incentives may be classified into two, viz., (i) individual financial incentives; and (ii) collective financial incentives.

(i) **Individual Financial Incentives:** Financial incentives include all such plans which stimulate an individual for higher output and to earn higher financial rewards. Taylor's differential piece-rate system, Rowans plan, Hasley's efficiency plan are examples of individual financial incentives.

(ii) **Collective Financial Incentives:** Incentives which help to induce individuals collectively are called collective financial incentives. It ensures higher productivity to the organisation and more income to the employees. Bonus, profit-sharing, pension plan, etc. are examples of collective financial incentives.

2. Non-financial Incentives: Non-financial incentives are required to satisfy the socio-psychological needs which cannot be gratified by money alone. It gives emotional satisfaction rather than financial satisfaction. This can be classified into three parts:

(i) **Individual Incentives:** The following are the various forms of individual incentives:

(a) **Status:** Status in general represents position in society. In an organisation, status means the ranking of positions, powers, rights and responsibilities of an individual. Status acts as an instrument of motivation.

(b) **Promotion:** Promotion means a movement to a higher position which result in an increase in pay and responsibilities of an individual.

(c) **Responsibility:** Challenging and responsible jobs satisfy the needs of people and thereby they complete the job efficiently.

(d) **Making Job Pleasant and Interesting:** The job is so designed that it allows the employees to work with zeal and thereby they satisfy their needs.

(e) **Job Rotation:** Job enlargement — increase number and type of work.

(f) **Job Enrichment:** Plan his own work.

(g) **Recognition of Work:** Recognition means evaluation and appreciation of the work of employees which they expect from the management.

(h) **Job Security:** Job security represents stability about the future, income and work. Security of job makes people free from worries and hence work with zeal.

(ii) **Collective Incentives:** The following are the various forms of collective non-financial incentives:

(a) **Team Spirit:** Developing team spirit by means of co-operation and co-ordination among the workers help to satisfy them and contribute their maximum.

(b) **Informal Groups:** The creation of informal groups provides social satisfaction to employees at work. Besides, it makes people feel to achieve a sense of belonging and security.

(c) **Social Importance of Work:** The management should give such type of work to an employee which is socially acceptable. By performing a job of high social importance, employees get job satisfaction.

(iii) **Institutional Incentives:** Institutional incentives are associated with the environmental factors of organisation. A good organisational climate motivates people. Institutional incentives includes good human relations, high morale, good discipline, better communication, workers' participation and the like.

VI. Theories of Motivation

The theories of motivation have been grouped into two categories, viz.:

(1) Theories, associated with human needs: (i) Maslow's theory; (ii) Herzberg's theory; and (iii) Douglas Mc Gregor's theory.

(2) Theories associated with expectancy of individuals — theories of Vroom, Porter and Lawler.

Theories relating to the first category are discussed here:

(a) Maslow's Need Hierarchy Theory: Abraham Maslow's need hierarchy theory, published in 1943, is one of the most popular theories of motivation. According to him, the behaviour of an individual is determined by his strongest need at a particular moment. Needs that are not satisfied motivate the behaviour. The needs once satisfied, do not serve as a motivator. The needs have a certain priority which can be arranged in the order of priority.

Fig. 15.1 shows the hierarchy of human needs. Step-by-step progression from the lower level needs to the higher level needs is the fundamental assumption of this theory.

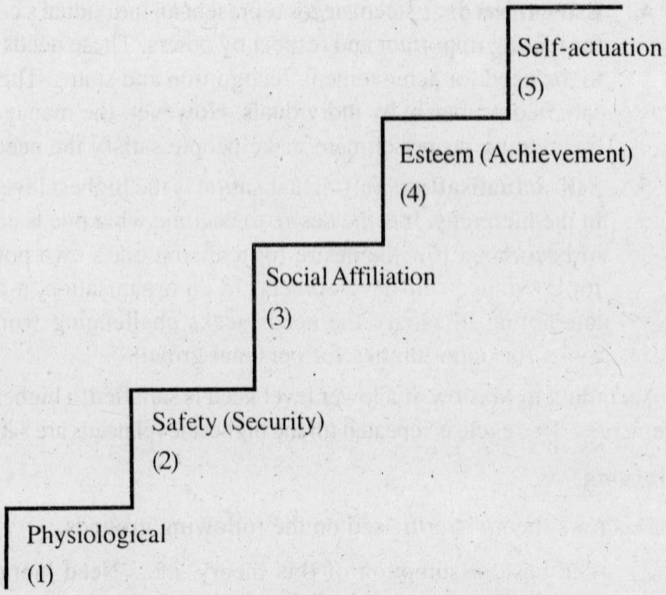

Fig. 15.1 Maslow's Hierarchy Needs

1. **Physiological Needs:** Physiological needs are biological needs required to sustain life itself. These needs include food, cloth, shelter, rest and exercise. These needs dominate when all needs are unsatisfied. As pointed out by Abraham Maslow; "Man lives by bread alone if there is no bread." So, these needs have the highest strength.
2. **Safety Needs:** Once the physiological needs are satisfied, the safety needs or security needs become predominant. These needs include:
   (i) protection from physiological dangers (fire, accident);
   (ii) economic security (job security, health and insurance programme, retirement plan etc.);
   (iii) desire for an orderly environment.
3. **Social Needs:** After the above named two types of needs are satisfied, social needs become an important motivator of behaviour. Since man is a social animal, he wants to belong and to be accepted by various groups. He wants to develop meaningful companionship and friendship with others. Social needs make the work enjoyable.

4. **Esteem Needs:** Esteem needs represent an individual's concern for feeling important and respect by others. These needs relate to the need for achievement, recognition and status. These are satisfied primarily by individuals. However, the management by creating proper climate make people satisfy the needs.

5. **Self-actualisation:** Self-actualisation is the highest level need in the hierarchy. It is the desire to become what one is capable of becoming. It is the desire for realising one's own potential for continued self-development. In an organisation, a person attempting to satisfy the needs seeks challenging work and looks for opportunities for personal growth.

According to Maslow, if a lower level need is satisfied, a higher level need emerges. This cycle is repeated till the highest level needs are satisfied.

Criticisms

Maslow's theory is criticised on the following grounds:

(a) The basic assumption of this theory, i.e., 'Need hierarchy,' does not hold good. Because every person has plenty of needs to be satisfied in some order which may not follow Maslow's need hierarchy.

(b) There is lack of direct cause and effect relationship between need and behaviour.

(c) It is only an empirical theory which is not scientifically tested.

(d) This theory does not cover some motivating factors such as perception, expectation, experience. So, it is not a scientific theory.

Though this theory has some limitations, the identification of basic needs has been fairly popular.

(b) Herzberg's Theory of Motivation: In the year 1959, managers of USA. were wondering why personnel policies and fringe benefits failed to increase employee's motivation on the job. To answer this question, a research study was conducted by Herzberg and his associates. Based on the research study, he developed a theory called "the dual factor theory or the motivation-hygiene of motivation" which is an extension of Maslow's theory of motivation.

According to this theory, man has two categories of needs which are independent of each other and affect behaviour in different ways. The first category of needs are called, "Hygiene factors" and the second category of needs are called "Motivators."

(i) **Hygiene Factors:** Herzberg viewed that hygiene factors create a zero level of motivation and if maintained at a proper level prevent negative type of motivation from occurring. In other words, hygiene factors act as a preventive measure that remove sources of dissatisfaction from the environment. Hygiene factors include 10 maintenance factors which are necessary to maintain a reasonable level of satisfaction among employees. Besides, these factors produce no growth in a workers' output but they prevent losses in performance due to work restrictions. The following are the 10 maintenance factors:

1. Company policy and administration;
2. Technical supervision;
3. Interpersonal relationship with supervisors;
4. Interpersonal relationship with peers;
5. Interpersonal relationship with subordinates;
6. Salary;
7. Job security;
8. Personal life;
9. Working condition; and
10. Status.

(ii) **Motivators:** According to Herzberg, motivational factors are essential to provide job satisfaction and to maintain high job performance. Motivators act as a stimuli that make people happy in the organisation. Motivators include the following six factors:

1. Achievement;
2. Recognition;
3. Work itself;
4. Responsibility;
5. Advancement; and
6. Growth.

An increase in these factors results in an increase in job satisfaction. However, a decrease in these factors does not affect the level of satisfaction. So, these factors are used to motivate employees for higher output. Besides, Herzberg identified the important variable, i.e., the significance of job content in work motivation which had been neglected previously.

Herzberg's Theory in a nutshell:

1. Hygiene Factors:

When absent — increase dissatisfaction.

When present — prevent dissatisfaction.

2. Motivators:

When absent — prevent satisfaction.

When present — lead to satisfaction and motivation.

Comparison of Maslow and Herzberg Models:

Both models concentrate on the factors which motivate employees' behaviour to achieve higher output. Maslow formulated the theory in terms of needs and Herzberg in terms of goals. However, Herzberg has refined the need hierarchy and developed a concept of work motivation (job enrichment). The similarities and differences between the two models are shown in the Fig. 15.2 and Table 15.1 respectively.

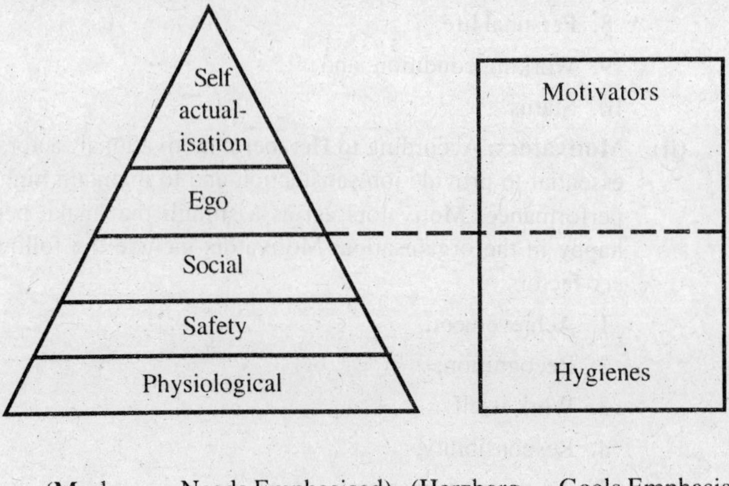

(Maslow — Needs Emphasised) (Herzberg — Goals Emphasised)

Fig. 15.2

Fig. 15.2 makes it evident that motivational factors are equivalent to Maslow's higher order level and hygiene factors are equivalent to lower order needs.

Table 15.1

Difference between Maslow's and Herzberg's 'Model

S.No.	Matter	Maslow's Model	Herzberg's Model
1.	Arrangement	Hierarchical arrangement of needs	No such arrangement of needs
2.	Concept	Unsatisfied needs encourage behaviour which cause performance	Satisfied needs cause performance
3.	No. of needs	Five needs	Sixteen needs
4.	Motivators	All needs are motivators	Only higher order needs are motivators
5.	Applicability	Need oriented – takes into account motivational problems of all workers	Work oriented – motivational problems of professional workers

(c) Douglas McGregor's Theory X and Theory Y: Douglas McGregor has made two sets of alternative assumptions about human behaviour in the organisation as Theory X and Theory Y. The assumptions of Theory X and Theory Y are presented in Table 15.2.

Table 15.2

Assumptions of Theory X and Theory Y

S. No.	Theory X	Theory Y
1.	People dislike work.	Work is as natural as play if the situation is positive.
2.	People do not accept responsibilities.	People are ready to accept responsibilities without fear.
3.	People are not achievement-oriented.	People are achievement-oriented.
4.	People are self-centred.	People are social.
5.	Motivation occurs at the lower order needs.	Motivation occur at the higher order needs as well as lower order needs.
6.	People must be closely controlled.	People can be self-directed and creative at work if properly motivated.

7.	People prefer *status quo* and security.	People dislike them but seek change and challenge in life and work.
8.	People are (likely to be) misled by unscrupulous people since they are simplistic.	People are alert and know the ways of the world.

Theory X

Theory X is a traditional approach of management which is based on the old time-honoured assumptions about behaviour. This theory regards that management must employ coercive methods and exercise tight control over employees to accomplish the objectives. Further, decision-making is the exclusive domain of the management and the workers have to follow the decisions made for them. Management is responsible for organising its elements of productive enterprise.

Theory Y

Theory Y is a modern approach of management. According to this theory, managers attempt to help their employees to develop and mature by exposing them to progressively less external control, allowing them to assume more and more self-control. This theory aims at creating opportunities, removing obstacles, encouraging growth and providing guidance for higher output.

(a) McClelland's Achievement Motivation (Three Needs Theory): According to David McClelland, "there are three major relevant, needs that lend an individual to work such as need for achievement, need for affiliation and need for power."

(i) **The Need for achievement:** The desire to excel, to achieve in relation to a set of standards and to strive to succeed belong to the need for achievement.

(ii) **The Need for affiliation:** The desire for friendly and close interpersonal relationship come under the need for affiliation.

(iii) **The Need for Power:** The desire to make others behave in a way that they would not have behaved otherwise come under the need for power.

Theories relating to the second category, (process theories) are discussed here.

(b) Victor. H. Vroom's Expectancy Model: V.H. Vroom and others have worked out yet another theory of motivation, known as the Expectancy theory. According to V.H. Vroom, motivation is the product of the anticipated values from an action and the perceived probability that these values will be achieved by the action. The anticipated probability is called the 'Valence', and the perceived probability is called the "expectancy". The valence is defined as the strength of a person's performance for the outcome in relation to others. The perceived probability is defined as the strength of belief that a particular act will be followed by a particular outcome. So, motivation is defined as the strength of drive towards action. It is expressed in the following:

Motivation = Valence × Expectancy

VII. Motivation and Morale

The term 'morale' conveys two distinct meanings. First, morale is essentially an individual matter. It refers to the total satisfaction experienced by an employee on his job. Total job satisfaction is composed of a number of factors like earnings, supervision, personnel policies and practices of the employer, job content, financial rewards etc. Secondly, morale is essentially group-oriented. It describes the overall climate prevailing among the members of a group. If they appear to feel good and happy, there exists a high morale. If they are quarrelsome, restless and critical, there may be low morale.

Morale varies from person to person and group morale is the resultant attitude of various levels of individual morale. In this context, Alexander H. Leighton defined morale as "the capacity of a group of people to pull together persistently and consistently in pursuit of a common goal."

As pointed out by Banerjee, "Motivation is intimately connected with morale. Good motivation leads to high morale. Poor morale is the manifestation of a weak or defective motivating process." Therefore, morale is a by-product of motivation.

Benefits of Morale: By building good morale in the organisation, the management enjoys the following advantages:

1. Good morale results in reducing the rate of personnel turnover and absenteeism;
2. Morale is a by-product of satisfaction and so it reduces waste, labour strikes and grievances;

3. Morale produces good discipline in the organisation. So, the task of supervision becomes easier and the company can enjoy the benefit of satisfactory relationship with the labour unions;
4. High morale improves the image of the company and thereby helps company in hiring better personnel;
5. Last but not the least, good morale ensures smooth and successful functioning of the organisation.

VIII. Morale and Productivity

Productivity is a function of four factors, such as, organisational factors, individual factors, attitudes and morale. Attitudes and morale, in turn, are determined by the satisfaction of individuals which is again effected by organisational and individual factors. Thus, productivity is a function of several variables. Of course, morale may be one of the important ones.

There is a belief that the morale and productivity go hand in hand and higher the morale higher the productivity and *vice versa*. But, in practice, it is not so. An increase of five per cent in morale does not guarantee a proportional increase in productivity. It is quite possible to increase morale with either favourable or infavourable shifts in productivity as shown in Figure 15.3.

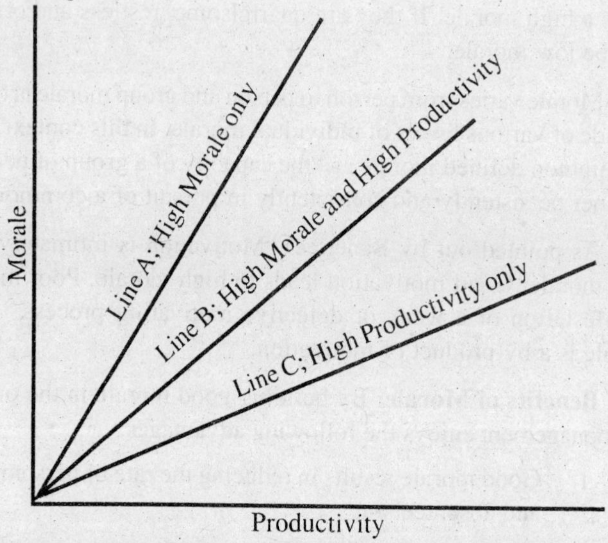

Fig. 15.3 Relationship between Morale and Productivity

(Adapted from Keith Davis, *op. cit.*, p. 67)

Model Questions

Section A

1. Define motivation.
2. What are the differences between motivation and satisfaction?
3. Distinguish between motivators and hygiene factors.
4. Is there a single best way to motivate the employees?
5. "Motivation is the core of management." Do you agree?

Section B

6. Explain the merits of motivation.
7. Explain the various methods to promote motivation.
8. Explain the theories of motivation.
9. Explain the concept of dual theory of motivation.
10. Distinguish between Maslow's and Herzberg's theories of motivation.

Section C

11. Explain the importance of motivation in an organisation.
12. Define morale. How is morale related with motivation?
13. Critically examine Maslow's hierarchy theory of motivation.
14. Briefly explain the assumptions of Theory X and Theory Y.
15. Explain the non-financial incentive method of motivation.

I. Multiple Choice

1. An individual's concern for feeling important and respect for others is known as

   (a) Physiological needs (b) Self-actualisation need

   (c) Social needs (d) Esteem needs

2. Hygiene factors when absent

   (a) Increase dissatisfaction (b) Prevents dissatisfaction

   (c) Prevents satisfaction (d) None of the above

3. Team spirit is a form of

   (a) Individual incentives (b) Collective incentives

   (c) Institutional incentives (d) All

4. Job security relates to
   (a) Psychological needs (b) Safety needs
   (c) Social needs (d) Esteem needs
5. People dislike work according to
   (a) Maslow's theory (b) Theory 'X'
   (c) Theory 'Y' (d) Expectancy theory

Answer

1.(d) Esteem need, 2. (a) Increases dissatisfaction, 3. (b) Collective incentives, 4. (b) Safety needs, 5. (c) Theory 'Y'

II. Say, 'True or False'

1. Motivation means a process of stimulating people to action to accomplish desired goals.
2. Psychological needs are biological needs required to sustain life itself.
3. Self actualization is the highest level need in the hierarchy.
4. The anticipated probability is called the valence and the perceived probability is called the expectancy.
5. Morale describes the overall climate prevailing among the members of a group.

Answer:

6. True, 7. True, 8. True, 9. True, 10. True

III. Fill in the Blanks

6. ____________ is an internal feeling.
7. Douglas McGregor developed theory 'X' and ____________.
8. V.H. Vroom and others have worked out theory of motivation, known as the __________
9. High morale improves the image of the ___________.
10. ___________ is a by-product of motivation.

Answer:

11. Motivation, 12. Theory 'Y', 13. Expectancy theory, 14. Company, 15. Morale.

Chapter 16

Leadership

Chapter Outline

Definitions — Characteristics of Leadership — Importance of Leadership — Functions of Leadership — Qualities of a Leader Leadership Styles — Theories of Leadership — Leadership as a Continuum — Model Questions

All successful organisations have one common attribute, i.e., leadership. Leadership is an important aspect of managing. By performing the functions of planning, organising, staffing and controlling, the managers can get some results. But managers could achieve better results by effective leadershipey. Lawrence A. Appley pointed out in 1955, that the time has come to substitute the word "leadership" for management. Leadership has become an inevitable aspect in industry during the past few decades.

Even a sick unit could be made a successful one by a good leader. Leadership is essential for the success of any business unit. The success of French Coal Combine, a sick unit, under the leadership of Henry Fayol is a classic example in this regard.

According to Peter Drucker, leadership is a characteristic of an individual. The history of the world has been made by able leaders like Napoleon Henry Ford of America, Winston Churchill, Mahatma Gandhi and so on. In the business world, leaders like Ford (General Motor Company, USA), Tata, Birla, Dalmia, Mafatlal, TVS, Nirma and so on have played a predominant role.

According to Keith Davis, "Leadership is something a person does, not something he has". In this context, it is viewed that leadership is the ability to guide, direct and lead people in an organisation towards the attainment of the organisational goals. Besides, leadership is the ability, capacity and potentiality to persuade and influence others to follow him.

Koontz and O'Donnell pointed out that leadership is the ability of a manager to induce subordinates to work with confidence and zeal. According to him, the essence of leadership is 'followership'. In other words, it is the willingness of people to follow him, makes a person a leader. A good manager should possess leadership qualities which make him achieve organisational goals effectively.

I. Definitions

1. **Keith Davis:** "Leadership is the ability to persuade others to seek defined objectives enthusiastically. It is the human factor which binds a group together and motivates it towards goals."
2. **George Terry:** "Leadership is the activity of influencing people to strive willingly for mutual objectives."
3. **Fielder F.E:** "Leadership is the task of directing and co-ordinating task-relevant group activities."
4. **Peter Drucker:** "Leadership is the lifting of man's vision to higher sights, the raising of man's performance to higher standards, the building of man's personality beyond its normal limitations."

II. Characteristics of Leadership

The following are the characteristics of leadership:

1. Leadership presupposes the existence of followers.
2. Leadership is fundamentally a personal quality which motivates the followers to be with the leader.
3. Leadership establishes a relationship between the leader and his team of workers.
4. Leadership deals with understanding the problems of his followers.
5. Leadership helps others in attaining specified goals to the maximum satisfaction of both the leader and the followers.
6. Leadership is a managerial process through which goals are achieved.

III. Importance of Leadership

Leadership is an important aspect of making business organisation successful. As pointed out by Koontz and O'Donnell, "subordinates want to be led and led effectively". So, they want an effective leader and without a good leader, an organisation cannot function efficiently. In this context, the following are the important aspects of leadership:

1. Leader Motivates People: A leader motivates employees for higher output through motivational techniques. So, the leader himself acts as a motivating factor.

2. Leader Counsels Employees: In an organisation, people need counselling to reduce their emotional disequilibrium and to remove barriers to effective performance. A leader solves such types of problems and makes employees happy. Thus, a leader acts as a counsellor to them.

3. Leader Develops Team Spirit: Keith Davis has pointed out that a leader develops team spirit which makes the organisation a success. A leader creates confidence in his subordinates and gains their faith and co-operation. Besides, the leader provides the environment conducive to work which results in team spirit.

4. Leader Aims at Time Management: As stated by Richard M. Hodgets, "Leader is in a position to utilise the time productivity in the organisation. In this context, there are three dimensions of time, viz., boss-imposed time, system-imposed time and self-imposed time. A leader gets things done by people by the proper time management".

5. Leader Strives for Effectiveness: A leader brings effectiveness to an organisation by providing the workers with the necessary resources in terms of money, methods, climate and work environment and soon. So, the effectiveness of the organisation depends on the leader.

IV. Functions of Leadership

A leader, in an organisation, performs many functions which are required to carry out the management process effectively. Crutchfield and his associates have developed 14 leadership functions which are grouped into two categories, viz.,

(a) Primary leadership functions; and

(b) Accessory leadership functions.

Primary leadership functions are essential to achieve the desired organisational goals. Accessory leadership functions are incidental functions which arise by virtue of the position of the leader. Table 16.1 shows the functions of a leader.

Table 16.1

Functions of a Leader

S.No.	Primary Leadership Functions	Accessory Leadership Functions
1.	Executive	Exemplar
2.	Planner	Symbol of the group
3.	Policymaker	Substitute for individual responsibility
4.	Expert	Ideologist
5.	External group representative	Father figure
6.	Controller of internal relations	Scapegoat
7.	Purveyor of rewards and punishments	----
8.	Arbitrator and mediator	----

Managership and Leadership

Managership and leadership are not synonymous. There are differences between them:

(i) Managership deals with drives and orders whereas leadership deals with advices and directions;

(ii) Managership believes in "I" whereas leadership believes in "We";

(iii) Managership associates with authority whereas leadership associates faith, confidence and zeal.

Types of Leaders

There are various types of leaders in business. Alford and Beatty classify them into six types:

(i) Intellectual leader,

(ii) Creative leader;

(iii) Persuasive leader;

(iv) Institutional leader;

(v) Democratic leader; and

(vi) Autocratic leader.

(i) Intellectual Leader: An intellectual leader is one who possesses rich knowledge and technical competence. So, all have to bow their heads down and listen and follow his advice because of his specialised intellectual authority. Financial advisor, special officer, legal advisor are examples of an intellectual leader.

(ii) Creative Leader: Follett has remarked that a creative leader uses the technique of 'circular response' to encourage ideas to flow from group to him and *vice versa*. He draws out the best in his followers and controls them with zeal to attain the goals.

(iii) Persuasive Leader: A leader who gains faith and confidence from the followers is called a persuasive leader. He possesses a magnetic personality which attracts followers which helps him to get work done by them effectively.

(iv) Institutional Leader: When a person becomes a leader by virtue of his position, he is called an institutional leader. The principal of a college, managing director of a company, president of an institution, etc. are examples of institutional leaders.

(v) Democratic Leader: A democratic leader is one who does not lead but is led by his followers. In other words, such leaders follow opinion of the majority of his followers and delegates most of his powers to them. Such leaders are loyal to his followers.

(vi) Autocratic Leader: An autocratic leader is one who dominates and drives his group through coercion and command. He institutes a sense of fear among his followers. Such leaders love power and never delegate their 'authority.

V. Qualities of a Leader

A good leader should possess certain qualities. The qualities which are necessary for a leader are elaborated here.

(i) F.M. Viscount Slim has chosen six qualities of a leader:

1. Courage;
2. Will-power;
3. Judgement;
4. Flexibility;
5. Knowledge; and
6. Integrity.

(ii) Ordway Tead has developed a set of 10 qualities which make a person a leader:

1. Physical and nervous energy;
2. Sense of purpose and direction;
3. Enthusiasm;
4. Love and affection;
5. Integrity;
6. Technical mastery,
7. Decisiveness;
8. Intelligence;
9. Technical skill; and
10. Faith.

(iii) Henry Fayol has considered both physical as well as mental traits of a leader. He has considered the following as the essential qualities of a leader:

1. Health and physical fitness;
2. Intelligence and mutual vigour;
3. Moral qualities;
4. Knowledge; and
5. Managerial ability.

But there is no agreement among the management thinkers on the essential qualities of the leader.

VI. Leadership Styles

The pattern of the behaviour which a leader exhibts while supervising subordinates in an organisation is known as leadership style. There are different styles of leadership identified by the management thinkers. But fundamentally there are three leadership styles, viz.:

1. Autocratic leadership style;
2. Democratic leadership style; and
3. Free rein leadership style.

1. Autocratic or Authoritative Style: An autocratic leader centralises decision-making power in himself. He designs the workload of his employees and exercises tight control over them. The subordinates are bound to follow his orders and directions. He demands strict obedience from the subordinates. People have little freedom working under him. He shows greater concern for work than for his workers.

Merits

1. This style of leadership permits quick decisions and it is effective in a crisis or emergency situation.
2. It provides strong motivation and reward to a manager exercising this leadership.
3. This type of leadership works well with employees who lack initiative and thrive under clear, detailed and achievable directives.

Demerits

1. In autocratic situations, conflict, frustration and low morale arise easily.
2. Today, most people resent authoritation style which reduces them to machine-like log without human dignity and importance.

2. Democratic or Participative Style: In a democratic leadership style, a manager decentralises and delegates his authority to his subordinates. He makes a final decision only after consultation with the subordinates. While delegating a lot of authorities to subordinates, he defines the limits within which people can function. Democratic leaders have a high concern for both people and work.

The participative leadership has certain distinct advantages:

1. The managers by including subordinates in the decision-making process can make better decisions.
2. As the subordinates are consulted and trusted, a positive relationship is developed between the followers and the leaders.
3. Democratic leadership style helps to motivate employees and improve upon their morale and provide organisational stability.

Limitations

1. The participative leadership style needs human relations skill which is not widely possessed.
2. It is a time-consuming process. Leaders find it difficult to provide an atmosphere to the subordinates to participate actively in the decision-making process.
3. Some leaders may use this style as a way of avoiding responsibility.
4. The leaders may lose control if this style is not used properly.

3. Free Rein or Laissez-faire Style: Under this style, a manager gives complete freedom to his subordinates. The entire decision-making authority is entrusted to them. There is least intervention by the leader and so the group operates entirely on its own. The manager does not use power but maintains contact with them. This style helps subordinates to develop independent personality. It is rarely used in organisations since it tends to permit various units of an organisation to proceed at cross-purposes which may lead to chaos. The *laissez-faire* leadership can work in organisations where subordinates are highly competent and duty-conscious and can do better without a leader.

The distinction between autocratic and democratic styles are as follows:

S. No.	Autocratic	Democratic
1.	Decision-making is centralised	Decision-making is decentralised
2.	Communication is one-way	Commumication is two-way
3.	It is task-oriented	It is follower-oriented
4.	It is called Theory X leader	It is called Theory Y leader

Apart from these three styles, there is one more leadership style, i.e., "paternalistic style". A paternalistic leader is one who helps, guides, protects and keeps his followers happy by working together as a member of a team. He looks after his subordinates the way a father does his family. He likes people to be team players but decides what the team will do, i.e., the leader wants to be in-charge but also wants the subordinates to follow his directions. Under the paternalistic style, the subordinates feel free to meet the leader, express their grievances and feel secure about their services. In many organisations, the paternalistic style is quite popular.

VII. Theories of Leadership

A manager is expected to have a thorough knowledge of the different theories of leadership and thereby to lead the group effectively. Researchers have developed many theories of leadership in order to identify the factors which makes a person a good leader. Broadly, the theories of leadership has been classified into the following three types:

1. Trait Theory;
2. Behavioural Theory; and
3. Situational Theory.

1. Trait Theory: This theory was popular between 1930 and 1950 According to this theory, leadership is the result of some traits which a leader possesses. Traits which represent the sum of total of the qualities of a person can either be inherited or developed through training and experience or both.

This theory aims at predicting the success or failure of potential leaders based on their traits. In this context, Ghiselli developed a list of traits that contribute to the leader's effectiveness. Fig. 16.1 shows the list of traits.

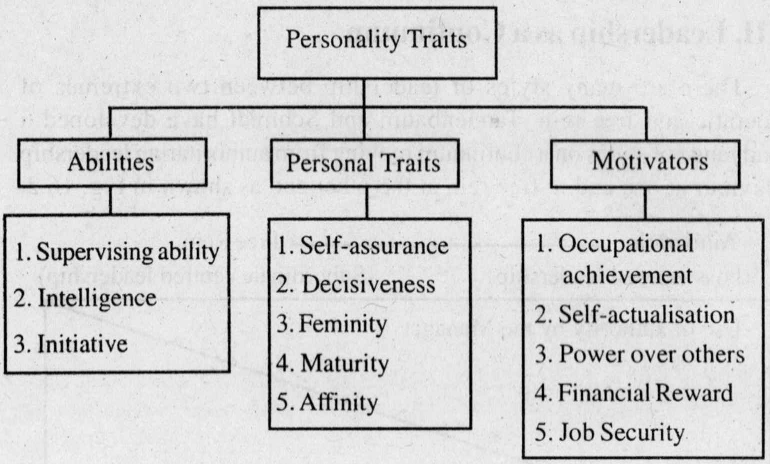

Fig. 16.1 Traits of Leadership Developed by Ghiselli

Though this theory is simple to understand, it fails to consider the whole environment of the leadership, of which trait is only one factor. However, this theory provides useful information regarding leadership qualities.

2. Behavioural Theory: According to this theory, leadership is the result of effective role behaviour. Leadership is shown by a person's acts more than by his traits. So, Michigan researchers replaced the role behaviour in the place of traits and developed two leadership styles, viz., employee-centred and production-centred, which influence performance and productivity. However, this theory fails to integrate the concern for production and people.

To overcome this problem, R.R. Black and Jane S. Mouton, industrial psychologists, developed a model called "Managerial Grid" which is more than a behavioural theory. This theory promises to turn the 'art' of managing into a 'science'. According to this theory, the concern for production and the concern for people should be integrated to achieve the results. This model is successfully applied in industry.

3. Situational Theory: The central idea of this theory is that the situation — the group, the problem and the environment will affect the type of leadership. A specific situation may make a person a good leader. A new leader would emerge on the specific demands of a situation. The thrust of this theory is that the style of leadership adopted to one situation may not be relevant to another situation. This theory states that there cannot be one best style of leadership universally applicable to all situations.

VIII. Leadership as a Continuum

There are many styles of leadership between two extremes of autocratic and free rein. Tannenbaum and Schmidt have developed a broad range of styles on a continuum moving from authoritarian leadership behaviour at one end to free rein at the other end as shown in Fig. 16.2.

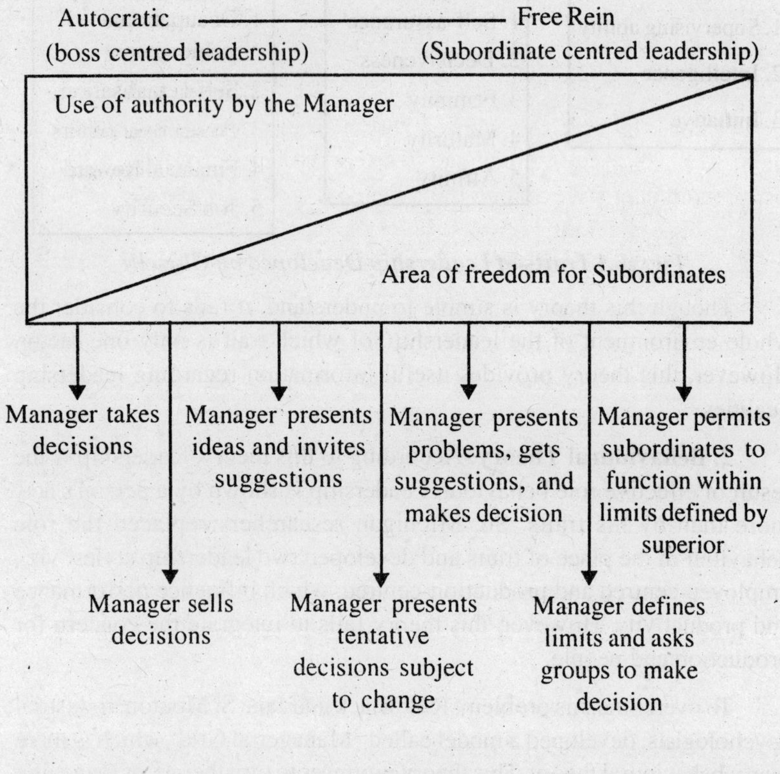

The figure shows a range of leadership behaviour available to a manager. Each type of action represents the degree of authority used by a leader and the degree of freedom which a subordinate enjoys in relationship to his superior. The left side shows a style where control is maintained by a manager and the right side shows the area of freedom. However, neither extreme is absolute as authority and freedom are never without limitations.

Leadership Styles in Indian Organisations

Indian Management is generally believed to be autocratic with subordinates closely supervised by their superiors and only a limited degree of participation is allowed to them. The findings of research studies on leadership styles in Indian industries are given below:

C.A. Myers studied the leadership behaviour of industrialists, government officers, labour leaders and managers in both India and foreign-owned organisations. He concluded that most Indian top managers are relatively authoritarian in their relationship with lower management and labour. This view is supported by Ganguli in his study of Leadership Behaviour in a State-owned Engineering Company.

P. Singh and G.S. Das studied 280 managers from two public and four private sector units and concluded that the bureaucratic style is the most predominant style among the managers. Rangaswamy in his study of leadership behaviour of 56 top-level managers has found that Indian managers are more employee-oriented as compared to their American counterpart.

The study of 120 managers by Jaggi concluded that prevailing leadership style appears to be between benevolent, autocracy and consultative type. The empirical studies available do not support the traditional view rather they present a mixed note.

Model Questions

Section A

1. Define leadership.
2. "A good leader is not necessarily a good manager." Do you agree?
3. Is there a single best style of leadership?
4. What is managerial grid?
5. "Leadership is situational." Do you agree?

Section B

6. "Leaders are not born but made." Discuss.
7. Enumerate the qualities of a leader.
8. "Good leadership is an integral part of effective direction." Discuss.
9. Explain the different leadership styles.
10. What are the different theories of leadership?

Section C

11. Discuss the nature and importance of leadership.
12. Describe the functions performed by a leader in an organisation.
13. In what sense are the trait and behavioural approaches to the study of leadership "two sides of the same coin"?
14. Discuss the advantages of participative leadership style. How is it superior to other styles?
15. What are the differences between autocratic and democratic leadership styles?

I. Multiple Choice

1. A leader who gains the confidence of the followers is called
   (a) Intellectual leader (b) Creative leader
   (c) Persuasive leader (d) Democratic leader
2. A manager gives complete freedom to his subordinates under
   (a) Free rein leadership style (b) Democratic leadership
   (c) Autocratic leadership (d) All
3. A specific situation makes a person leader according to
   (a) Trait theory (b) Behavioural theory
   (c) Situational theory (d) None
4. Quick decisions are possible under
   (a) Democratic leadership style
   (b) Autocratic leadership style
   (c) Free rein leadership style
   (d) None

5. Leadership is a
   (a) Managerial process (b) Personal quality
   (c) Task of directing (d) All

Answer:

1. (c) Persuasive leader, 2. (a) Free rein leadership style, 3. (c) Situational theory, 4. (b) Autocratic leadership style, 5. (d) All

II. Say, 'True or False'

6. The essence of leadership is followership.
7. Leadership counsels employees.
8. A leader who gains faith and confidence from the follower is called a persuasive leader.
9. Communication is two-way in autocratic leadership.
10. Managership believes in 'we' and leadership in 'I'.

Answer:

6. True, 7. True, 8. True, 9. False, 10. False

III. Fill in the blanks

11. Primary leadership functions are essential to achieve the desired organisational _______.
12. _______ leader is one who possesses rich knowledge and technical competence.
13. In a ___________ leadership style, a manager decentralises and delegates his authority to his subordinates.
14. R.R. Black and Jane S. Mouton developed a model called ___________.
15. Leadership presupposes the existence of _________.

Answer:

11. Goals, 12. Intellectual, 13. Democratic 14. Managerial Grid, 15. Followers

Chapter 17

Communication

Chapter Outline

Definitions — Features of Communication — Elements of Communication — Importance of Communication — Types of Communication — Forms of Communication — Barriers to Communication — Making Communication Effective — Ten Commandments of Effective Communication — Model Questions

The word 'communication' is derived from the Latin word 'communis' which means 'common' that stand for sharing of ideas in common. The term 'communication' has varied meanings. It refers to various means of transmitting information from one person to another or from one place to another. It also refers to the act of inducing others to interpret an idea in the manner intended by the writer or the speaker.

Chester Bernard was the first man who recognised the need for communication as early as in 1938. According to him, the first executive function is to develop and maintain a communication system in an organisation. He was of the view that it was communication which linked together all the employees within the organisation. Therefore, communication is one of the fundamental aspects of all human interaction. The ability to communicate effectively has enabled human beings to build organisations, societies and other social groups that make for survival and better living.

According to Ordway Tead, "No business can exist without communication". Communication is a management skill and it is an indispensable part of any management. The management succeeds through effective and purposeful communication. Communication plays the same role in a business organisation as the nervous system in a human body.

I. Definitions

The following are some of the definitions of communication:

(i) **Louis A. Alien:** "Communication is the sum of all the things one person does when he wants to create understanding in the minds of another. It is a bridge of meaning.' It involves a systematic and continuous process of telling, listening and understanding."

(ii) **Charles E. Redfield:** Communication is, "the broad field of human interchange of facts and opinions and not the technologies of telephone, telegraph, radio and the like."

(iii) **M.W. Gumming:** "Communication is the process of conveying messages (facts, ideas, attitudes and opinion) from one person to another so that they are understood."

(iv) **Newman-Summer:** "Communication is an exchange of facts, ideas, opinions or emotions by two or more persons."

(v) **Theo Haimann:** "Communication, fundamental and vital to all managerial action, is the process of imparting ideas and making oneself understood by others."

(vi) **William Scott:** Communication a process which involves the transmission and accurate replication of ideas ensured by a feedback for the purpose of eliciting actions which will accomplish organisational goals."

II. Features of Communication

The following characteristics of communication are derived from the above definitions:

(i) Communication is the process of transfer or transmission of information between two or more persons;

(ii) It is a bridge between two or more people;

(iii) Communication provides for a feedback mechanism;

(iv) Communication facilitates human interaction and aims at achieving the organisational goals.

III. Elements of Communication

According to Redfield, the following are the elements of communication ,process:

(i)	A communicator	—	A person who passes on the information.
(ii)	Transmission		It is the actual issue of orders or information.
(iii)	Stimuli	—	It is the message, order, report or information.
(iv)	A communicatee	—	A person who receives the information.
(v)	Response	—	It is the reply or feedback or reaction of the receiver.

To be an effective communicator, a manager should understand the above basic framework of the communication process.

Fig. 17.1 shows the elements of the communication process.

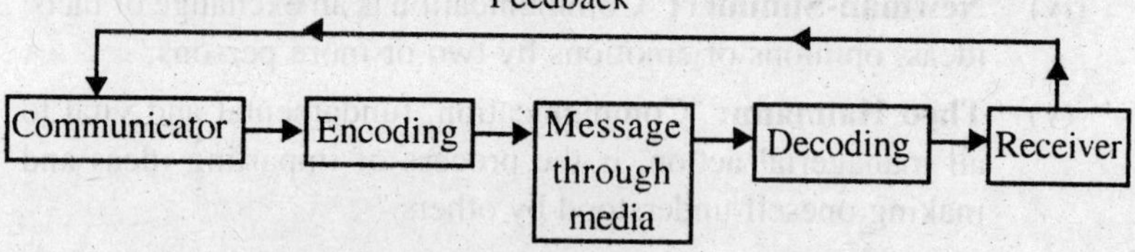

Fig. 17.1 Communication Process

IV. Importance of Communication

(i) Efficient Functioning of the Organisation: The efficient functioning of the organisation totally depends on the effective communication system. Communication helps everyone in the organisation to understand his role clearly and provides a path through which an enterprise can attain the objectives of the organisation.

(ii) Quick Decision and Implementation: A continuous flow of information enables the executives to take decisions quickly and implement them without delay. Therefore, effective communication is a prerequisite for solving managerial problems.

(iii) Good Industrial Relations: It is always desirable on the part of management to avoid disputes rather than finding solutions after they occur. In this context, communication plays a vital role. It provides reliable and accurate information and thereby prevents disputes and promotes good industrial relations in an organisation.

(iv) **Develops Managerial Skill:** According to modern management thinkers, communication which is a learning process helps executives to acquire more knowledge. It also facilitates executives to share the acquired knowledge with their subordinates which results in increase in the overall managerial skill of people in the organisation. Thus, proper communication system develops managerial skill.

V. Types of Communication

Broadly, communication may be divided into following categories:

(i) Formal and Informal,

(ii) Oral and Written,

(iii) Downward and Upward,

(iv) Horizontal,

(v) Communication Network.

(i) Formal and Informal Communication: This type of communication is based on a formal relationship that exists in the formal organisation. It is generally associated with the particular position of the communicator and the receiver. In other words, communication through official channels is known as formal communication. These include the following types, namely:

(i) Departmental meetings;

(ii) Conferences;

(iii) Company news bulletins; and

(iv) Special publications.

Informal communication is unofficial and based on an informal relationship that develops in an organisation. The informal communication, also known as grapevine, is the result of social forces at the workplace. The term 'grapevine' was used for the first time during the days of US Civil War. At that time, intelligence telephone lines were strung loosely from tree to tree in the manner of a grapevine and the message thereon was often distorted. Today, the term 'grapevine' is applicable to all informal communication. Communication grapevine is quite fast and enjoys a high degree of credibility in the organisation. But the message communicated is generally distorted and degenerates into a rumour.

(ii) Oral (Verbal) and Written Communication: Oral communication refers to the communication made through the word-of-mouth. The popular forms of oral communication include speeches, discussions, seminars etc. The following are the merits and demerits of oral communication.

Merits	Demerits
1. Oral communication saves time and money.	It is not suitable when message is long and technical.
2. It gives a personal touch.	It is temporary and not verifiable.
3. It gets immediate feedback.	It may not be a reliable one.
4. Oral communication is informal. and more flexible.	It allows no thinking on the part of receiver.

Written communication refers to the communication in the written form. In of ther words, communication when put in black and white becomes a written communication. Reports, leave letters, memos, commercial letters, orders are examples of written communication.

Merits

1. Written communication is a record and is verifiable when disputes arise.
2. Where the message is lengthy, a written communication is suitable.
3. It is a permanent and tangible evidence and is valid in a court of law.
4. It is formal and official.

Demerits

1. Written communication is time-consuming and seldom flexible.
2. There is no in-built mechanism for feedback which is generally late.
3. There is a possibility of red-tapism.
4. It is expensive.

(iii) Downward and Upward Communication: Downward communication flows from the top management to the lowest level in the organisation. Orders and instructions, directions about a job and its relations, organisational policies, etc. are included in this category. It stands out as a force for initiating, influencing and controlling activities of the members of the organisation.

Upward communication flows from the subordinates to the superior positions. It includes work performance of subordinates, feedback, understanding of orders, clarification of orders opinions and attitudes, criticisms, suggestions etc.

(iv) Horizontal Communication: Horizontal communication, also known as crosswise or lateral or diagonal communication, takes place between two managers or two supervisors of the same status or of the same rank. Communication between two departmental managers like the sales manager and production manager is an example of horizontal communication. This type of communication is based on the concept of 'gangplank' advocated by Henry Fayol. Fig. 17.2 shows the communication channel, i.e., information flows from A to B to C to D and feedback in the same way. If 'D' wishes to communicate to 'A', the communication will have to be channelled from D to C to B and to A.

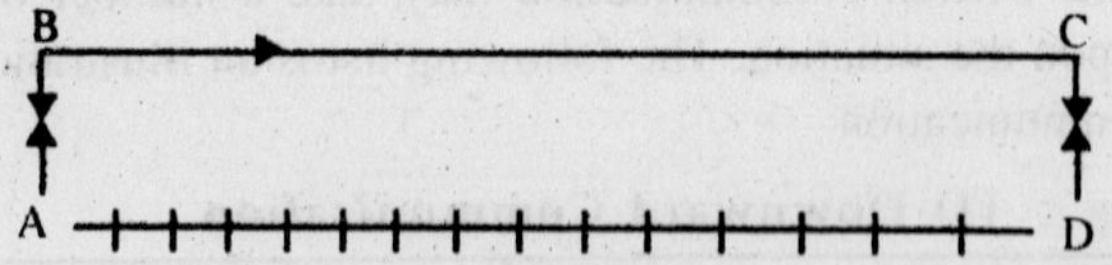

(+++++. --"Gangplank" — not permitted)

Fig. 17.2 Communication Channel

("Gangplank" — not permitted)

To overcome this lengthy process, Henry Fayol has suggested that 'D' can directly communicate to A. This idea is coined as 'Gangplank' which is popular in a modern organisation.

(v) Communication Network: The route through which communication flows from the communicator to the receiver is called 'communication network' or 'route'. A number of such networks exist in the organisation. Three types of networks are shown in Fig 17.3 (a), (b) and (c).

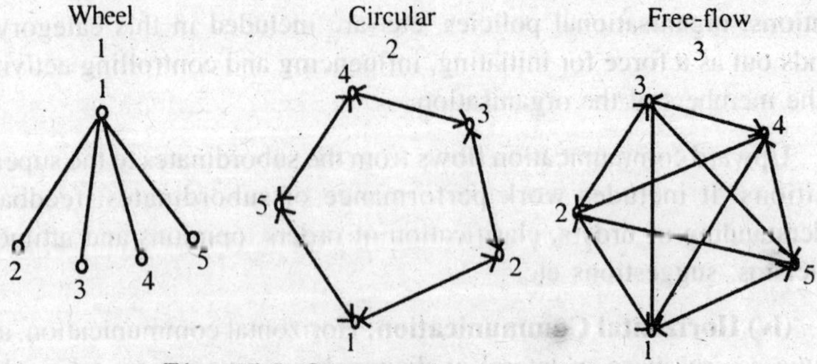

Fig. 17.3 Communication Network

In the wheel network, four persons can communicate with only a central fifth person. In the circular network, each person can communicate with his two neighbours only. In the free-flow or all channel communication network, every person is allowed to communicate with others.

VI. Forms of Communication

Oral and written communication may take a number of forms, depending upon the situation. The following list is an illustration of the forms of communication:

(1) Downward Communication

Oral	Written
1. Personal instructions	1. Orders and instructions
2. Lectures, conferences and meetings	2. Letters, memos and circulars
3. Interviews and counselling	3. Bulletin and notice board
4. Social and cultural affairs	4. Posters
5. Grapevine	5. Handbook and manuals
	6. Annual reports
	7. Union publications

(2) Upward Communication

Oral	Written
1. Face-to-face conversation	1. Reports
2. Interviews	2. Personal letters
3. Meeting and conferences	3. Grievances
4. Social and cultural affairs	4. Suggestion system
5. Grapevine	5. Complaint system
6. Union Channels	6. Attitude and morale surveys
7. Telephone and other devices	7. Union publications

(3) Horizontal Communication

Oral	Written
1. Lectures, conferences and meetings	1. Letters, memos and reports
2. Telephone and other devices	2. Handbooks and manuals
3. Social and cultural affairs	3. Annual reports
4. Grapevine	4. Union publications

VII. Barriers to Communication

There are a number of factors that impede the flow of communication in the organisation. They may be classified as follows:

(a) External barriers;
(b) Organisational barriers;
(c) Mechanical barriers; and
(d) Personal barriers.

(a) External Barriers

External barriers are those barriers which affect the communication network in any context. The following are the elements of external barriers: (i) semantic barrier, and (ii) emotional or psychological barrier.

(i) Semantic Barriers: In the communication process, the receiver is expected to understand the message in the same way as the communicator. In the process of receiving and understanding of the message, certain obstructions are caused due to the capacity of the parties involved to understand it. Such obstructions are called 'semantic barriers.'

The following are the semantic barriers:

1. **Badly Expressed Message:** The sender of communication may have a clear idea in his mind. But the message may not be communicated properly if there is no clarity and precision in it; Poorly chosen words, lack of coherence, bad organisation of ideas, awkward sentence structure, repetition, use of jargon etc. make the message badly expressed.
2. **Faulty Translation:** Faulty translations lead to distorted messages. So, the communicator should use words appropriate to the framework in which the receiver operates.
3. **Unclarified Assumptions:** The message may be specific but the assumptions may not be clear to the receiver. The unclarified assumption may result in confusion.

(ii) Emotional or Psychological Barriers: Emotional and psychological status of the communicator and receiver is an important barrier to the effective communication. The following are some of the psychological barriers:

1. **Premature Evaluation:** The receiver makes judgement about the worth of the message prior to receiving the entire communication. Such judgement may be based on the past experience of the receiver. A manager may pay little attention to a memorandum from the union leader because "he is always up against something".
2. **Inattention:** The preoccupied mind of the receiver makes him not to pay attention to the message.
3. **Loss by Transmission and Poor Retention:** In a series of transmission from one person to the next, the message becomes less accurate. A study has found that the employees retain about 50 per cent of the information they receive and supervisors only 60 per cent. Poor retention of the information is a major reason for this problem.
4. **Distrust and Fear:** Distrust and fear of the communicator is another barrier to effective communication. In a climate of distrust and fear, there will not be open and honest communication.

(b) Organisational Barriers

1. **Organisational Policy:** The organisational policy serves as a guideline to the members in the organisation. If the policy is not supportive to the flow of communication, the flow would be affected.
2. **Organisational Rules and Procedures:** Organisational rules and procedures prescribe the channel through which the communication is to flow and the subject-matter to be communicated. These rules and procedures act as barriers, thereby delaying the message and also restricting the flow of communication.
3. **Status and Position:** 'Status' refers to the attitude of members of the organisation towards a position and its occupant. Status arises on account of the formal position in the hierarchy. Persons enjoying higher positions generally do not share information with their subordinates. Subordinates also feel reluctant to report their shortcomings to them for fear of loss

of prestige. Thus, the difference in position in terms of status acts as a barrier to the smooth flow of communication.

4. **Organisation Structure:** Effective communication depends, to a large extent, on the organisational structure. If it involves several layers of supervision, long communication lines, complex relations among the personnel and a long distance between the management and the workers, the communication gets distorted. At every layer of the structure, a, set of information is cut off and the communication becomes ineffective.

(c) Mechanical Barriers

The flow of communication is also affected by mechanical barriers. Inadequate provisions made for transmitting messages, poor organisational layout, defective communication network and media, etc. hinder the communication system.

(d) Personal Barriers

Communication is basically an interpersonal process. So, the person involved in communication — the sender and the receiver — act as barriers in a number of ways:

1. **Attitude of Superiors:** The attitude of superiors towards communication and their subordinates act as barriers. Insistance on passing information through the formal channels, withholding information to cover their weaknesses, lack of confidence in the competence and capacity of subordinates, lack of awareness about the significance of the message, etc. hinder the flow of communication.

2. **Attitude of Subordinates:** The attitude of subordinates to withhold information which is likely to affect them adversely or which can control purposes and also modify the information to protect his own interest, etc. prevent the free flow of communication.

VIII. Making Communication Effective

Considering the importance of communication, it is necessary to take steps to overcome the above barriers and make communication effective. The following are some of the suggestions in this regard:

1. **Clarity in Idea:** The communicator should be clear about the message he wants to communicate.

2. **Use Simple Language:** The communicator should use the language which is understandable by the receiver. Use of simple language with appropriate words, avoiding ambiguous words and complicated jargon will make the communication effective.
3. **Choose Media and Channel Carefully:** The communication channel should be selected and employed carefully. For important messages, more than one channel may be used. A judicious combination of formal and informal communication will help in achieving effective communication.
4. **Empathy in Communication:** 'Empathy' refers to projecting oneself into the viewpoint of the other person. When the sender looks from the point of view of the receiver, much of the problems will be avoided. The sender should be sensitive to the needs, feelings and perceptions of the receiver so that communication can be effective.
5. **Restating the Flow of Information:** Regulating the flow of communication ensures an optimum flow of information. The principle of 'Management by exception' may be followed so that managers will not be overburdened and concentrate on the messages of high priority. The message may be condensed or edited and arranged in the order of merit. This will burden the subordinates with minimum and necessary information so that work is not hampered.
6. **Good Listening:** Hearing is passive and listening is active and is an intellectual process. Good listening removes communication barriers.

Keith Davis has suggested ten principles to improve listening:

(i) Stop talking;
(ii) Put the listeners at ease;
(iii) Show the talker that you want to listen;
(iv) Remove distraction;
(v) Empathise with the speaker;
(vi) Be patient;
(vii) Hold your temper;
(viii) Do not argue;
(ix) Ask questions; and
(x) Stop.

7. **Providing Adequate Provisions for Feedback:** It is imperative that the management should always promote a two-way communication for the full understanding of the message. In other words, management must provide adequate facilities for the free flow of communication and follow-up by establishing a good communication system.

8. **Providing Communication Training:** Effective communication can be achieved by providing communication training facilities to people working in organisation. It aims at improving speaking skill, listening skill, hearing skill and writing skill. Improvement of such skills results in effective communication.

9. **Providing the Right Organisational Climate:** Organisational barriers can be removed by providing the right climate. In other words, while communicating, the physical and human setting should be considered. For example, one of the ways to build up good human relations is that the managers praise people in public and scold them in private. This technique is called physical and human setting of communication which promotes better communication.

IX. Ten Commandments of Effective Communication

Communication can be improved by the following suggestions made by the American Management Association:

1. Clarify ideas before attempting to communicate.
2. Examine the purposes of communication.
3. Understand the physical and human environment when communicating.
4. In planning communication, consult others to obtain their support as well as the facts.
5. Consider the content and the overtones of the message.
6. Whenever possible, communicate something that helps or is valued by the receiver.
7. Communication, to be effective, requires continuous follow-up.
8. Communicate messages that are of short-run and long-run importance.
9. Actions must be congruent with communication.
10. Be a good listener.

Model Questions

Section A

1. Define communication.
2. What do you mean by grapevine?
3. What is communication network?
4. What is a gangplank?
5. "Communication is sharing of understanding," Do you agree?

Section B

6. Distinguish between oral and written communication.
7. What are the elements of communication?
8. Explain the importance and characteristics of communication.
9. Explain the ten commandments of effective communication.
10. "Half-way communication gets half-way results." Comment.

Section C

11. Discuss the communication process in an organisation.
12. What are the barriers to effective communication? How can the barriers be removed?
13. Explain the various types of communication. Discuss the comparative advantages of verbal and written communication.
14. Explain the requisites for making communication effective.
15. "Management is like a two-way traffic. It is based on an effective machinery of communication." Discuss.

I. Multiple Choice

1. The communication that takes place between two managers of the same rank is called
   (a) Downward communication
   (b) Upward communication
   (c) Horizontal communication
   (d) None
2. Faulty translations are
   (a) Semantic barriers (b) Organisational barriers
   (c) Personal berriers (d) All
3. Loss by transmission and poor attention is
   (a) Emotional barriers (b) Mechanical barriers
   (c) Personal barriers (d) None

4. The actual issue of orders or information is called
   (a) Transmission (b) Stimuli
   (c) Response (d) None
5. The grapevine communication is
   (a) Formal (b) Informal
   (c) Written (d) Horizontal

Answer:

1. (c) Horizontal communication, 2.(a) Semantic barriers, 3. (a) Emotional barriers, 4. (a) Transmission, 5. (a) Informal

II. Say, 'True or False'

6. Department meetings are informal communication.
7. Communication is the process of conveying messages from one person to another.
8. In the circular network, each person cannot communicate with his two neighbours only.
9. Reply to the message is called response.
10. Faulty translations lead to distorted messages.

Answer:

6. False, 7. True, 8. False, 9. True, 10. True.

III. Fill in the blanks

11. A person who receives the information is called __________.
12. ____________ communication flows from subordinates to supervisors.
13. The word communication is derived from the Latin word "communis" which means ___________.
14. Projecting oneself into the viewpoint of other persons refers to __________.
15. The flow of communication is affected by ____________ barriers due to defective communication network.

Answer:

11. Communicatee, 12. Upward, 13. Empathy, 14. Gangplank, 15. Mechanical.

Chapter 18

Controlling

Chapter Outline

Definitions — Characteristics of Control — Control Vs. Controls — Importance of Control — Control Process — Requirements of an Effective Control — Techniques of Control — Model Questions

Control is a fundamental managerial function which follows other functions such as planning, organisation and direction. Plans do not lead to automatic accomplishment. With a view to complete the plans and achieve the organisational objectives, managers have to exercise control.

Control is concerned with securing individual and organisational performance. This is effected through setting standards, measuring and evaluating the performance against the standards and taking corrective action, whenever necessary.

Control is the effective counterpart to planning. Planning starts and controlling ends the whole sequence of the management process. As pointed by Newman and Warren, "Planning without corresponding control are apt to be hollow hopes". Control involves keeping the organisation activities on the right track and is aligned with plans and goals. Hence, control is not only closely linked with planning but also linked with other managerial functions.

I. Definitions

1. **Koontz and O'Donnell:** "Control, like planning, is ideally forward looking and the best kind of managerial control corrects deviations from plans before they occur."
2. **Peter Drucker:** "Control maintains an equilibrium between the ends and means, output and efforts."
3. **George R. Terry:** "Controlling is determining what is being accomplished, that is, evaluating the performance and, if necessary, applying corrective measures so that the performance takes place according to plans."
4. **S.S. Chatterjee:** "Controlling is an executive process involving three elements — standards, evaluation and corrective action."
5. **E.F.L. Breach:** "Control is checking event performance against predetermined standards contained in the plans, with a view to ensuring adequate progress and satisfactory performance."

II. Characteristics of Control

On the basis of the above definitions, the following characteristics are identified.

1. Control forces event to conform to the plan. So, control and plans are closely interrelated. Control has similar characteristics of the plan such as unity, continuity, flexibility etc.
2. Control involves constant revision and analysis of standards in the light objectives of the organisations. So, it is a continuous process.
3. Control is the function of every manager. However, the scope of control varies among managers. The top level management is concerned with administrative control and the lower level management is concerned with operational control. So, control is an essential managerial function at every level.
4. Effective control depends on the organisation structure, proper direction, flow of communication and feedback. So, control is an all-pervasive function.

Control Vs. Controls

In management science, control means measurement whereas controlling is the process of collecting and feedback of information. Peter

F. Drucker has given the following differences between the term 'control' and 'controls':

(i) Control refers to direction whereas controls refer to measurement;

(ii) Control pertains to an end whereas controls pertain to the means;

(iii) Control deals with the future events whereas controls deal with the past events; and

(iv) Control is normative whereas controls are analytical. Thus, control is not controls.

III. Importance of Control

The controlling function may result in the following benefits:

1. Increases Efficiency: Controlling is exercised to standardize performance for increasing efficiency and reducing cost by way of time and motion studies, inspections, written directives and the like. All these result in an increase in the overall performance of the organisation.

2. Helps to Measure Job Performance: Controlling is used to measure the job performance by way of special reports, budgets, internal audit, interpersonnel communication and the like. This leads to an increase in labour efficiency and decrease in labour turnover.

3. Keeps a Balance in Managerial Activities: Control helps the top management for keeping the various plans and programmes in balance through the master budget, policy and organisational manual and management consultants. This results in the effective utilisation of financial resources which every organisation expects from the controlling function.

4. Facilitates Co-ordination: Control keeps all activities and efforts within their fixed boundaries and makes them move towards goals through co-ordinated activities. Thus, control facilitates co-ordination.

5. Ensures Achievement of Objectives: The function of control is to regulate the activities in such a way as to conform to the predetermined objectives. So, control eliminates the risk of non-conformity and ensures achievement of objectives.

6. Enhances Employee Morale: Control motivates personnel to work more through promotions, rewards for suggestions, profit-sharing and other methods. Control is vital to the strength of the company.

IV. Control Process

According to Koontz and O'Donnell, the control process involves the following three steps:

1. Establishing standards;
2. Measuring performances; and
3. Correcting the deviations.

1. Establishing Standards: Establishment of standards is the first step in the controlling process. Standards are criteria for judging the results. Standards are the performance expectations, as pointed by R.M. Copeland and P.E. Dascher. In other words, standards may be defined as measured quantities which should be attained in connection with some particular operation or activity. Standard is a measuring rod in attaining goals. Fred Luthans viewed that "in essence, standards are used to control objectives, objectives are used to control goals, and goals are used to control purpose." Thus, standards are the yardsticks of performance and as such must be established.

While establishing standards, the manager is expected to consider the following questions and find out the answers:

(a) What are the types or standards required?

(b) How to set the standard?

(c) Which strategic points should be selected?

(a) Types of Standards: In an organisation, there are many types of standards. But broadly, it is divided into quantitative and qualitative standards. Normally, standards are expressed in terms of physical, monetary and time. Physical standards include the quantity of production, number of customers and quality of the product etc. Monetary standards include gross profit, net profit, and sales etc. Time standard refers to the speed with which the job is to be done. For example, a particular typist is considered to be efficient, depending on his typing speed per minute, i.e., 80 words per minute.

(b) How to Set the Standard: While setting standards, due consideration should be given to the characteristics of the work, since it differs from one operation to another. Therefore, the manager must collect all the relevant information in this regard.

(c) Strategic Points: Management should select some strategic points that reflect the total operation. For example, output, inventory and efficiency in operation are examples of strategic points. Besides, limited points and control points should be selected which act as a measurement device. In this context, Prof. Newman has suggested four guides for selecting strategic points as below:

(i) The control points should be timely so that they may be able to reveal significant deviation in time thereby saving further losses.

(ii) Control points should be such as to permit economic observation and report.

(iii) Control points, especially for executives at higher levels, should provide comprehensive coverage.

(iv) Control points should be such as would promote balanced performance.

2. Measurement of Performance: After standards are established, the next step in the control process is the measurement of performance. While measuring the performance of standard, the following questions should be kept in mind:

(i) What and how to measure?

(ii) Why to measure?

(iii) When to measure? and

(iv) How to check the performance?

Measurement of performance is an easy task when the standards and methods of measuring performance are clear. Peter Drucker pointed out that it is very much desirable to have clear and common measurements in all key areas of business. For example, the performance which is quantitative, can easily be measured in terms of production units, sales units, gross profit, whereas the qualitative performance such as morale, human relations, job satisfaction, etc., cannot easily be measured because of lack of standards. Some techniques are used to measure standards, such as personal observation, sampling surprise visit, managerial accounting tools and so on.

While measuring performance, comparison of the actual and standard performance should be made in order to find out the deviations and the causes of such deviations. This enables better control and ensures better performance.

3. Correcting the Deviations: The final step in the controlling process is correcting the deviations. Correction of deviations may be done by adopting the following control action:

(i) Review of plans and goals and change therein on the basis of such review;

(ii) Change in the assignment of tasks;

(iii) Change in the existing techniques of direction;

(iv) Change in the organisation structure; etc.

Corrective actions are necessary to avoid the occurrence of unfavourable deviations in future. Corrective actions make control effective and inculcate a sense of responsibility and discipline among the employees.

V. Requirements of an Effective Control System

The goals of organisation are achieved through an effective control system. So, the manager should have an effective control system. The following are the prerequisites for an effective control system:

1. Suitability: The control system should reflect the nature and needs of the company. The control system differs from company to company, and department to department. A large company calls for controls different from a small company. In the same way, the tools of control used in the sales department is different from those used in the personnel department. So, the manager should select the right tool for control which results in controlling actions according to the plan. In other words, the control system should reflect both the nature of activity and organisational pattern.

2. Tailored to Individual Manager: A manager is the controller who is expected to have effective control over all departmental activities. In this context, the management should provide adequate facilities to managers to be thoroughly aware of the control techniques to be used in the organisation. Therefore, the system of control should be well-organised only after consulting the managers.

3. Control by Exception: An effective control system calls for the application of the principle of management by exception. Significant deviation from the standard constitute exceptions. Managers should pay immediate attention to the exception to make the control effective.

4. Flexibility: The system of control should be flexible so as to accommodate all changes or failures in plans. In other words, controls must remain workable in the face of changed plans. Flexibility in control is generally achieved through flexible budgets.

5. Economical: Controls should be worth their cost. In fact, economy is a relative concept since the costs and benefits vary from one operation to another. However, the control system can be made economical by tailoring controls to the job and the size of the organisation.

6. Objective: It should be objective and definite, otherwise many subjective elements enter into the process which catch the controller and controlled on a wrong fooling. Besides, objective control should be determinable and quantifiable.

7. Lead to Corrective Action: The control system facilitates managers to identify the deviations from the standard. Once the deviations are identified, it should be reported without loss of time so that corrective action can be initiated immediately. This is done through the management information system.

8. Simplicity: The control system should be easy to understand and operate. A complicated control system will cause unnecessary confusion and frustration among employees. Proper understanding of the system will ensure its implementation.

9. Time Element: Effective control system attaches importance to the time element. A good control system should report the deviations as promptly as possible. Appropriate action should be taken without loss of time especially in matters like cash management, inventory management etc.

10. Forward Looking: An effective control system always aims at future. Control through feedback provides a framework within which planning can be undertaken. So, control always looks forward, of course through planning.

VI. Techniques of Control

In an organisation, a variety of control techniques are used in controlling the operations. These techniques are useful in measuring the overall performance of the organisation. Broadly, the techniques of control are classified into two heads, viz., budgetary and non-budgetary control techniques. The following chart shows the classification of control techniques.

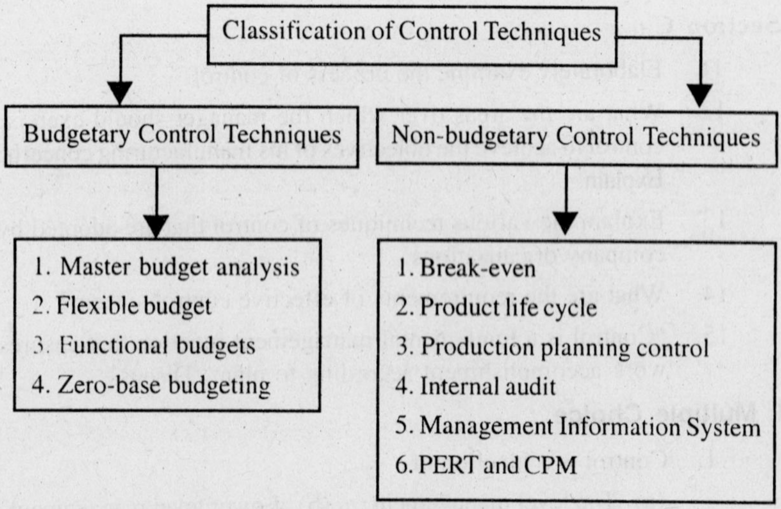

Fig. 18.1

The choice of selecting the control techniques depends on the nature and size of business. However, in a big organisation, all control techniques are used to achieve the desired goals.

Model Questions

Section A

1. Define control.
2. What is feedback control?
3. What is feed forward control?
4. What do you mean by standard?
5. Distinguish between control and controls.

Section B

6. Enlighten the correlation between planning and control.
7. Explain the importance and characteristics of control.
8. Explain the procedures for establishing standards.
9. "Planning is the basis, delegation is the key, information is the guide and action is the essence of control." Discuss.
10. "Control is an all-pervasive function." Discuss.

Section C

11. Elaborately examine the process of control.
12. What are the areas over which the manager should exercise control to achieve the objectives of his manufacturing concern? Explain.
13. Explain the various techniques of control that are adopted by company organisations.
14. What are the requirements of effective control system?
15. "Control is a fundamental management function that ensures work accomplishment according to plan." Discuss.

I. Multiple Choice

1. Control is a function of
   (a) Top level management (b) Lower level management
   (c) All managers (d) None
2. Number of customers is a
   (a) Physical standard (b) Monetary standard
   (c) Time standard (d) None
3. The requirement of an effective control system is
   (a) Flexible (b) Objective
   (c) Suitable (d) All
4. Effective control depends on
   (a) Organisation structure (b) Proper direction
   (c) Flow of communication (d) All
5. Zero-base budgeting is one of the budgeting control
   (a) Techniques (b) Times
   (c) Texts (d) None

Answer:

1. (c) All managers, 2. (a) Physical standard, 3. (d) All, 4. (d) All, 5. (a) Techniques

II. Say, 'True or False'

6. The final step in controlling process is measuring performance.
7. Controlling is an executive process involving three elements.
8. Control facilitates co-ordination.

9. Monetary standards do not include net profit and sales.
10. Break-even analysis is one of the non-budgetary control techniques.

Answer:

6. False, 7. True, 8. True, 9. False, 10. True.

III. Fill in the blanks

11. Control refers to direction whereas controls refer to __________.
12. __________ standard refers to the speed with which the job is to be done.
13. Standards are the yardsticks of ____________.
14. The control system facilitates managers to identify the deviations from the ______.
15. An effective control system requires the application of management by _______.

Answer:

(11) Measurement, (12) Time, (13) Performance, (14) Standard, (15) Exception

Chapter 19

Control Techniques

Chapter Outline

Introduction — Budgetary Control — Characteristics of Budgetary Control — Advantages of Budgetary Control — Budgetary Control Techniques — Types of Budgets — Non-Budgetary Control Techniques — Operations Research — Model Questions

I. Introduction

Control has a regulatory effect. For better performance and better results, certain means of control have been evolved. These are called control techniques. The control techniques are classified into two broad categories such as, budgetary control techniques and non-budgetary control techniques.

II. Budgetary Control

A budget is an anticipated financial statement of revenue and expenses for a specified period. Budgeting refers to the formulation of plan for a given period in numerical terms.

According to Floyd H. Rowland and William H. Barr, "Budgetary Control is a tool of management used to plan, carry out and control the operation of business. As a further explanation, it establishes predetermined objectives and provide the basis for measuring performance against these objectives."

According to Cecil Gillespie, Budget is "a plan of operations integrated and co-ordinated, comprising all phases of business activities and summarised to show the financial results of carrying out the plan".

The above definitions point out that budgeting is an aid to planning and control.

III. Characteristics of Budgetary Control

The following are the characteristics of Budgetary Control:

1. **Planning:** It helps to plan all activities of each department of the enterprise.
2. **Co-ordination:** It ensures co-ordination among all the departments with a view to prepare a master budget.
3. **Recording:** It enables to keep up-to-date records of all activities of the business unit as a whole.
4. **Control:** It aims at comparing the actuals with projected estimates and finding out the deviations.
5. **Corrective Actions:** It ensures corrective actions on the basis of deviations for better results.

IV. Advantages of Budgetary Control System

The following are the advantages of budgetary control system:

1. Budgetary Control integrates and ties together all activities of the enterprise right from planning to controlling.
2. It is an effective method of controlling activities of the business unit since it provides standards against which actual performance is measured.
3. It is a useful tool in profit planning. It helps in setting targets for profits and related matters.
4. Control helps to eliminate or reduce unproductive activities and minimising waste.
5. Control makes everyone accountable for their work, as it defines the responsibility for performances.
6. It helps in directing, counselling, guiding and supervising in a co-ordinated manner. So, this improves the overall performance of the business unit.

V. Budgetary Control Techniques — Types of Budgets

Every business unit has large variety of plans such as, production plan, sales plan, financial plan and the like. When these plans are projected in advance, they are called budgets. The budgets may be classified on the following basis:

1. Coverage of function	Master budget and Financial budget.
2. Nature of activities	Capital and Revenue budgets.
3. Period	Long and Short-term budgets
4. Flexibility	Fixed and Flexible budgets.
5. Preparation of budget method	Performance and Zero base budget.

A description of major budgets is given below:

1. Master Budget: The Master Budget is a budget which covers all types of budgets such as sales, production, costs, profit and appropriation of profit. It deals with the summary budget incorporating various functional budgets.

2. Flexible Budget: A budget which is designed to change in accordance with the activities of the organisation is known as flexible budget. It is quite useful for control as well as for planning purposes in uncertain environments.

3. Functional Budgets: The functional budgets have a number of classification depending upon the type of functions performed and budgeting practices adopted by an organisation. Therefore, there can be budgets for each major functions and sub-functions like Materials budget, Production budget, Financial budget, Marketing budget, Sales budget, Research and Development budget, Personnel budget and the like.

4. Zero Base Budget (ZBB): Zero base budgeting was originally developed by Texas Instruments of USA in 1970s. The key element in ZBB is future-objective orientation of past objectives. Instead of taking the last year's budgets and adjusting them for finding out the future level of activity and preparation of budget therefrom, ZBB forces the managers to review the current, ongoing objectives and operations. Hence, ZBB is a type of budget that requires managers to rejustify the past objectives, projects and budgets and to set priorities for the future. ZBB has three steps such as Decision Package, Ranking and Resources allocation.

Decision Package summarises the scope of work and provides a running commentary of all the activities in a particular project. Then, Decision Packages are ranked on the basis of benefits to the total organisation. Resources are then allocated to the packages according to preferential rank in the organisation. Therefore, ZBB provides an opportunity for the managers to carefully and critically examine, evaluate and prioritise each organisational activity.

VI. Non-budgetary Control Techniques

The control techniques included under this category are as follows:

S. No.	Area	Techniques
1.	Cost Control	Break-even analysis (BEA)
2.	Production Control	Production planning and control (PPC)
3.	Quality Control	Statistical quality control (SQC)
4.	Inventory Control	Economic order quantity (EOQ)
5.	Marketing Control	Marketing research
6.	Financial Control	Ratio analysis
7.	Information Control	Management information system
8.	Operations Research	PERT and CPM

Among the above techniques, few techniques have been explained below:

1. Break-even Analysis: Cost control is essential for the survival of a business unit. Cost analysis shows how efficiently an organisation is managed. Break-even analysis is one of the cost control techniques. Break-even analysis is a function of three factors, i.e., sales volume, cost and profit. It aims at classifying the dynamic relationship existing between total cost and sales volume of a company. Hence, it is also known as cost-volume-profit analysis.

Break-even analysis helps to know the operating conditions that exist when a company 'breaks even', that is, when sales reaches a point equal to all expenses incurred in attaining that level of sales. In other words, it indicates 'No loss no profit point'. Beyond this point, the company makes profit on additional sales. Hence, it is used as invaluable planning and controlling technique. It is based on marginal costing concept. Hence, it deals with Marginal Costing equation and its statement is shown below:

Sales	=	xxx
Less: VariableCost	=	xxx
Contribution		xxx
Less: Fixed cost		xxx
Profit		xxx

Two Approaches to Study Break-even Analysis: There are two well-known approaches to calculate the break-even point: (a) algebrical and (b) graphical approach. A company is said to be in break-even position when the contribution has just enough the fixed costs at the break-even point. An illustration is worked out below:

Sales ₹ 10.000/-		**Solution:**
Variable Cost ₹ 5,000/-		Break-even Sales
Fixed Cost ₹ 3,000/-	=	$\frac{\text{Fixed Cost}}{\text{Contribution}} \times \text{Sales}$
Find out the Break-even point from the above data		
	=	$\frac{3000}{10,000 - 5,000} \times 10,000$
	=	6,000

Under the graphical approach, break-even chart is constructed as in Fig. 19.1.

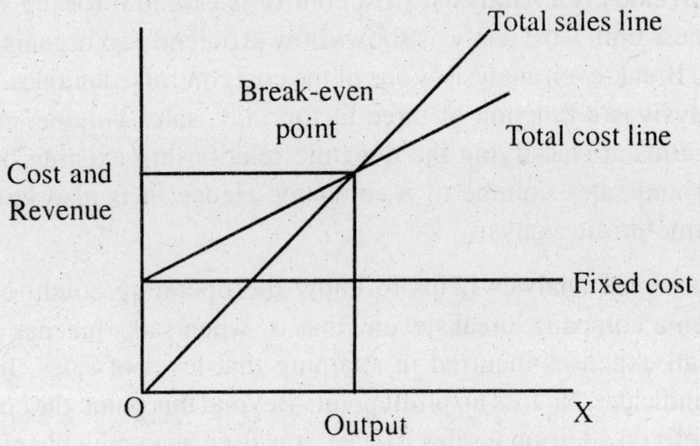

Fig. 19.1 Break-even chart

'X' axis represents the output and 'Y' axis represents costs and revenue. The total cost line and total sales line are drawn and the point of intersection is called break-even point.

Break-even analysis enables the analyst to know the expected amount of sales to have a desired level of profit. Hence, it is widely employed in industrial organisations.

2. Production Planning and Control (PPC): Production planning and control is a yardstick which helps to overcome problems of modern production. In other words, it refers to a decision with regard to quantity, quality and time of production and it helps in the control of the entire production process.

According to Alford and Beatty, "production planning and control comprises the planning, routing, scheduling, despatching and follow-up functions in the productive process so organised that the movement of material, performance of machines and operation of labour, however, subdivided are directed and co-ordinated as to quantity, quality, time and place".

The elements of production planning and control are shown in Fig. 19.2.

Elements of Production Planning and Control

Pre-planning function	**Regulatory function**	**Control function**
1. Forecasting the demand and volume sales.	1. Routing.	1. Inspection.
2. Determining the quantity of production.	2. Scheduling.	2. Evaluation.
3. Determining the production procedure.	3. Despatching.	
4. Laying out of plans.	4. Follow-up.	
5. Materials management.		
6. Research and development.		
7. Internal transport planning.		

Fig. 19.2

Production Control is done through regulating functions such as routing, scheduling, despatching and follow-up.

(i) Routing: According to Kimball and Kimball, "routing is the selection of paths and/or routes over which each piece is to travel in being transformed from raw materials into finished product." In other words, it involves planning of where and by whom work shall be done, the determination of path that work shall follow and the necessary sequence of operations.

(ii) Scheduling: According to G.L. Lendy, "work scheduling consists of the assignment to starting and completion times for the various operations to be performed."

(iii) Despatching: It is a doing function of production control and initiates actual manufacturing in accordance with work of routing and scheduling. Direction of distribution of production work, issue of raw materials, plants, etc., and issue of instructions come under despatching function.

(iv) Follow-up: Follow-up action is essential to get the work completed according to plan in time.

3. Management Information System (MIS): It is an integrated technique for gathering relevant information from whatever source it originates and transferring it into reusable form for the decision-makers in management. MIS provides working tools for all the management personnel in order to take the best possible action at the right time with respect to the operations and functions of the enterprise for which they are largely responsible.

MIS performs a useful triple service function to management, i.e., data generation, data processing and information transmission. Hence, MIS enhances the manager's ability to plan and control and take corrective action. Besides, it provides more specialised and technical kind of information for better results. Hence, MIS has become one of the control techniques which facilitates better performance..

4. Ratio Analysis: The term "ratio" means one number expressed in terms of another. It describes in mathematical terms the relationship which exists between two numbers. Ratio analysis is the process of determining and interpreting numerical relationship based on financial statements. It is a financial control technique. It is considered to be the best guide for the efficient execution of the finance functions like financial planning, forecasting, control, etc.

Classification of Ratios

Accounting ratios may be classified as follows:

1. Classification According to Statements.
2. Classification According to Time.
3. Classification According to Nature.
4. Classification According to Function.

The following Fig. 19.3 shows the classification of ratios according to functions:

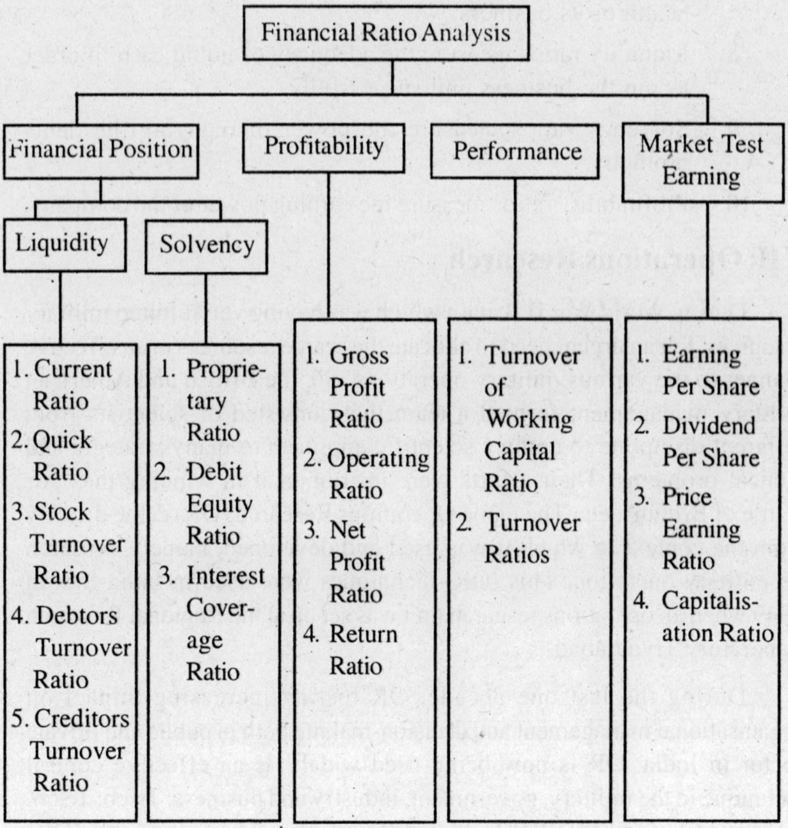

Fig 19.3 Financial Ratio

Advantages of Ratio Analysis

1. Accounting ratios are commonly used for management control purpose.

2. It is one of the media to link between the past and the future.
3. It is useful to assess features of business like liquidity, solvency, profitability, etc.
4. The ratios are also used as measure of efficiency.
5. It is the main tool of analysis for inter-firm and intra-firm comparisons.
6. Ratios serve as a tool for control of performance as well as control of cost.
7. Ratio analysis helps the management to understand the financial health of its business.
8. Liquidity ratios measure the adequacy of liquid cash in order to run the business unit successfully.
9. Solvency ratios measure the power of repaying the debts promptly.
10. Profitability ratios measure the earning power of the company.

VII. Operations Research

During World War II Britain which was having very limited military resources, felt an urgent need to allocate the scarce resources in an effective manner to the various military operations. So, the British and American military management formed a team that consisted of scientists from different discipline to apply a scientific approach to many strategic and tactical problems. Their efforts were instrumental in winning the "Air Battle of Britain", etc. The name Operations Research (OR) came directly from the context in which it was used and developed, namely, research on military operation. This (OR) techniques were used in India first in 1949 when an operations research unit was set up at the Regional Research Laboratory, Hyderabad.

During the last one decade,. OR had an increasing impact on organisational management and decision-making both in public and private sector in India. OR is now being used widely as an effective control technique in the military, government, industry and business. Tisco, Telco, Hindustan Lever Ltd., BHEL, Indian Railways etc. have used this (OR) techniques to make optimum use of their limited resources to maximise the profit.

Textile mills like OCM and DCM apply linear programming techniques in Cotton blending. RCON, NBCC, etc. are making use of PERT/CAM techniques for effective control of their construction projects. Many business enterprises are using OR techniques for solving problems relating to staffing, blending, production planning control, product mix, investment mix, advertising, inspection, transportation etc.

1. Definition

The term "Operations Research" refers to the application of scientific methodology of several different disciplines to problems related to the functioning of business units.

Besides, OR is a scientific approach to decision-making and is an integral part of the multidisciplinary area of management philosophy.

1. **Morse and Kimble:** "A scientific method of providing executive department with a quantitative basis for decisions regarding the operations under this control."
2. **Charchman:** "OR is the application of scientific methods, techniques and tools to problems involving the operations of systems so as to provide those in control of operations with optimum solutions to the problem."
3. **T.L. Saaly:** "OR is the art of giving bad answers to problems, to which otherwise have worse answers."
4. **Ackoff and Sasient:** "OR is the application of scientific method by interdisciplinary teams to problems involving the control for organised systems so as to provide solutions which best serve the purpose of the organisation as a whole."

2. Characteristics of OR

1. It is an interdisciplinary team approach.
2. OR is a continuous process.
3. Operations research is a decision-making science.
4. OR increases the creative ability of a decision-maker.
5. It acts as a control device for solving managerial problems.

3. Methodology of OR

Due to the complications involved, OR project is divided in the following phases:

1. Perception and formulation of the problem.
2. Setting out or construction of a model of decision process.
3. Specification of alternative courses open.

4. Solution of the model evaluating the outcome of each course of action on the basis of given criterion.
5. Selection of a particular course and resolution of the decision process.
6. Pre-test and establishment of control over the solution with a degree of precision.
7. Implementation of the decision reached.

4. OR and Managerial Decision-making

Decision-making is a key managerial responsibility of today's managers under intense competition than ever before. Therefore, the need for effective decision-making in business is more apparent. OR provides the executive with quantitative basis for decision-making to solve every-day problems of running a business with greater efficiency and confidence. The merits of OR in management decision-making may be ramified into four categories such as:

(a) Better control

(b) Better co-ordination

(c) Better decision

(d) Better system.

5. Techniques of Operations Research

The following are the techniques of operations research used by a progressive manner in this decision-making process:

1. Probability	Analysing the uncertainties
2. Decision Theory	Analysing the monetary value of utility from a given a set of situation
3. Linear programming	Selecting an optimum combination
4. Dynamic programming	Equation developed for each individual situation
5. Sequencing	Measuring effectiveness in terms of cost, time, etc.
6. Game theory	Dealing with the situation where two or more individuals are making decisions
7. Inventory control	Analysing the levels of stock and cost of inventory control

8. Queueing Theory	Dealing with the waiting lines at service centre and reduction of waiting time
9. Network analysis	Aiming at misinformation of total cost, total time, idle resources, production delay, etc.

6. PERT and CPM

Programme Evaluation Review Technique (PERT) was developed by Booz, Alien and Hamilton to the needs of US Navy in 1950 for one effective control method for large multifaceted development programmes. It provides a high degree of visibility in programme planning and control and stresses the time required to perform the activities necessary for a given event to occur. Almost at the same time, engineers at Du Pont company, USA also developed Critical Path Method (CPM). PERT and CPM utilise the same principles. The basic difference between PERT and CPM is that PERT emphasises time and provides a way of computing the most probable time whereas CPM emphasises costs as well as time.

A programme which consists of several activities should be completed in a proper sequence and in allotted time. For this purpose, a network is developed to show the sequence, time taken and time of start of particular activities. The whole process is the function of PERT/CPM. The following are the steps in the preparation of PERT:

1. Identification of activities;
2. Sequential arrangements of activities;
3. Time estimates of activities;
4. Network construction; and
5. Preparation of critical path.

Here is given an example of the applicability of PERT utilised in setting up a project for manufacturing 1,000 TV sets per annum in an organisation. The whole project is divided into the following activities:

1. 1-2 Acquiring land and construction of building.
2. 2-3 Hiring of technical staff.
3. 2-4 Select suppliers and place orders.
4. 4-5 Start commercial activities.
5. 5-6 End activity.

Based on the above information, a PERT chart is shown in the diagram given below. It also indicates the critical path.

refers to activity
0 refers to event

(a) Critical path 1-2-3-5-6
(b) Critical path 1-2-4-5-6

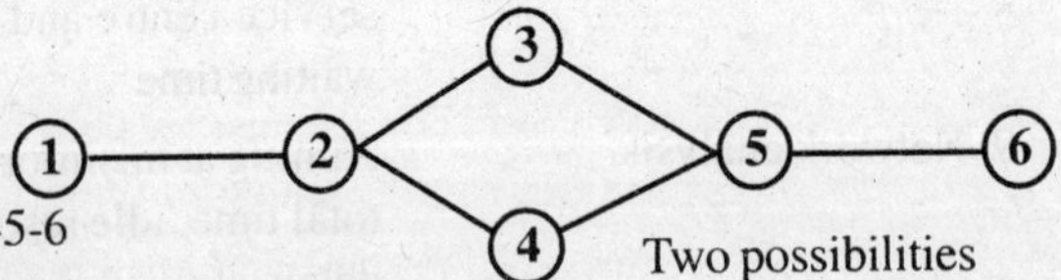

Two possibilities

The building of Polaris Missile was the first application of PERT. The unique contribution of PERT as a form of network analysis is that it provides a means of obtaining a probability estimate of the expected time to complete activities that have not been performed previously. Hence, it is useful as a best tool in the hands of top management which has overall managerial responsibility of a project.

PERT Vs CPM

SI. No.	PERT	CPM
1.	It is applied for planning and scheduling research.	It is used for construction and business problems.
2.	It is a probabilistic model.	It is a deterministic model.
3.	It uses the weighted average of three-time estimates.	It uses only one-time estimate.
4.	It emphasises time and provides a way of computing the most probable time.	It deals with cost as well as time. It also introduces concept the of "critical path"

Model Questions

Section A

1. Define Budget.
2. What is budgetary control?
3. What is Zero base budgeting?
4. What is PERT and CPM?
5. What is Master Budget?
6. Define Operations Research.

Section B

7. Discuss the objectives of budgetary control.
8. Define Production Planning and Control. What are its elements?
9. Explain the various tools of budgetary control.
10. Narrate the scope and objectives of OR.

Section C

11. What steps would you suggest in the organisation of a budgetary control system for an industrial undertaking?
12. Explain the non-budgetary control techniques briefly.
13. Define Break-even point. Explain its uses.
14. Explain the different techniques of OR.

I. Multiple Choice

1. A budget designed to change in accordance with the activities of the organizations is known as
   (a) Master budget (b) Flexible budget
   (c) Functional budget (d) Zero base budget
2. Capital and revenue budgets relate to
   (a) Period (b) Flexible
   (c) Nature of activity (d) Coverage of function
3. The path over which the raw materials travel to be transformed into finished products is known as
   (a) Routing (b) Scheduling
   (c) Despatching (d) Follow-up
4. CPM emphasises
   (a) Time (b) Cost
   (c) Cost as well as time (d) None
5. BEP is a function of
   (a) Sales volume (b) Cost
   (c) Profit (d) Sales volume, cost and profit

Answer:

1. (b) Flexible budget, 2. (c) Nature of activity, 3. (a) Routing, 4. (c) cost as well as time, 5. (d) Sales volume, cost and profit

II. Say, 'True or False'

6. Budgeting refers to the formulation of plan for a given period in numerical terms.
7. Budgetary control plan system integrates all activities of the enterprise right from planning to controlling.

8. Ratio analysis is the process of determining and interpreting numerical relationship based on the financial statements.
9. Operations research is a scientific approach to decision-making.
10. The building of Polaris Missile was the second application of PERT.

Answer:

6. True, 7. True, 8. True, 9. True, 10. False.

III. Fill in the blanks

11. A budget is an anticipated financial statement of ______ and ______ for a specific period.
12. Budgetary control system is a useful tool in profit ____________.
13. A budget which is designed to change in accordance with the activities of the organisation is known as ___________ budget.
14. Zero base budgeting involves ___________ steps.
15. Linear programming is one of the techniques of ____________.

Answer:

11. Revenue, Expenses, 12. Planning, 13. Flexible, 14. Three 15. Operations research.

Chapter 20

Co-ordination

Chapter Outline

Concept of Co-ordination — Definitions — Characteristics of Co-ordination — Essentials of Co-ordination — Types of Co-ordination — Principles of Co-ordination — Co-ordination vs. Co-operation — Techniques of Co-ordination — Problems of Co-ordination — Steps for Effective Co-ordination — Advantages of Co-ordination — Model Questions

In a modern organisation, managers synchronise and harmonise various departmental activities to achieve the desired goals. To ensure the smooth and successful functioning of an organisation, all the departmental activities should be linked together. At the same time, managers should be careful in avoiding managerial problems which might affect and destroy the unity of command and direction. Co-ordination provides the key to all these activities.

Co-ordination is the process of integrating the various departmental activities of an organisation. It deals with the task of blending efforts for the successful attainment of the objectives of an organisation. So, it is rightly said that "Co-ordination is the heart of management."

I. Concept of Co-ordination

The traditional management thinkers like Louis Alien, Henry Fayol, James Mooney, etc. have viewed that co-ordination is a "separate function of management." They contended that managers should try to Co-ordinate the organisational goals. Later, the classicists advocated that "co-ordination is achieved automatically," while all the managerial functions are performed effectively.

According to Follett. "co-ordination starts from the very first stage of managerial functions." Moreover, Harold Koontz and O'Donnell described co-ordination as "the essence of managership."

But the modern management thinkers do not conform to the thinking of Koontz and O'Donnel. Modern thinking is that co-ordination is not an independent function which can be performed separately. So, the modern thinkers said that co-ordination is a continuous process by which managers can achieve the integrated patterns of group efforts towards common goals.

II. Definitions

Co-ordination is defined differently by different authors.

1. **Henry Fayol:** "To co-ordinate is to harmonise all the activities of a concern in order to facilitate its working and its success."
2. **Alan C. Reiley and James D. Mooney:** "Co-ordination is an orderly arrangement of group effort to provide unity of action in pursuit of a common purpose."
3. **Wiliam Gulick:** "Co-ordination is a set of human and structural mechanisms designed to link the parts of the enterprise together to achieve the specified objectives."
4. **James L. Lundy:** "Co-ordination involves the development of unity of purpose and harmonious implementation of plans for the achievement of the desired ends."
5. **Daltom McFarland:** "Co-ordination is the process by which managers achieve integrated patterns of group and individual effort. To co-ordinate is to develop unity of action in common purposes."
6. **William H. Newman:** "Co-ordination deals with synchronising and unifying the actions of a group of people. A co-ordinated operation is one in which the activities of the employee are harmonised, dovetailed and integrated towards a common objective."

III. Characteristics of Co-ordination

The above definitions point out the following chief features of co-ordination:

(i) Co-ordination is a continuous process.

(ii) It refers to an orderly arrangement of group activities.

(iii) It depends on unity of action and group effort.

(iv) Co-ordination aims at the attainment of common purposes.

IV. Essentials of Co-ordination

According to Chester Bernard, "the quality of co-ordination is the crucial factor in the survival of the organisation." In an organisation, as pointed out by Brech, the need for co-ordination arises from the diversity of tasks to be undertaken and of persons to carry them out. Co-ordination is essential for the following reasons:

(i) Co-ordination minimises conflicts between the line and the staff.

(ii) Co-ordination pulls together all the functions and activities.

(iii) Co-ordination ensures the smooth flow of resources into productive units.

(iv) Co-ordination results in the accomplishment of organisational goals.

(v) Co-ordination helps to improve the effectiveness of management.

V. Types of Co-ordination

Broadly, co-ordination is divided into the following two types:

1. Internal co-ordination; and
2. External co-ordination.

1. Internal Co-ordination: Internal co-ordination exists within the organisation. It is the establishment of interpersonnel relationship with a view to co-ordinate the activities of all departments. The following are the various forms of internal co-ordination:

(i) Co-ordination between different groups of employees of the same department.

(ii) Co-ordination between managers and workers at different levels.

(iii) Co-ordination between Board of Directors and departmental managers.

Normally, internal co-ordination isclassified as follows:

(i) Vertical internal co-ordination; and

(ii) Horizontal internal co-ordination.

Vertical internal co-ordination refers to the co-ordination of relations and activities between the superior and subordinates and *vice versa,* e.g., co-ordination between the marketing manager, and the marketing superintendent. On the other hand, horizontal internal co-ordination refers to the co-ordination of relations and activities among the authorities and employees of the same status. Co-ordination among the different departmental heads, supervisors of different sections are examples of horizontal co-ordination.

(2) External Co-ordination: External co-ordination refers to the establishment of relationship with outsiders. The enterprise must establish such relations and co-ordinate its activities for the benefit of the enterprise as a whole. Normally, the function of external co-ordination is assigned to the public relations officer in a modern organisation.

Apart from these two types of co-ordination, there is one more type, i.e., self-co-ordination. It is the effort of independent responsibilities to achieve harmonious or reciprocal performance of their own responsibilities. It is applicable to a simple situation. Under this concept, people at work manage themselves according to the work of others.

VI. Principles of Co-ordination

Co-ordination is a continuous process by which managers achieve the integrated patterns of groups towards a common goal. Co-ordination is essentially the managerial responsibility. Mary Parker Follett has advocated the following four principles of co-ordination:

1. Principle of direct contact,
2. Principle of early stage,
3. Principle of reciprocal relationship, and
4. Principle of continuity.

1. Principle of Direct Contact: Co-ordination can effectively be achieved by direct contact among the responsible people concerned. But in a large organisation, every time direct contact may not be possible. To overcome this difficulty, mechanical devices are provided for the effective personal communication through which better co-ordination can be achieved.

2. Principle of Early Stage: Co-ordination starts right from the beginning of the planning process. The success of co-ordinating activities depends on the early stage itself. Lack of co-ordination in the early stage may result in business failure. So, the general manager should try to co-ordinate all departmental activities right from the beginning of the management process.

3. Principle of Reciprocal Relationship: This principle indicates that all factors in a situation are reciprocally related. In other words, all the aspects or parts are influenced by other aspects or parts. For example, the financial manager co-ordinates with the production manager and the production manager, in turn, co-ordinates with the marketing manager and other managers. Each one of the four finds himself influenced by others and influenced by all people in the total situation.

4. Principle of Continuity: Co-ordination is a continuous process. Co-ordination is a never-ending exercise of management. If anywhere it stops, a derailment is the only possibility which in turn can harm the whole enterprise. Hence, much care should be taken by the top executives regarding this aspect.

VII. Co-ordination Vs. Co-operation

The terms "co-ordination" and "co-operation" are widely used in business organisations. Co-operation indicates the willingness of people to help others. However, co-ordination is not co-operation. The main distinctions between co-ordination and co-operation are given below.

Table 19.1

Differences between Co-ordination and Co-operation

Co-ordination	Co-operation
1. Co-ordination is one of the functions of management. So, it enjoys the status of a separate function.	Co-operation indicates only the attitude of an individual or group than anything else. So, it does not enjoy such status.
2. Co-ordination is said to be a broader concept. Because it is necessary for the success of the organisation.	Co-operation is said to be a narrower concept. Because it is necessary for effective co-ordination.
3. The basic principle of co-ordination is to co-ordinate the efforts of groups towards a common goal.	The basic principle of co-operation is a spirit of dedication and service with absolute honesty.

4. The basic objective of co-ordination is the synchronisation of efforts of groups.	The basic objective of co-operation is to protect the interests of members of a co-operative group.
5. It is an official and deliberate effort.	It is a voluntary service.
6. Co-ordination is basically achieved through the performance of other activities.	Co-operation is basically achieved through the motto and spirit. "Each for all and all for each."
7. Co-ordination arises compulsorily out of the limitations of organisational structure. So, it is inevitable necessity for the success of the enterprise.	Co-operation arises out of the willingness of the employees in the organisation to co-operate with each other.

VIII. Techniques of Co-ordination

In an organisation, managers use a variety of techniques to achieve co-ordination. Some of important techniques of co-ordination are as follows:

1. Co-ordination by Order and Command: In an organisation, order and command are the most important techniques of effective co-ordination. A manager, with well-formulated rules and procedures,can issue orders and commands to their subordinates and thereby achieve effective co-ordination. He can also define the work of subordinates, their functions, and thiming of performance in order to achieve co-ordination. The modern management thinkers do not consider this as a good technique since the significance of human relations is neglected.

2. Co-ordination by Goals or Targets: Sometimes, the general manager fixes targets or goals for each departmental manager. The departmental managers reassign the same targets to their subordinates to facilitate co-ordination. The setting of goals and targets facilitates co-ordination.

3. Co-ordination by Departmentation: Departmentation is a means of dividing the large organisation into smaller administrative units. Departmentation is done on the basis of function, product, customers, territory and the like. Departmentation facilitates co-ordination better than others. Product departmentation is an effective technique of co-ordination since it reduces the degree of interdependence.

4. Co-ordination by Communication: To facilitate effective co-ordination, a perfect system of communication is essential. Any communication gap might affect the free flow of communication and result in ineffective co-ordination. So, adequate facilities for good communication should be provided.

5. Co-ordination by Committees: Formation of departmental committees is another technique to ensure effective co-ordination. The committees usually comprise of representatives from all departments. The committees meet periodically and discuss various managerial problems and find solutions to these problems. Thus, committees solve many managerial problems and serve as a sound technique of co-ordination.

6. Co-ordination by Meetings and Conferences: Periodic meetings of staff of various levels of management is an effective technique of co-ordination. Such staff meetings and conferences provide a forum for discussing the various problems encountered by the different departments and taking suitable decisions. This enables effective co-ordination.

7. Co-ordination by Special Co-ordinators: In a big industrial organisation, along with the various managers, a project co-ordinator is appointed. His main function is to co-ordinate the various activities relating to a particular project. Sometimes, a co-ordinator cell may be established to facilitate effective co-ordination. The main function of such a co-ordination cell is to collect information and send them to the various departments. Such cell paves the way for the smooth co-ordination and ultimate success of the enterprise.

The choice of selecting the technique of co-ordination depends on the size, volume and objectives of the organisation. The organisation may adopt any one or a combination of any of the above techniques of co-ordination to achieve the desired results.

IX. Problems of Co-ordination

Co-ordination is essential for the smooth and successful functioning of the organisation. However, there are certain problems in co-ordination.

1. Natural Hazards: Effective co-ordination is not achieved due to natural hazards. Natural hazards like floods, earthquakes, fires, cyclones, changes in the behaviour of individuals and groups affect effective co-ordination.

2. Lack of Administrative Skill: Failure to recurit the right persons for the right jobs leads to lack of administrative skill. Added to this, lack of proper understanding of the administrative procedures prevent people from co-operating with others.

3. Lack of Techniques of Co-ordination: Major co-ordination problems arise due to the lack of techniques of co-ordination. Management itself limits the number of techniques of co-ordination thinking that it is good enough for the organisation. But, in practice, a number of techniques of co-ordination are required to avoid co-ordination problem.

4. Confused and Conflicting Objectives and Ideas: The knowledge of the managers about the conflicting objectives and ideas also act as a constraint on effective co-ordination.

5. Lack of Understanding among Personnel: Very often, problems of co-ordination arise due to the misunderstanding among the personnel working in the organisation. The persistent conflict between the line and staff is an example in this regard.

X. Steps for Effective Co-ordination

To overcome the above limitations and to achieve effective co-ordination, the following steps may be considered:

1. Delegation of authority and imposition of accountability through all levels of management in a balanced and integrated manner.
2. Departmentalisation of activities in tune with the size of the organisation.
3. Formulation of consistent policies, procedures, rules, methods etc.
4. Establishing an effective communication channel.
5. Introduction of a reporting system.
6. Introduction of a reward system for workers.
7. Encouraging the workers to take part in meetings, conferences and committees.
8. Encouraging the interpersonal interaction on an informal basis.
9. Proper training to managers in the area of leadership, communication, co-ordination, and personality development.

XI. Advantages of Co-ordination

The following are the advantages of co-ordination:

1. Increases the Effectiveness of Management: Co-ordination increases the effectiveness of management. It pulls all the departmental activities together. In the absence of co-ordination, the 5Ms, i.e., men, materials, methods, machines and money may not be fully utilised. Co-ordination brings unity of direction and action in the organisation. It ensures not only resolving managerial problems but also the smooth flow of resources into the productive units. That is why co-ordination is said to be the essence of management.

2. Increases the Profitability and Productivity: Co-ordination resolves all types of managerial problems and helps to reduce the overall cost of production which results in increase in the profitability and productivity in an organisation.

3. Helps to Achieve the Desired Goals: Co-ordination results in the accomplishment of organisational goals. It tries to link all the managerial activities towards the common goals. It helps not only in achieving the desired goals but also paves the way for future goals.

4. Increases the Morale of the Workers: Co-ordination ensures the smooth flow of resources that results in the successful functioning of the organisation. This situation not only protects the workers but also increases the welfare of workers in terms of promotion, security, incentives, increments, higher position and the like. This encourages the employees to work harder and to achieve success. This naturally boosts the morale of the workers.

Model Questions

Section A

1. Define co-ordination.
2. What do you mean by self-co-ordination?
3. Is co-ordination a separate function?
4. Can co-ordination be achieved automatically?
5. "Co-ordination is the practical purpose of management." Do you agree?

Section B

6. Explain the various principles of co-ordination.
7. Describe the characteristics of co-ordination.
8. How is co-ordination different from co-operation?
9. What are the essentials of co-ordination?
10. "Systems approach ensures better co-ordination." Discuss.

Section C

11. Describe the various types of co-ordination. Explain them briefly.
12. Explain briefly the elements and advantages of co-ordination.
13. Explain the various techniques of co-ordination.
14. Explain the problems of co-ordination and how management overcomes these problems.
15. "Co-ordination is the essence of management." Discuss.

I. Multiple Choice

1. Co-ordination among different heads of departments is an example of
   (a) Horizontal co-ordination (b) Vertical co-ordination
   (c) External co-ordination (d) All
2. The heart of management is
   (a) Planning (b) Organizations
   (c) Controlling (d) Coordinating
3. Co-ordination starts from
   (a) Planning (b) Starting
   (c) Organising (d) Motivation
4. Co-ordination is a
   (a) Deliberate effort (b) Voluntary service
   (c) Both (d) None
5. Co-ordination resolves all types of managerial
   (a) Problems b) Process
   (c) Progress (d) None

Answer:

1. (a) Horizontal co-ordination, 2. (d) Co-ordination, 3. (a) Planning
4. (a) Deliberate effort, 5. (a) problems.

II. Say, 'True or False'

6. Co-ordination is stage of managerial function process.
7. Co-operation indicates the willingness of people to help others.
8. Mary Parker Follett has advocated four principles of co-ordination.
9. Problems of co-ordination arise due to the misunderstanding among the staff.
10. Formation of departmental committee is a technique to ensure effective co-ordination.

Answer:

6. False, 7. True, 8. True, 9. True, 10. True

III. Fill in the blanks

11. __________ is the process of integrating the various departmental activities of an organisation.
12. Co-ordination minimises conflicts between the line and the __________
13. The function of external co-ordination is assigned to the __________________ in a modern organisation.
14. Co-operation is basically achieved through the motto and spirit "Each for all and _________ for each".

Answer:

11. Co-ordination, 12. Staff, 13. Public Relation Officer, 14. All.

Chapter 21

Functional Management

Chapter Outline

Personnel Management — Financlal Management — Production Management — Marketing Management — Model Questions.

The General Manager of a company enjoys a distinct place in its management hierarchy. He performs not only the basic duties, but also functions as a co-ordinating und connecting link between different levels of management. The effective and efficient discharge of these duties require the General Manager to possess the basic knowledge of the nature and scope of different functional areas of management, such as:

1. Personnel Management
2. Financial Management
3. Production Management
4. Materials Management
5. Marketing Management

The different functional areas of Management and their scope are described here.

I. Personnel Management

Today, labourers are considered no more as workers but as an important part of the business. The management can run the business successfully when it gets the wholehearted co-operation of the personnel. So, a manager, executive or supervisor has to follow the essentials of good personnel management.

1. Definitions

Some of the important definitions of personnel management are given below:

(i) **Edwin B. Flippo:** "The personnel function is concerned with the procurement, development, compensation, integration and maintenance of the personnel of an organisation for the purpose of contributing towards the accomplishment of that organisation's goals or objectives."

(ii) **E.F.L. Brech:** "Personnel Management is that part of management process which is primarily concerned with the human constituents of an organisation."

(iii) **Dale Yoder:** "Manpower management effectively describes the process of planning and directing the application, development and utilisation of human resources in employment."

(iv) **Pigors and Myres:** "Personnel administration is a method of developing the potentialities of employees so that they get maximum satisfaction out of their work and give their best efforts to the organisation."

2. Features of Personnel Management

The above definitions convey the following features of personnel management:

(a) Personnel management aims at developing human resources required by a business unit.

(b) It aims at achieving the organisational objectives.

(c) Personnel administration motivates the personnel to contribute to the overall efficiency of management.

(d) It helps the management to maintain industrial peace, safety and health.

(e) Personnel management is a managerial function.

3. Objectives of Personnel Management

According to Michael J. Jucius, personnel management aims at:

(a) Attaining economically and effectively the organisational goals.

(b) Serving to the highest possible degree the individual goals such as income, power, satisfaction, etc.

(c) Preserving and advancing the general welfare of the community.

4. Functions of Personnel Management

The personnel management consists of two functions, such as (i) Basic managerial function and (ii) Operative function. The following Fig. 21.1 shows the various functions of personnel management.

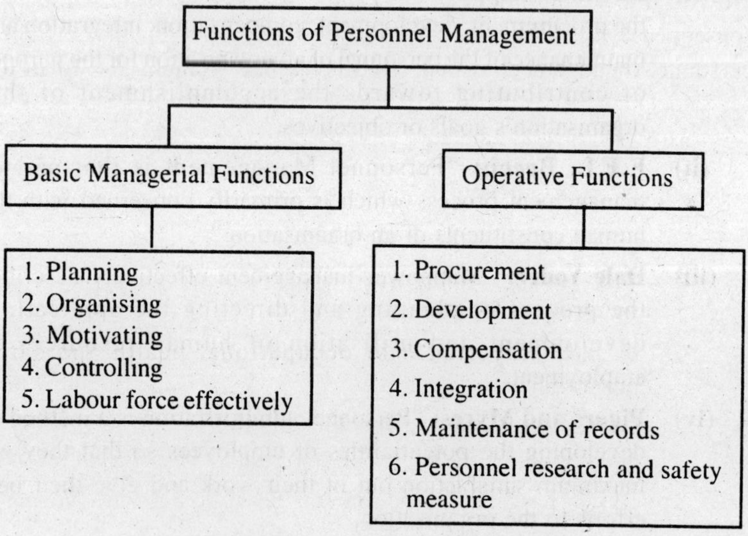

Fig. 21.1 Personnel Functions

The above Figure shows that the task of personnel management begins with the recruitment of staff and ends with the provisions of welfare service and safety measure. In the light of its coverage, the following are the notable functions of Personnel management:

1. to advise and assist the top management in formulating and developing personnel policies.
2. to advise and assist the management in recruitment, selection, training, promotion and compensation of employees.
3. to assist the management in maintaining discipline and in developing grievance procedure and negotiating with trade unions and employees.
4. to undertake personnel research in order to render a better service to the top management.
5. to help maintaining industrial safety and health.

From the above, it is clear that the personnel department of business unit shoulders a heavy responsibility.

5. Future of Personnel Management in India

The present traditional management will surely yield place to professional management in which the decision-making process will rest with professional managers. This will create climate favourable for the growth and development of personnel management in India. As a consequence, the following changes are likely to occur in the field of personnel management which will give a new content and form to a personnel manager:

1. Greater involvement in development planning.
2. Change in personnel policies.
3. Change in sources of manpower.
4. Retraining of workers.
5. Increasing Government role.
6. Greater importance of occupational health and safety programmes.
7. Greater attention to the human problems of adjustment to change.
8. Better performance appraisal devices and new forms of compensation.

In short, it can be said that "although no fundamental changes are expected to take place in future in the personnel manager's present role as a file clerk, a housekeeper, a social worker and a firefighter," yet due to the above changes his prestige and power are likely to increase manifold in India.

II. Financial Management

Finance is regarded as the lifeblood of a business enterprise. Therefore, the success of a business unit is closely linked with efficient management of its finances. In general, finance deals with the provision of money at the time it is needed. In other words, it deals with the procurement of funds and their effective utilisation. Financial Management may be defined as the planning, organising and controlling of funds and allocation and use of these funds scientifically.

1. Definitions

(i) **Guthmenn and Dugall:** "Business finance can broadly be defined as the activity concerned with planning, raising, controlling and administering of the funds used in the business."

(ii) **Soleman:** "Financial Management is concerned with the efficient use of an important economic resource, controlling and administering of the funds used in the business."

(iii) **James Van Home:** "Financial Management is concerned with the acquisition of funds and effective utilisation of these funds".

(iv) **S.C. Kutchhal:** "Financial Management is an integral part of overall management rather than a separate function concerning with funds raising".

(v) **Phillippalus:** "Financial Management is concerned with the managerial decisions that result in the acquisition and financing of long-term and short-term credits of the firm."

2. Objectives of Financial Management

The above definitions pinpoint the following objectives:

1. Maximisation of profit is the basic objective of Financial Management. However, it is subject to criticism in recent times. Maximisation of profit is replaced by maximisation of wealth. Hence, wealth maximisation is the main objective of Financial Management.
2. Financial Management aims at a fair return to shareholders.
3. Building up reserves for growth and expansion is another goal of financial management.

3. Scope of Financial Management

There are two approaches to study the scope of financial management, such as:

1. Traditional approach
2. Modern approach.

According to Traditional approach, financial management deals with raising and administering of funds needed by the corporate enterprises to meet their financial needs. However, this approach has ignored to consider the other side of finance function, i.e., effective utilisation of funds raised.

According to Modern approach, financial management deals with both acquisition of funds as well as their allocation and effective utilisation. The modern approach is an analytical way of working at the financial problems of a business unit. Besides, its scope may be defined in terms of the following questions:

1. How large should the firm be and how fast should it grow?
2. What should be the composition of the firm's assets?
3. What should be the mix of the firm's financing?
4. How should the firm analyse, plan and control its financial affairs?

The above questions relate to four broad decision areas of financial management, such as:

1. Funds requirement decision
2. Financing decision
3. Investment decision.
4. Dividend decision.

These decisions can also be termed as functions outlining the scope of financial management.

4. Functions of Financial Management

According to S.C. Kutchhal, the functions of financial management can broadly be classified into two categories such as:

(a) Executive Finance Functions

(b) Clerical Finance Functions.

The Executive finance function is so called because it requires executive skill whereas clerical finance function is so called because it requires clerical skill in order to carry out these functions. The following Fig. clearly shows the various functions of financial management. From the Figure 21.2, it is clear that the executive finance function includes three decisions. Further, these decisions have been divided into six sub-functions as shown below.

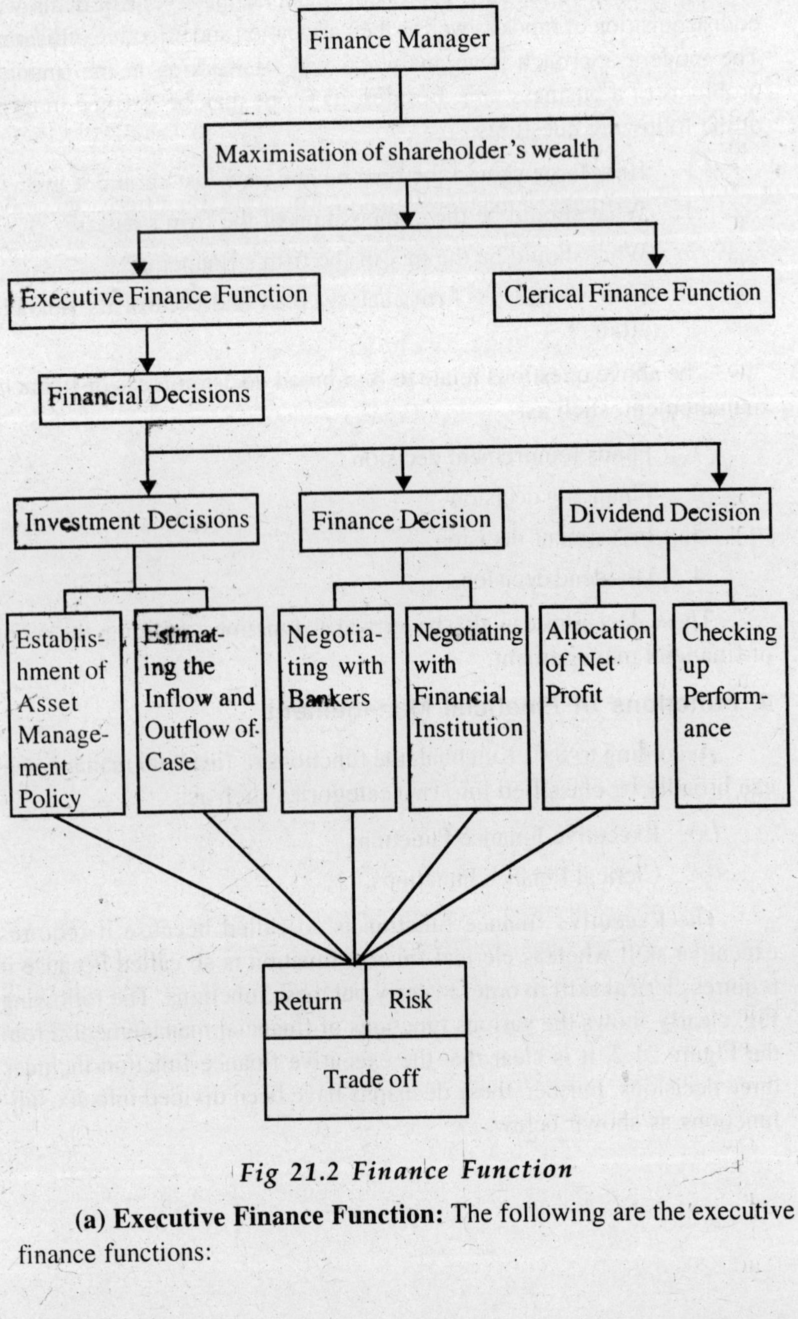

Fig 21.2 Finance Function

(a) Executive Finance Function: The following are the executive finance functions:

(i) **Investment Decision:** This comprises decisions relating to investment in both fixed and current assets. The investment in fixed assets depends on the asset management policy pursued by the business unit. The investment in current asset depends on the credit and inventory policies. So, the financial manager has to establish a sound asset management policy and thereby the financial manager can utilise the available funds effectively. Besides, the financial manager has to estimate the inflow of cash and outflow of cash in order to meet the day-to-day business expenses in the form of working capital.

(ii) **Financing Decision:** It deals with the decisions relating to the provision of funds required at the proper time. The financial manager has to identify the sources from which the funds can be raised. For this purpose, financial manager has to negotiate with the lenders.

(iii) **Dividend Decision:** It involves the allocation of net profit to equity shareholders. In other words, it deals with the determination of the percentage of profit to be paid to its owners. This decision also involves issue of bonus shares and right issues.

To put it in a nutshell, the executive finance function covers six sub-functions such as:

1. Establishment of asset management policy
2. Estimating inflow and outflow of cash
3. Negotiating with bankers for raising finance
4. Negotiating with financial institutions
5. Allocation of net profit
6. Checking up the financial performance.

(b) Clerical Finance Function: It deals with the following activities:

1. Looking after tax affairs such as, income tax, sales tax, excise duty, etc.
2. Preparation of payroll
3. Maintaining and safeguarding important documents
4. Preparing confidential financial reports
5. Maintaining cash register and cash box and the like.

5. Financial Tools

The following are the important financial tools used by financial manager for the purpose of evaluating the overall performance of a business unit:

1. Financial leverage is a tool which helps in increasing the return equity shareholders.
2. Capital budgeting helps to select the best capital investment proposals from among various alternatives.
3. ABC analysis, cash management models, debtor's turnover ratio etc. help in effective management of current assets.
4. Ratio analysis helps in evaluating the performance of business unit.
5. Fund and cash flow analysis techniques help in determining whether the funds have been procured from the best available source and they have been used in the best possible way.
6. Cost of capital helps in deciding about the sources of raising funds and in determining the optimum capital structure.

6. Organisation of the Finance Function

A company must give proper attention to the structure of its finance department. It differs from company to company depending on their repective needs and the financial philosophy.

Generally, in most companies, Vice-President Finance has under him two officers looking after the two important finance functions such as:

(a) An officer who performs the accounting functions is regarded as controller and

(b) An officer who does the finance function is designated as Treasurer.

The following Fig. 21.3 shows the various functions performed by a controller and treasurer in a large business unit.

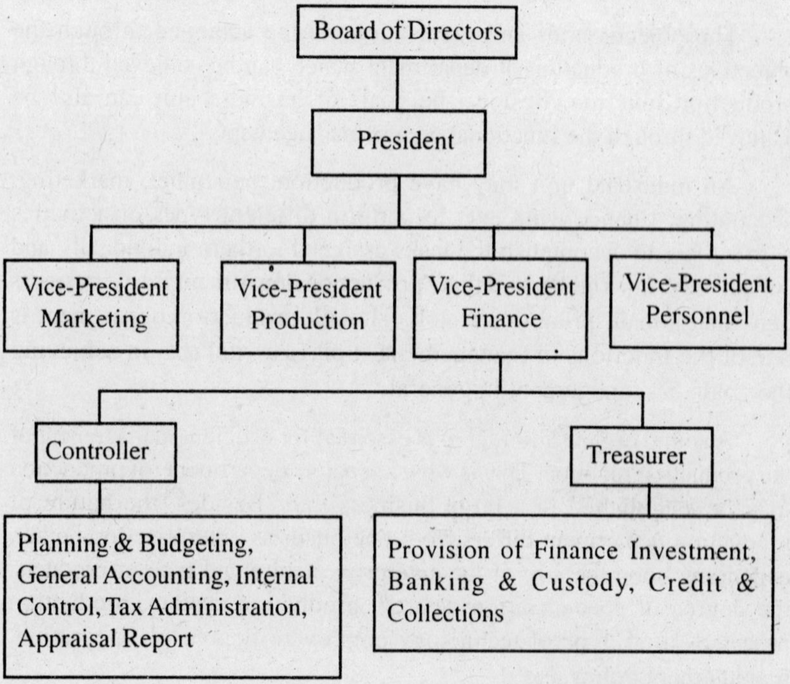

Fig. 21.3 Finance Department

7. Conclusion

As Collins Brooks has pointed out, "Bad production management and bad sales management have slain in hundreds, but faulty finance has slain in thousands." So, sound financial management is inevitable in both profit and service organisations. Besides, it is indispensable for any organisation since it helps in profit planning, capital spending, measuring cost, controlling inventories, accounts receivables, etc. Finally, it essentially helps in optimising or maximising the wealth to shareholders.

III. Production Management

Production is one of the important functions of management. In the modern money-oriented economy, production is the basic foundation of all kinds of the economic activities. It is the master key which provides the process of transforming inputs into outputs for sale. Hence, it is rightly said that business enterprise needs production to generate more money. Moreover, the success of a business unit depends upon the effective and efficient functioning of production department.

The objectives of an organisation can be achieved through the objectives of production of department which can be achieved through production function. Besides the goals of business unit can also be achieved through the functional area of management.

An industrial unit may have production, personnel, marketing, accounting, finance wing, etc. to perform different types of activities with a view to accomplish the tasks assigned to them individually and collectively. It is rightly said that "production department is to a business unit what a mainspring to a watch. Though production department is one of the functions of management, it plays a vital role in achieving the goals of management in general.

A sound organisation setup is essential for efficient management of the production function. That is why, a separate department for production may be established in a large business unit. Besides, the nature of production department differs from one business enterprise to another, depending upon the size of the enterprise, nature and type of products, the degree of specialisation desired, production system, production processes used, type of technology employed, degree of integration, management policy, etc.

1. Definitions

In general, production may be defined as the creation of goods and services to satisfy human wants and needs. Production involves the transformation of inputs into outputs. Some of the authoritative definitions are as follows:

(i) According to **Prof. Gart Hayel,** "Production is the process of transforming raw materials into finished products for sale".

This definition has pointed out that the conversion process while adds to the value or utility of products, the value added is the difference between the value of outputs and the value of inputs.

Value Added = Value of outputs – Value of inputs

(ii) According to **Prof. G.J. Stigler,** "The production function is the name given to the relationship between the rates of inputs of productive services and the rates of outputs of products." Algebraically, production function is written as:

$$q = f(a, b, c, d, \ldots..)$$

where, 'q' is the quantity of output; a, b, c, d etc. stand for the quantity of inputs.

This definition has pointed out that production is associated with factory which includes in its purview all activities that create utility or increase utility for individuals and society.

From the above two definitions, one can define the production concept in two ways, such as: (a) Narrow view and (b) Wide view.

In narrow sense, production deals with factory production. But, in wide sense, production is the process of producing something useful with the object of satisfying human wants and needs. Hence, production function takes place in all profit and non-profit business enterprise including public agencies, e.g., banks, hospitals, factories etc.

2. Productivity

There is a close relationship between production and productivity. The ratio between input and output is known as productivity. It is nothing but reduction in wastage of resources.

In the wide sense, productivity is defined as "the rate of available goods and services to the potential resources of the community or the country." In a narrow sense, it is the ratio between the output of wealth produced and the input of resources used up in the process of production.

$$\text{Productivity} = \frac{\text{Output}}{\text{Input}} = \text{or } P = \frac{O}{I}$$

It is the quality that indicates how well labour, capital, materials and energy are used in production process.

3. Production Management

From the various definitions of the term production given above, it can be concluded that the term production mainly involves transforming inputs into outputs keeping in view the overall objectives of business unit. This requires great caution and wisdom on the part of management. The management makes use of various tools of production, devices, methods, process, etc. for administering the affairs of production of the firm in the most effective and efficient way. Production management, therefore, means the entire gamut to managerial efforts devoted to the management of production — inputs into outputs — of the business unit.

Production management is concerned with planning, organising, directing and controlling of production system so as to produce goods of desired quality at minimum cost and the right time. It deals with decision-making concerning production processes.

According to E.L.F. Brech, "Production management then becomes the process of effectively planning and regulating the operations of that part of an enterprise which is responsible for all actual transformation of materials into finished products."

Thus, production management is mainly concerned with the conversion of inputs into outputs of sale. The production manager must see that the production process are arranged in a manner that the risk, cost and control considerations are properly balanced in given a situation and there is optimum production in the factory.

4. Objectives of Production Management

The following are the objectives of production management:

(i) To manufacture high quality products at minimum cost.

(ii) To eliminate duplication of work and overlapping efforts, leading to increased efficiency.

(iii) To increase productivity.

(iv) To minimise the cost of production which generates more revenue to the company.

(v) To facilitate product planning an6develppment which results in the development of new product development.

(vi) To fix responsibility of each employee in the production department which facilitates co-ordination between different activities.

5. Scope of Production Management

The scope of production management can be studied under the following three heads:

(a) **Manufacturing:** Processing of the product is the conversion of raw materials into finished products. To achieve this objective, production processes and production systems are developed.

(b) **Ancillary Functions:** It deals with the activities supporting manufacturing such as purchases, storage, maintenance etc.

(c) **Advisory Functions:** It covers the activities that provide advice and guidance in the form of work study, quality control, production cost control etc.

The scope of manufacturing analysis is very wide and it comprises the following all activities right from product design and layout of production facilities till finishing the products for despatch to warehouse or customers:

(i) Plant location and layout

(ii) Product design and development

(iii) Plant engineering — equipment and tool design, manufacturing techniques and process design

(iv) Industrial engineering — work study, method study, time study etc.

(v) Capacity management — demand and supply of products

(vi) Production planning control — planning, scheduling (routing) despatching and follow-up

(vii) Production quality control — inspection and testing

(viii) Materials management — purchases, stores, records etc.

(ix) Maintenance — services, replacement, preventive checking

(x) Automation — modern methods, machines etc.

The above said scope of manufacturing analysis/production management can be achieved by setting up of a sound production department in a manufacturing business unit.

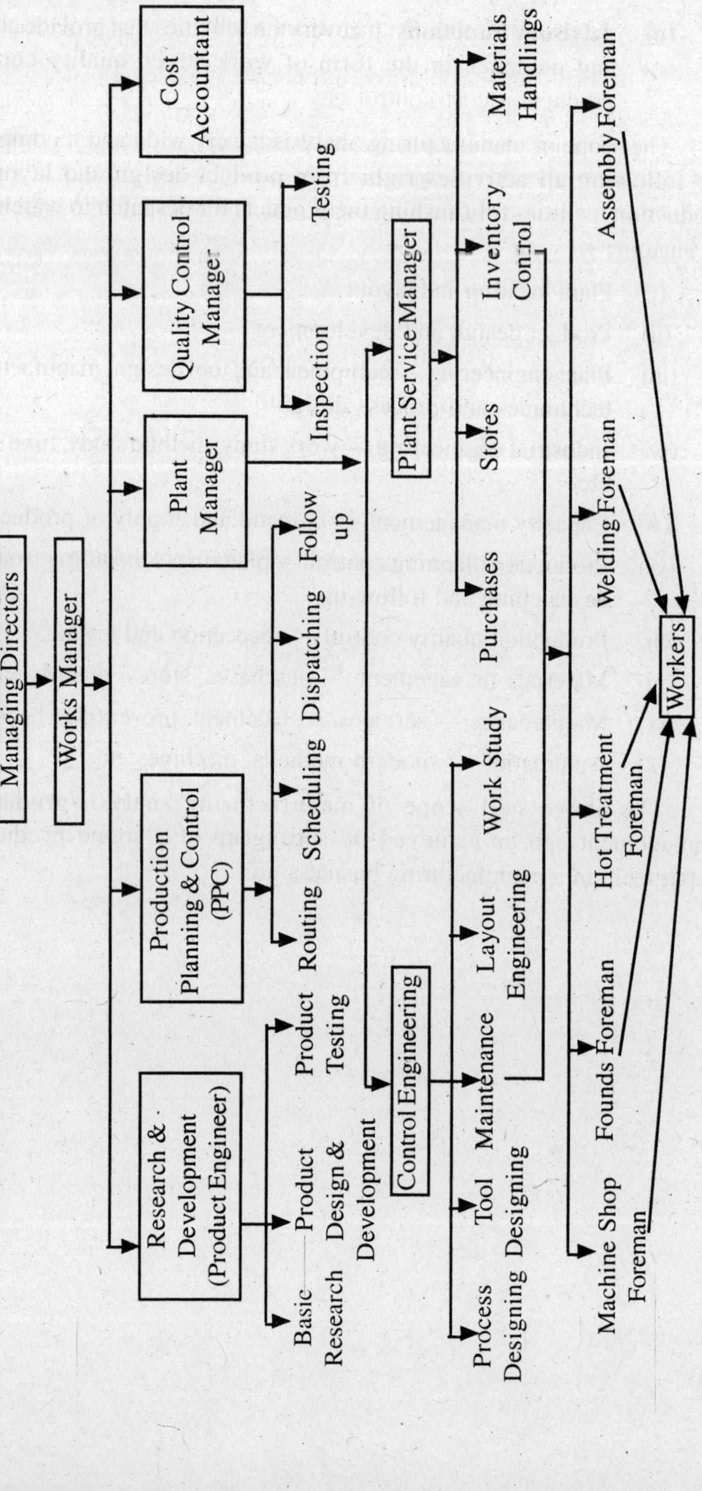

Fig. 21.4 Organisation of Production Department

6. Organisation of the Production Function

A business unit should give proper attention to the structure and organisation of its production department. The role of different production personnel should be clearly defined in order to avoid conflict and overlapping of functions. Organisation of production department differs from company to company depending upon the respective needs and the production policy. For example, a large firm may have a separate research and development section which may not be possible for a small firm.

A typical organisation of production is shown in Fig. 21.4. This diagram indicates he production functions rather than the titles of the persons carrying the activities. Production function may be organised on line, functional or line staff principles. Generally, functional production department is established in many business units.

7. Modern Production Management

The modern approach is an analytical way of looking at the production problems of a business unit. The main contents of the new problem are as follows:

(i) What is the total volume of production an enterprise should commit?

(ii) What specific products should an enterprise produce?

(iii) How should the needs and wants of customers be satisfied?

(iv) How should high quality products be produced at minimum cost? etc.

The above questions relate to four broad production decisions, such as:

1. Product research, designing and development decision
2. Production engineering decision
3. Production planning and control decision
4. Production cost and quality control decision.

These four decisions, which can also be termed as functions outlining the scope of production management, are shown in the next page.

The functions of production management are shown in Fig. 21.5.

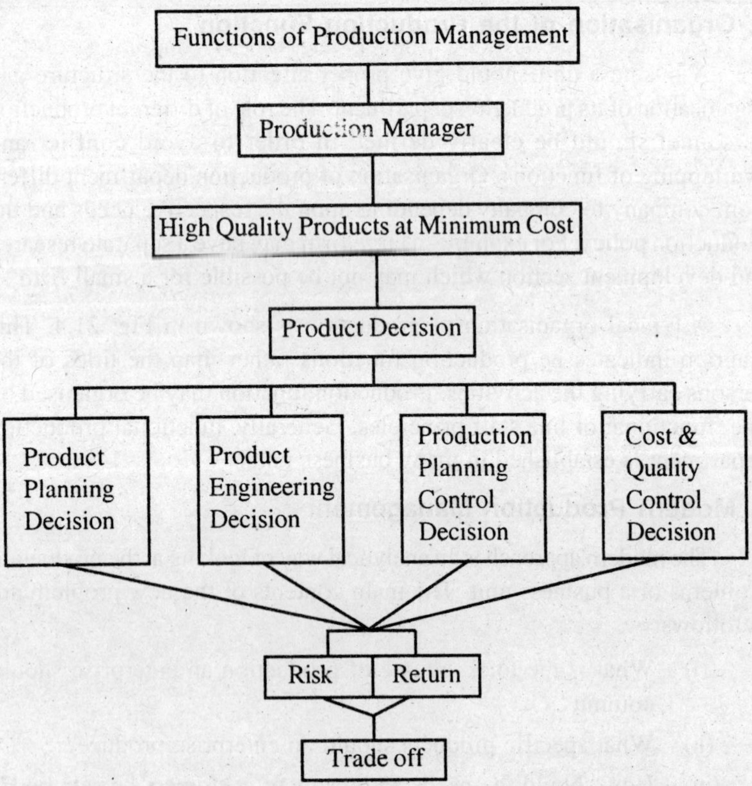

Fig. 21.5 Functions of Production Management

1. Product Research, Design and Development Decision: The primary objective of production management is to produce a product that can be sold at a satisfactory profit. Hence, product research, design and development is a very important decision in production. The design of the product should be modified from time to time in order to cope with the changes in customer's need and wants. To satisfy the customers, the production manager has to understand the product research project in order to translate customer's needs into a physical product.

Product research or product planning is the process of searching ideas for products, screening them scientifically, transforming into products and introducing the new products in the market.

Product planning and development is a vital function in production management due to the following reasons:

(a) To replace absolute products due to new technology
(b) To maintain and increase the growth rate or sales revenue for the company
(c) To utilise spare capacity
(d) To employ surplus funds
(e) To diversify risks and face competition
(f) To introduce new products
(g) To improve the existing products
(h) To facilitate the profitability and growth of the company
(i) To satisfy the needs and wants of customers etc.

Product planning process consists of a sequence of six stages as given below:

(a) **Product Exploration:** It deals with the generation of ideas for new products.

(b) **Product Screening:** It involves a preliminary evaluation of products ideas to select the most processing ideas.

(c) **Detailed Business Analysis:** It deals with the technical, financial and economic feasibility of a new product.

(d) **Development:** It deals with the preparation of the design of the product.

(e) **Test Marketing:** A sample of the product is tested in the market to get opinion from consumers about the new products.

(f) **Commercialisation:** It deals with the introduction of the new product in the market.

Hence, the development of a new product involves a heavy commitment in financial and technological terms. Further, product planning and development is a never-ending or ongoing process which covers product engineering, product design, product specification, product standardisation, product simplification, and diversification.

2. Production Engineering Decision: Production engineering decision is the second function of production management. This decision deals with plant engineering, industrial engineering, etc. However, the production engineering decision consists of two main subsystems such as: (i) Plant Engineering and (ii) Plant Service Engineering.

(i) Plant Engineering: It is concerned with the determination of appropriate techniques and manufacturing process. The plant engineer decides the most efficient methods of operating production facilities with due consideration to quality and cost. The following are the various elements of plant engineering:

(a) Production process
(b) Production system
(c) Machine tools and machines
(d) Plant layout
(e) Plant location
(f) Maintenance
(g) Work study.

(a) Production Process: It deals with the transformation of inputs into outputs. It is of three groups, such as fabrication, metal and machining processes. In production processes, several activities are involved. For instance melting, offering, drilling, milling, etc., are examples of production activities Production process differs from one product to another. Hence, the production manager has to design the production process keeping in view the volume to be produced, degree of variety and other output characteristics.

(b) Production System: It is the framework within which the production activities are carried out. Inputs, transformation process, outputs, storage transportation and information are the various elements of production system. It depends upon the volume of output, quality and standard equipments and machines. Production systems is of two types, such as continuous and intermittent production systems which are used to produce greater volume of output.

(c) Machine Tools and Machines: In addition to production processes and systems, the production manager has to employ the wide varieties of machines and machine tools in order to produce mass production of standardised products. Hence, the different types of machines are grouped into categories such as, general purpose machines and special purpose machines. For example, drilling, milling, grinding machines are general purpose machines whereas hobbing and honing are special purpose machines.

(d) Plant Layout: Layout refers to the arrangements of facilities in a particular workstation. It may be plant layout, office layout, etc. Plant layout implies the physical arrangement of machines, equipments and other industrial facilities on the factory floor in such a manner that they may be handled efficiently. According to Riggs, the overall objectives of plant layout is "to design a physical arrangement that most economically meets the required output quantity and quality." There are four broad categories of plant layout such as product layout, process layout, fixed position layout and group layout. While planning the plant layout, the following factors should be kept in mind, such as plant location, nature of product, type of industry, plant environment, management policy etc. Of late, computer programs are developed to guide the layout engineer in planning the best possible layout.

(e) Plant Location: First of all, it is the duty of production manager to select the site at which the factory is to be located. In deciding plant location, availability of men, materials, methods, machines, transport and other facilities is to be taken into account. These factors grouped into four categories such as input costs, location of output market, transportation cost and agglomeration. To put it in a nutshell, the objective for choice of location is profit maximisation for economic activities according to Mr. Buffa.

(f) Maintenance: It refers to the upkeep and protection of plant, machinery and other fixed assets. Maintenance engineering is concerned with keeping the physical facilities in good operating condition. The main objective of plant maintenance is to preserve and prolong the working life of plant and equipment. It is of four types such as planned maintenance, preventive maintenance, routine maintenance and breakdown maintenance. It is one of the components of plant engineering.

(g) Work Study: Work study is the study of human work in all aspects in order to improve productivity. In other words, it is the systematic and analytical study of work process and work methods with the objective of increasing efficiency and reducing cost. The main objective of work study is the optimum use of plant and equipment with the help of human efforts. Work study consists of two categories, *viz.,* method analysis and work measurement. Work study is a vital tool of measuring productivity and cost-effectiveness. It makes improvement in the areas of plant layout, employee safety, work environment etc.

(ii) Plant Service Engineering: The production process requires frequent loading, unloading, transfer and movement of materials through the various stages. To carry out this process, the production engineer has to render many plant services, such as purchases of raw materials, storage of materials, materials control, materials handling, etc. Materials handling is the art and science of moving, packing and storing of materials in any form. Plant service engineering is an essential sub-function of production management.

3. Production Planning and Control Decision: While a product is to be produced, the production should be planned perfectly so as to achieve the goals of production management. At the same time, the production should be controlled to ensure that the planned output is constantly maintained. These fanc tions are known as production planning and production control respectively. Production planning deals with the management decision relating to how much to produce, what materials, tools and parts would be needed etc., whereas production control deals with implementation of production plans by co-ordinating different activities.

Production and control consists of the following steps:

(a) Estimating
(b) Routing
(c) Loading
(d) Scheduling
(e) Despatching
(f) Progressing or follow-up.

Estimating involves deciding the quantity of output to be produced. Routing is the process of determining the sequence of operations to be performed in the production process. Loading is the process of assigning specific jobs to men and machines on the basis of their relative capacities. Scheduling involves fixing priorities for different jobs and laying down the starting and finishing dates for each jobs. Despatching deals with giving necessary authority to start the work as per the schedule. Finally, progressing or follow-up deals with the ensuring of the completion of work and delivery of the output as planned. Hence, production planning and control is acting as an effective tool of production management.

(4) Production Cost and Quality Control Decision: It is the fourth function of production management in a large business unit. It deals with "the fitness for use" of products which is known as quality. While deciding the quality of the products, a producer has to reconcile two conflicting trends, namely, customer satisfaction and cost of production. Higher is the quality greater is the satisfaction of customer. But every improvement in quality means additional costs. Hence, it is the responsibility of management to build a quality level which provides reasonable customer satisfaction at economical cost. The level of quality depends upon the following factors such as market, materials, technology, labour management, etc. Besides, the level for quality has a direct correlation with the purchasing power of customers. Therefore, the production manager has to maintain the level of quality, for which quality control is refused. Quality control is an overall function designed to ensure that manufactured products meet meaningful specification. It deals with the recognition and removal of identifiable causes or defects and variations from the set standards quality. Quality control may be defined as "an effective system for integrating the quality development, quality maintenance and quality improvement effects of the various groups in an organisation so as to enable production and service at the most economical levels which allow for full customer satisfaction. Hence, it includes all the activities performed to fulfil the quality objective of a business unit. Thus, the production manager of a large firm carries out the above four production decisions as his duties and responsibilities.

8. Responsibilities of the Production Manager: The primary responsibility of the production manager is to ensure that right type of products are produced at the right time and at the minimum cost. In addition to this primary responsibility, the production manager is responsible for the quantity and cost of the plant's output. The quality of products and cost of production are affected by production processes and system. Hence, a production manager is concerned with plant location, layout, materials handling, work study, quality and cost control etc. Production Manager who is an executive head of the production department is expected to maintain close human relations with other departments of an organisation.

A model of organisational setup is given for easy understanding.

According to M.K. Starr, "Modern production management cuts across departments and divisional lines. It recognises the existence of other viewpoints such as those of marketing and financial management. In addition, it is cognizant of the fact that these other points of view cut across many elements that are fundamentally in the domain of production." Hence, there is an interrelationship between production and marketing department of a large business unit. This situation makes a production manias a liaison officer.

IV. Marketing Management

In a simple and non-technical language, marketing is explained as a business function entrusted with the creation and satisfaction of customers to achieve the aims of business itself. At the same time, marketing management deals with product planning, sales organisation, physical distribution, advertisement, marketing research, etc. towards attainment of marketing goals.

1. Definitions

1. **American Marketing Association:** It defines Marketing Management as, "the performance of business activities that direct the flow of goods and services from procedure to consumer or user."
2. **Cundiff and Still:** "Marketing is the business process by which products are matched with market and through which transports of ownership are affected."
3. **Huegy and Mitchell:** "Marketing includes all the activities involved in the creation of place, time and possession utilities."
4. **William J. Stanton:** "Marketing Management is the marketing concept in action".
5. **Cundiff and Still:** "Marketing management is a branch of the broad area of management. It is concerned with the direction of purposeful activities towards the attainment of marketing goals."

2. Objectives of Marketing Management

The above definitions convey the following objectives:

1. It ensures satisfaction of customer's need.
2. It increases the sales volume.
3. Marketing Management finally helps in increasing the level of profit of a business unit.

3. Importance of Marketing

Marketing is a potential force that commands high significance in the society as a whole. William J. Stanton says that "Marketing is a total system of interaction of business activities designed to plan, price, promote and distribute wants satisfying products and services to present and potential customers." Yet another writer has pointed out "Nothing happens in the world economy until somebody sells something." The following are the importance of marketing:

1. It converts latent demand into effective demand.
2. It acts as a source and channel of new ideas.
3. It provides employment and decreases distribution cost.
4. Marketing enables the firm to earn more profit.
5. It increases national income and stabilises economic conditions.
6. Marketing is the delivery of standard of living to society.

4. Modern Concept of Marketing

William J. Stanton's definition of Marketing brings out clearly the, modern concept of marketing. He states that the customer's want satisfaction is the economic and social justification of a company's existence. His view is supported by Philip Kotler and he expresses that the market concept is customer orientation backed by integrated marketing. The main components of modern concept of marketing are as follows:

1. Customer orientation,
2. Integrated marketing, and
3. Profitable sales through customer's satisfaction:

In the case of customer orientation concept, the business unit has to produce what the people want and not what the business unit can sell. According to Charles G. Mortiner, "Look at the company through the customer's eyes — The customer is at the top of the organisation chart."

In the case of integrated marketing concept, there is an intelligent adoption and co-ordination of the four 'P's of product, price, place and promotion to build up a strong exchange relationship with customers.

The third pillar of the marketing concept is the customer satisfaction. The business enterprise should strive to maximise customer satisfaction.

5. The Study of Marketing and Its Aims

The following aims can be achieved by studying marketing:

1. To develop an intelligent appreciation of modern marketing practices.
2. To provide guiding policies regarding marketing procedure and its implementation.
3. To study marketing problems according to the circumstances and to suggest solutions.
4. To understand the shortcomings in an existing pattern of marketing.

5. To enable successful distribution of land products, mineral wealth and factories.
6. To enable the managers to assess and decide a particular course of action.

6. Approaches to the Study of Marketing

The following are the different approaches to the study of marketing:

1. **Commodity Approach:** It undertakes the study of marketing on thebasis of a commodity or product.
2. **Institutional Approach:** It studies the various marketing institutions particularly the middleman who performs the marketing functions.
3. **Functional Approach:** It was originally developed by A.W. Shaw. Later, it was further developed by L.D.H. Weld by ramifying the field of marketing into separate functions, such as, buying, selling, transportation, storage, standardisation, grading, financing, risk taking and marketing research, etc.
4. **Management Approach:** Is based on the fact that marketing is purely a management function and it combines certain features of the other three approaches.
5. **Legal Approach:** Emphasises only one aspect, i.e., transfer of ownership to buyer.
6. **Economic Approach:** Deals with problems of supply, demand and price.
7. **System Approach:** Can be defined as "a set of objects together with the relationships among them and their attributes."
8. **Societal Approach:** Is originated recently. The marketing process is regarded as a means by which society meets its own consumption needs. Here, attention is paid to ecological factors.

7. Organisation of Marketing Function

Marketing system is concerned with interrelating and co-ordinating the activities of manufacturers and their distributors with the wants and needs of consumers. Hence, the system supplies all management level with the desired information according to R.M.S. Wilson. This situation points out that marketing must be managerially organised. The following Figure shows the numerous marketing management functions carried out by a marketing manager in a large business unit.

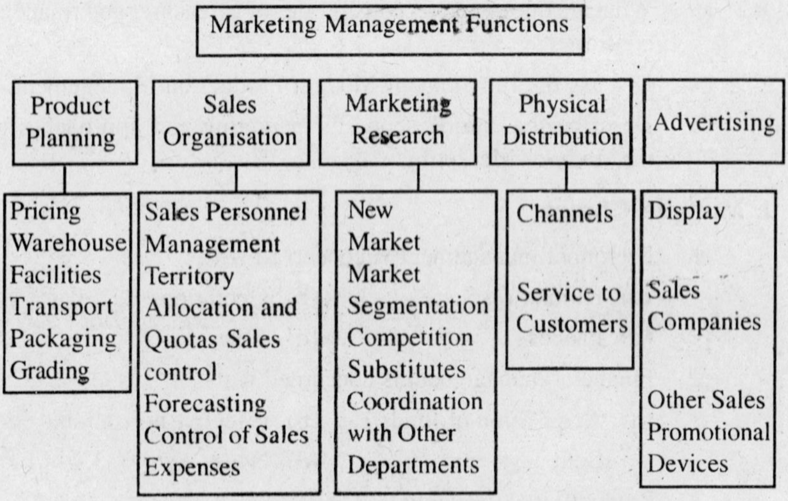

Fig. 21.6 Marketing Management Function

The above chart shows that the role of a marketing manager is very wide.

Model Questions

Section A

1. What is Personnel Management?
2. Define Financial Management
3. What is Production Planning Control?
4. Define Marketing Management.
5. What is Scheduling?
6. What is Test Marketing?
7. What is Marketing Mix?

Section B

8. Explain the scope and objectives of Personnel Management.
9. Narrate the importance and nature bf Financial Management.
10. What are procedures in establishing the production department?
11. Describe the functions performed by a Marketing Manager.

Section C

12. Explain the various functions preferred by a personnel department in a modern business unit.

13. What are duties and responsibilities of a treasurer and financial controller?
14. Discuss the functions of Modern Production Management.
15. Describe the nature, scope of marketing and approaches to the study of Marketing.

I. Multiple Choice

1. Personnel management is concerned with
   (a) Human resource (b) Operations
   (c) Process (d) None
2. Financial management is concerned with
   (a) Acquisition of funds (b) Effective utilisation
   (c) Both (d) None
3. Productivity is equal to
   (a) Output/Input (b) Input/Output
   (c) Both (d) None
4. Which marketing approach deals into problem of supply, demand and price ?
   (a) Functional approach (b) Institutional approach
   (c) Management approach (d) Economic approach
5. The arrangement of facilities in a particular work situation is called
   (a) Plant location (b) Plant layout
   (c) Production process (d) None

Answers:

1. (a) Human resource, 2. (c) Both, 3. (a) Output/Input, 4. (d) Economic approach, 5. (b) Plant layout.

II. Say, 'True or False'

6. Personal management is a managerial function.
7. Finance is regarded as the lifeblood of a business enterprise.
8. Maximisation of profit is replaced by maximisation of wealth.
9. Three is a close relationship between production and productivity.

10. Marketing is the delivery of standard of living to society.

Answers:

6. True, 7. True, 8. True, 9. True, 10. True.

III. Fill in the blanks

11. The personal management consists of two functions such as basic managerial function and ____________ function.
12. Dividend decision deals with the determination of the percentage of profit to be paid to its __________.
13. Product planning and development is a vital function in ____________.
14. The functional approach to study marketing was developed by _____ originally.
15. _________ approach undertakes the study of marketing on the basis of a commodity or product.

Answers:

11. Operative, 12. Shareholders, 13. Production, 14. A.W. Shaw, 15. commodity.

Chapter 22

Social Responsibility of Business

Chapter Outline

What is Social Responsibility? — Arguments for Social Responsibility — Arguments against Social Responsibility — Dimensions of Social Responsibilities — The Indian Scene — Social Audit —Model Questions

Traditionally, the responsibility of the business firm has been to produce and distribute goods and services in return for a profit. The profit motive has provided necessary incentive to business to make the goods and services as efficiently as possible.

For quite a long time, it was held that the sole objective of business was maximisation of profit.

The modern concept of business has changed radically. The profit maximization is no longer an universally valid business objective. A profit is still a necessary part of the total picture but is not the primary purpose. Business objective has transcended the profit motive and recognised social responsibility.

The contemporary thinking is that organisations operate only because society grants them the right to do and so the right will continue so long as the society is satisfied with its results. The business should not work on the narrow ground of what is best for the shareholders alone but from the point of view of what is best for the community at large. It must contribute to the promotion of social and community welfare and healthy growth of the society.

I. What is Social Responsibility?

The term 'social responsibility' is generally defined as "those obligations a business firm has to the society in which it operates. It is concerned with how organisations and managers deal with issues and problems confronting the society".

Keith Davis and Robert Blomstorm define social responsibility as follows:

"Social responsibility is the obligation of the decision-makers to take actions which protect and improve the welfare of the society as a whole along with their own interest".

The primary obligation of a business firm which accepts social responsibility, is to ensure that its decisions and operations meet the interest of the constituent groups in the society, i.e., employees, consumers, shareholders and the community.

II. Arguments for Social Responsibility of Business

The case for social responsibility of business has been put forward by business executives and modern writers on various grounds. The major arguments for the acceptance of social responsibility are as follows:

1. The business is no longer a private arrangement for enriching shareholders. It has become a joint enterprise in which workers, management, consumers, the locality, Government and all play a part.
2. The operations of business enterprises affect a wide spectrum. The impact of business operations is felt by many a people who are in no way connected with the business. So, it has to consider whether the actions are likely to promote social good.
3. The business makes use of resources of the society and depends on society for its functioning. Hence, it has an obligation to promote the welfare of the society.
4. As an organisation grows, there is increasing public interest in its policies and actions. If the management of large enterprises do not react to changes in social demands, the society will either force them to do so through laws or will not permit the enterprise to survive.
5. The image of the company is linked to the extent to which it fulfils the expectations of its shareholders. With a view to

enhance the image and goodwill of the business, it has to accept social responsibility.

6. By helping society, business actually serves its own long-term interest. It is to be noted that long-term interest of business can best be served when management assumes social responsibility.
7. Business has the resources. It can use the human and capital resources to solve some of society's problems.
8. By voluntarily assuming social responsibility, a company can reduce the need for introducing new corporate laws by the government regarding social involvement. The result is greater freedom and more flexibility in decision-making.

III. Arguments against Social Responsibility

The important arguments against social responsibility are given below:

1. According to Milton Friedman,"there is only one social responsibility of business, that is to use its resources and engage its activities designed to increase profits". Social matters are not the immediate concern of the business.
2. Investment in social activities will result in curtailment of investment in productive activities and fall in productivity which are the sources of real gain.
3. The business is not equipped to handle social activities. The managers do not have the required skill and expertise to deal with social problem. Concern for social activities also implies the diversion of attention from the primary objective.
4. Entrusting management with power to use the enterprise resources for social good rather than upholding the owner's interest would amount to conferring management with arbitary and politically dangerous powers.
5. The cost of social involvement of business is ultimately passed on to the consumers. In such a case, the society gets no gain but a net loss.

IV. Dimensions of Social Responsibilities

The business which assumes social responsibility must take into account the claims of various sections of the society and balance it from the point of view of what is best for the society at large.

The dimensions of social responsibility can be studied with reference to the management's responsibility towards shareholders, consumers, workers, government, community and the society.

Responsibilities towards Owners

1. Earn sufficient profit and assure a fair and reasonable rate of return on capital.
2. Commitment of funds in best possible manner,
3. Build adequate reserves to declare dividend during lean period.
4. Consolidate and improve its competitive position by innovation and diversification.
5. Fair and honest reporting of business operations.
6. Ensure public image so that shareholders can feel proud of their company.

Responsibilities towards Employees

1. Fair and reasonable rate of pay.
2. Create healthy working conditions.
3. Provide labour welfare facilities.
4. Proper training and education of workers.
5. Recognition, appreciation and encouragement of special skills a capabilities of workers.
6. Changes for accomplishment and promotion.
7. Maintain harmonious relationship between superior and subordinates.
8. Opportunity to participate in managerial decision making.

Responsibility towards Consumers

1. Supply of quality goods at reasonable price.
2. Provide sufficient information about the produce *viz.*, content maximum retail price, possible adverse effects, risks etc.
3. Avoid false and highly exaggerated advertisements.
4. Ensure perfect system of distribution by preventing hoarding, black marketing, profiteering by middlemen.
5. Provide the required after sales service
6. Do research and development to improve quality of existing products and introduce better and new products.
7. Provide opportunity for being heard and redress grievances.

Responsibility towards Government

1. Pay taxes honestly.
2. Obey the laws of the country.
3. Discourage unhealthy practices like corrupting public servants for selfish ends.
4. Follow fair trade policies and practices.

Responsibility to the Community

1. Develop constructive relationship with those in the community.
2. Participate in the community activities and promote community welfare.
3. Provide safe, livable communities with housing, transportation, school, hospital etc.
4. Rehabilitate the population displaced by the operations of the business.

Responsibility to the Society

1. Provide equal employment and educational opportunities to all regardless of sex, caste, religion, region etc.
2. Set up industrial units in backward and less developed areas.
3. Prevent enviornmental pollution and preserve ecological balance.
4. Protect natural enviornment including forest, lakes, rivers, wildlife etc.
5. Help alleviation of poverty and provide quality health service.

V. The Indian Scene

In India, many large industries have undertaken social responsibility.

The Tata Iron and Steel Company (TISCO) has been in the forefront with regard to corporate social responsibilities.

It launched a programme of community development and social welfare as early as 1949 for the Adivasi population living in and around Jamshedpur.

TISCO started a rural development programme in 1979 with the object of raising the standard of living in villages within a periphery of 10 to 15 kilometres from Jamshedpur.

The Cement Corporation of India has adopted villages close to the operating units. It has provided medical and educational facilities to the locals and contributed towards improvements to the infrastructure nearby.

The Lupin Group launched upon Rural Support Programmes in Rajasthan in 1988 to provide infrastructure so that the benefits to government programmes reach the rural poor.

The Birla Group has built the Birla Planetarium and the Birla Science and Art Museum in Calcutta and three institutes of Technology and Science for promoting technical education.

The Hindustan Ciba Geigy started in 1990 a project to eliminate leprosy from Goa by 2000.

The Lupin Laboratories launched 'Life for Life Programme' in 1993 to control tuberculosis in India.

The Finolex Industries started the Hope Foundation for the detection and treatment of cancer.

TISCO had in 1970, voluntarily incorporated in its Articles of Association, its social and moral responsibilities to consumers, employees, shareholders, society and the local people. CCI has made special mention of social responsibility being one of the objectives in its state of objectives. The public sector is yet to prove its social responsibility.

VI. Social Audit

The acceptance of social responsibility raises the question of how social performance should be evaluated?

This led to the development of the concept of social audit.

Social audit refers to the evaluation or assessment of a company's performance against planned goals in the areas of social responsibility.

Bowen defines social audit as a commitment to a systematic assessment of and reporting on some meaningful definable domain of a company's activities the have social impact'.

Beesley and Evans define social audit as "a retrospective review of the impact or contribution of a company in the recognised social dimensions."

The above definitions reveal that the term social audit means a comprehensive evaluation of the way in which a business discharges its responsibilities to the owners, customers, employees, government and the society.

Features of Social Audit

1. Social audit includes all the activities of management which produce an impact on the relationship between the business and the various groups in society.
2. It is difficult to measure the impact of social performance of an enterprise as it occurs mostly outside the organisation.
3. Social audit can be conducted either by internal auditors or external bodies or both.
4. Both quantitative and qualitative data are used in social audit.

Limitations of Social Audit

1. It is difficult to determine the areas to be included in social audit.
2. Collection of data from outside an organisation is a problem.
3. Presentation of data in a way that accurately reflects social involvement of a business is not easy.
4. There may be resistance within the company to conduct social audit because of the time, effort and difficulty involved in it.

Despite difficulties, many organisations in USA conduct social audit. The concept of social audit is yet to receive attention of business enterprise in India.

Model Questions

1. What is social responsibility of business?
2. Write short notes on 'Social Audit'.
3. State the arguments for and against social responsibility of business.
4. Analyse the responsibilities of business to shareholders and employees.
5. What are the social responsibilities of business towards the community and society?
6. Explain the concept of social responsibility of business. How do business adhere to social obligation towards various shareholders?

I. Multiple Choice

1. Social responsibility of business is
   (a) Duty (b) Obligation
   (c) Legal one (d) All
2. Preventing environment pollution is a responsibility towards
   (a) Consumers (b) Community
   (c) Society (d) Government
3. Avoiding false and exaggerated advertisement is a responsibility towards
   (a) Employees (b) Government
   (c) Owners (d) Consumers
4. The evaluation of social responsibilities of business is called
   (a) Financial audit (b) Social audit
   (c) Art audit (d) Performance audit
5. Creating healthy working conditions is one of the social responsibilities towards
   (a) Employees (b) Employers
   (c) Earnings (d) None

Answer:

1. (b) Obligation 2. (c) Society 3. (d) Consumers, 4. (b) Social audit, 5. (a) Employees.

II. Say, 'True or False'

6. Social responsibility is the obligation of the decision-makers to take actions which protect and improve the welfare of the society.
7. Business objective has transcended the profit and recognised social responsibility.
8. The cost of social involvement of business is ultimately passed on to the customers.
9. Social audit can be conducted either by internal auditors or external bodies or both.
10. Investment in social activities will not result in curtailment of investment productive activities.

Answer:

6. True, 7. True, 8. True, 9. True, 10. False

III. Fill in the blanks

11. The dimension of the social responsibility can be studied towards shareholders, employees, customers and _________.
12. __________ refers to the evaluation or assessment of a company's performance against planned goals in the areas of social responsibility.
13. Paying taxes honestly is the social responsibility towards _______.
14. Providing the required after-sales service comes under the responsibility towards _______.
15. Assuring a fair and reasonable rate of return on capital is the basic social responsibility of business towards _________.

Answer:

11. Community, 12. Social audit, 13. Government, 14. Consumer, 15. Shareholders.

Chapter 23

Modern Management Thinker

Chapter Outline

Peter F. Drucker and His Contribution — Management Practices in Various Countries — Japanese Management and US Management — Model Questions.

I. Peter F. Drucker and His Contribution

P.F. Drucker was bom in Vienna in 1909. He started his career as a newspaper correspondent and was also serving as an economist for an International Bank in London. Later, he was working as a consultant for many American corporations. Finally, he worked as a professor of management. So, he was a professor, leading management consultant and a great management thinker. He has written more than 20 Management books which are sharp, incisive and thought-provoking. His contribution to management is remarkable and discussed below.

1. Peter Drucker on Management

P.F. Drucker is against bureaucratic management. He treats tasks and innovation as management. He also treats management as a discipline. According to him, people are important. He emphasizes *performance* and *practice*. So, he feels that management is a practice and universal.

2. P.F. Drucker on Organization

The world, today looks for all major social tasks to be performed by organisation. So, he has emphasised the role of *autonomous institutions* for achieving the business goals.

3. P.F. Drucker on Federalism

He has advocated the concepts of *decentralisation.* He calls decentralisation as "Federal Principle". It created a new "Constitution" and a new "Ordering Principle". He states "In a Federal Organization, local Managements must also participate in the decisions that establish their own local business and that set the limits of their own authority".

4. P.F. Drucker on Manager

According to Drucker, a manager must be an *able administrator* and entrepreneur. He emphasised that a manager should look after the three functions without fail, such as:

(a) the specific purpose and mission of Institution.

(b) making work productive and the worker achieving.

(c) managing social impacts and social responsibilities.

Besides, Drucker has attached great importance to the formulation of objectives of management. In his opinion, objectives of performance must be in eight areas, such as:

1. Market standing
2. Innovation
3. Productivity
4. Physical and financial resources
5. Profitability
6. Manager performance and development
7. Worker performance and attitude
8. Public responsibility.

5. P.F. Drucker on MBO

The concept of Management by Objective is regarded to be one of the major contributions of Drucker to the management science. MBO is basically a process in which the *superior and the subordinate jointly* identify the objectives desired to be accomplished by the subordinate in terms of the overall results expected and use the same to measure and evaluate the subordinate's performance.

II. Management Practices in Various Countries

The recent trends in management practice in various countries are quite fascinating. In Germany, the authoritarian approach is replaced by participative approach. This principle is called co-determination principle which gives opportunities to employees to participate in the supervisory board and executive committee.

In Britain, individualism, resourcefulness and logic are highly valued. In USA, there is an upsurge of foreign managers from Japan and other countries. Italians are highly competitive like group decision-making. In Australia, managing is influenced by that country's moralistic stance.

III. Japanese Management and US Management

The basic principles of Japanese management are two, such as:

(a) Lifetime employment and

(b) Consensus Decision-making

The individual employee, his seniority and his lifelong employment are important in Japan. That is why the Japanese have succeedeed in their profession and occupied the first position in the world business today. Besides, one-third of the Japanese employees are well under the cover of job security system. The practice of decision-making is built on the concept that change and new ideas come primarily from low level. Since it is a group decision-making, the Japanese are slow in making decision but fast in implementing. When wrong decision is taken, the blame is shared by all. However, in the case of US management, decisions are taken at the top. Individual takes decision. When the decision goes wrong, it becomes an affair of fixing blame on the individual superior, In short, the Japanese, i.e., participative management has attracted the businesspeople all over the world.

Model Questions

Section A

1. "Management is a practice and universal." Discuss.
2. Is it necessary to manage a business unit by objectives?
3. What is a manager's letter?
4. What are the principles of Japanese Management?

Section B

5. Discuss Drucker's contribution towards MBO?
6. What is Drucker's contribution on a Manager's task?
7. What is Federalism? Explain its principles.

Section C

8. Discuss Peter F. Drucker's contribution to the Management philosophy.
9. Explain the several benefits of Peter F. Drucker's contributions to Management.
10. Discuss the various principles of Japanese Management and US Management?

I. Multiple Choice

1. Peter F. Druker advocated the concept of
   (a) Federal Principle (b) Centralisation
   (c) Delegation (d) None
2. The process of MBO starts with
   (a) Setting up of obligation (b) Fetron plan
   (c) Review (d) All

Answer:

1. (a) Federal Principle, 2. (a) Setting up of Obligation

II. Say, 'True or False'

3. Peter. F. Drucker feels that management is a practice.
4. MBO is a process in which the superior and the subordinate jointly identify the objectives of the business unit.
5. According to P.F. Drucker, the objectives of management must be in 10 areas.

Answer:

3. True, 4. True, 5. False

III. Fill in the blanks:

6. P.F. Drucker has emphasised the role of _________ institution for achieving the business goal.
7. According to Drucker, a manager must be an able _________.
8. P.F. Druker was a professor, management consultant and management _________.

Answer:

6. Autonomous, 7. Administrator, 8. Thinker.

Chapter 24

Modern Techniques in Functional Management

Chapter Outline

Human Resource Monagement — Operations Managemtnt — Marketing Management — Financial Management — Systems Management — Strategic Management — Model Questions

Management should take into account both the external and internal system, especially the internal system and apply the modern techniques and tools. Knowledge of internal system requires an understanding of the physical, human, financial and technological make-up of the organisation. It includes all the functional areas that operate as subsystem of the organisation system, such as Human Resource, Production, Marketing, Finance and other areas that can effectively contribute to the achievement of organisational goals.

I. Human Resource Management (HRM)

The emergence of HRM as a distinct field of management which gives the employee management function the importance deserves. HRM approach is considered a commitment, competence and co-ordination. It is more of proactive investment in employees, since in this paradigm employees are the organisation's greatest assets.

1. Meaning and Definition of HRM

The proactivity of the HRM approach as compared to traditional personnel management is the ability to sense the contextual changes and keep the internal system fit to take on the changes. Conceptual perspective for HRM came from varied disciplines like sociology, economics, psychology, political science and organisation theory.

According to Schuler and Jackson (1995), HRM has become an umbrella term covering different dimensions:

- Specific practices like recruitment, performance appraisal, rewards etc.
- Formal policies which act as guidelines for managerial decision-making and are important in practice formation and organisational justice perspectives.
- A human resource philosophy which specifies the results that guide the policy and practice.

From the above definitions, it is understood that the practice of HRM is to enable employees to create sustainable competitive advantage through building skill and internal tacit system like to change, organisational culture and performance-reward system.

2. Customer Service Approach to HR (Customer Service Model)

The challenge of HRM is to ensure that the people who deliver business excellence are prepared to deploy the competencies to build sustainable competitive advantage. To achieve the above challenge and promise, a dimension to be considered is fair play in HRM, covering distributive, procedural and interactional justice. In this context, a line of thinking advocates that HR department should treat all employees as internal customers and should do everything to satisfy them which is popularly known as customer service approach to HR. This approach can be self-destructive and lead to lower self-esteem and reputation for the profession.

3. Human Resource Accounting Approach —Measurement of HR Impact

Of late, attention both at practice and concept level has been given to measuring HR. The Human Resource Accounting approach has gained currency in placing a currency equivalent of employees in the balance sheet, even though the applicability of this information for managerial decision-making is doubtful.

It may be viewed as a part of the process of managing people in the organisation. The conservational accountants may agree to managing employees or Human Resources as assets if they are convinced that future benefits are associated with expenditures on human resources.

4. Work to Live or Live to Work — Achieving a Work-life Balance

Work-life balance is not just about women juggling a home and family. But it is about adjusting working patterns so that everyone, regardless of age, race or gender can find a rhythm that enables them more easily to combine work with their other responsibilities or aspirations. Work-life is becoming more integrated and embedded into HR. Work-life is playing a critical role in recruitment and retention strategies. While implementing work-life policies in order to achieve the goal of HRM, the following factors have been considered by companies at international level such as Flexible hour, Term-time working, Job share, Part-time work, Home-working, Tele centre working etc. Therefore, there is a relationship between HR and Work-life balance.

5. Human Resource Profession — Challenges of Opportunities

The emergence of globalisation, technical advancements, telecommunication growth, IT growth, growth of knowledge-based workforce and intense competition, etc. have changed in style of HRM in organisations. In this context, the major competitive challenges faced by execution are as follows:

- building and operating customer responsive organisation
- profitability through cost and growth
- redefining organisational capabilities for sustained and integrated individual competencies.
- focusing on transportation to create fundamental and enduring change, making technology a viable and productive part of work setting
- attracting, retaining as well as measuring intellectual competence.

These challenges and changes in organisational structure and workplace practices necessitate changes in style of HRM. Besides, the role of HR professionals in the future would be pivotal as business strategists. This will require considerable business acumen and the ability to contribute effectively to strategic decision-making.

Ulrich (1997) has developed a model of multiple roles for HR professional. This model covers four major HR roles such as:

1. Management of strategic HR: Translating business strategies into HR priorities through organisational diagnosis.

2. Management of firm infrastructure: HR professionals should design and deliver efficient HR process for selecting, training, appraising, rewarding, promoting and managing the flow of employees in the organisation.

3. Management of employee contribution: HR professionals should involve themselves in day-to-day problems, concern and needs of the employees.

4. Management of transformation and change: HR professionals should add value to a firm to manage transformation and change by altering the culture.

Therefore, the significance of HR and HR professionals have grown after the realisation that the "people" aspects really matter and it can make a difference. With shifting priorities, HR professionals are moving to leadership position and organisation depends on them to improve other performance (Kemske, 1998). So, HR professionals have to look for opportunities to acquire influence within the world of organisation and to make top management understand the paramount of HR.

6. Future Vision of HRM and HR Professionals

Corporate HR managers have to work with the senior executive team and business unit leaders to create a shared mindset. They serve as the repository and monitor the organisation's knowledge asset management system and the development of its intellectual capital. However, HR professionals should realise that future lies with strategic HRM. Besides, HR professionals can make strategic contribution while continuing to engage in administrative practices. Therefore, it is effective management of the human capabilities that will ensure the continued success of an organisation, and the knowledge and expertise of the professionals, through strategic HR policies and practices which can provide an ideal platform to do this in order to realise the goals of HRM and HR professionals.

II. Operations Management

1. Introduction

Operations Management deals with the use of various tools of production, devices, methods, process, etc... for administering the affairs of production of the firm in the most effective and efficient way. Operations management covers both the functions of materials and production. Management experts have developed many modern tools of operations management in order to achieve the goals of organisation, i.e., maximisation of profit with minimum cost. Some of the techniques of operations management implemented and used successfully by companies at National and International levels are given below.

- Total quality management (TQM)
- Six Sigma
- Quality circles (QC)
- Just-in-time (JIT)
- Kaizen model
- ISO 9000
- Value Engineering.

A brief discussion of the above techniques is given in the subsequent pages.

2. Total Quality Management

The principles of Total Quality Management (TQM) are now recognised characteristics of most successful business all over the world. Customer's changing demands, the awesome penetration of Japan and its pacific Rim neighbors, viz., south Korea, Taiwan, Singapore and Hong Kong into the US and Western markets and the need for stringent cost management in fluctuating environments, make TQM a practice of paramount importance for every enterprise, big or small.

"TQM should be a simple blend of charisma and process discipline to be effective,"said Yotaro Kokayashi, President of Fuji Xerox, Japan. His model requires a continuous harnessing of three forces: vision, sensitivity, and technology. This is named as Fuji Xerox model. This model was the fountain-head for Xerox-wide leadership through total quality movement.

It is possible to achieve total quality in an organisation systematically and scientifically by understanding the six concepts such as, customers (external and internal), never-ending improvement, control of business processes, 'upstream' preventive management, ongoing preventive action, leadership and teamwork management addressing six management elements and launching of six stage plan.

(i) Statement of intent
(ii) Awareness — directors
(iii) Diagnosis
(iv) Initial strategy
(v) Management consensus
(vi) Launch.

3. Six Sigma

Six Sigma is converting defect-prone business into powehouse of perfection. It is invented at Motorola, perfected at General Electric (GE), and now practiced by a handful of corporations in India. The main objective of six sigma is to design, operate and control every one of the processes of the company in such a way that none of them yields more than 3.4 defects out of every one million units of output. There are four phases or steps in six sigma such as measurement, analysis, improvement and control.

Six Sigma offers two approaches — one is to change the design of the product in which this component is used and the second approach is to make improvements in the process itself so that the chances of defects are lowered. By using the two approaches, six sigma is implemented in Indian companies.

For example, Wipro, Goderej, Maruthi, Hero Motors, Bajaj Auto, Modi Xerox etc.

4. Quality Circle

Quality Circle is a small group of employees in the same work area or doing similar type of work who voluntarily meet regularly for about an hour every week to identify, analyse and resolve work-related problems, leading to improvement in their total performance and enrichment of their work life.

Quality Circle is a philosophy but not a technique. Quality Circle has a bottom-up approach but not a top-down approach.

In India, Quality Circle was first initiated in an engineering company — Bharat Heavy Electrical Limited (BHEL). At present, companies like NTC, JK Jute Mills, Crompton Greaves, Air India, Indian Airlines, Apollo Hospital etc. have implemented Quality Circle successfully.

5. Just-in-Time (JIT)

JIT is an approach to minimise in manufacturing in the form of time, materials, energy and errors. It seeks to claim all sources of waste in production activities by producing the right component part at the right time and at the right place. It is called a philosophy because it goes beyond inventory control. JIT production simply requires little use of computer and in some industries can provide tight control on inventory than are attainable through the American western computer-based approach.

JIT system results in much less inventory, lower cost and better quality than in the JIC approach (Just-in-case). It leads to significant quality and productivity and provides visibility for results so that worker's responsibility and commitments are improved. So, it is alternative to MRP system (Material Reguitrituion Planning).

It aims at reducing the setup times, lot sizes and inventory cost. It helps to achieve 'zero defects'. The primary objectives is to eliminate waste and all non-value adding activities. The following are the elements of JIT system, i.e., market schedule, setup time, multiple function. workers, layout of plant, emphasis on quality, vendor's relation, and stabilising the master schedule.

Sell One, Make One (SOMO) is the philosophy of NISSAN and TOYOTA, Japan, which focusses on lean production. Lean production is the second greatest industrial revolution. JIT was originated from Japan. Finally, JIT is a broad philosophy of pursing to inventories, zero transactions and zero disturbances, i.e., execution of the schedule day in day out.

6. Kaizen Model

Kaizen is Japanese word meaning "improvement over improvement". In other words, Kaizen means improvement and ongoing improvement involving all people. Management of job function in Japan is perceived as having two main components such as maintenance and improvement.

Maintenance means activity directed towards maintaining current technologies, managerial and operating standards. Improvement means activities directed towards improving current standards. It is seen that improvement can further be broken down into Kaizen and innovation. Innovation involves drastic improvement in the status quo as a result of large investment in new technology and equipment.

Management makes concerted efforts to involve employees in Kaizen through suggestions. Suggestions made by workers is regarded as the improvement criterion. Workers provide 1.5 million suggestions a year in Toyota Motor Company in Japan. 95% of these suggestions are put to practical use. In Kaizen model, the following 3 Mu's should be avoided.

Muda (Waste)
Muri (strain) } 3 Japanese words
Mura (Discrepancy)

In India, Eicher Tractor Limited is practicing this Kaizen Model successfully.

7. ISO 9000

International organisation for standardisation (ISO 9000) is a set of fine worldwide standards that establish requirements for the management of quality. Unlike product standards, these standards are for quality management system. It is used by 12 Nation European Economic Community (EC) to provide a universal framework for quality assurance — preliminarily through a system of internal and external audit.

European community has adopted ISO 9000 in the year 1989 to integrate the various technical norms and specification of its member status. By 1991, ISO compliance became part of hundreds of product safety laws all over Europe. A British government survey revealed that 89% of ISO 9000 registered companies reported greater operational efficiency.

8. Value Engineering

Value engineering is a management technique that targets the best functional balance between the cost and the performance of a product or project without compromising the reliability of the same. According Prof. Woodward, "Value Engineering is a system of techniques of accelerating identification and modification of unnecessary costs in a production or service. In other words, Value Engineering is the process of determining the value of a product and/or service during various stages of the product life cycle. Therefore, it is a powerful tool of cost reduction which the present-day industrial business has necessarily to exercise in order to survive as a viable enterprise.

The term value engineering and value analysis is interchangeably used in practice. L.D. Miles defined value analysis "as an organised creative approach which has for its purpose the efficient identification of unnecessary cost, i.e., cost which provides neither quality, nor use, nor life, nor appearance, nor customer feature" (1961).

It is usually difficult to specify value mainly because value changes from person to person. The value of a cane of water to a thirsty man varies with the man's distance from the source of supply. In general, there are 7 classes of value, such as economic, moral, aesthetic, social, political, religious and judicial. Of these, only the economic classification which can be considered to be objective are four subdivisions, such as use value, esteem value, cost value and exchange value. Value can be measured in a mathematical way, i.e.,

Value = function/cost

Value Engineering aims at reducing cost without reducing quality. Besides, it helps to increase value without increasing cost and at the same time it increases value for the given cost. Most of the Indian companies like Tata, Birla, Mafatlal, etc., have implemented this concept successfully in their organisations.

III. Marketing Management

1. Introduction

Marketing on the 21st Century (Change or Die Policy)

The new economy is based on the Digital revolution and the management of information. The digital revolution has placed a whole new set of capabilities in the hands of consumers and business. Today's companies need fresh thinking about how to operate and compete in the new economy. Today's economy is made up of old and new economy and is essentially a hybrid.

- Companies are increasingly subcontracting activities to outsourcing firms.
- Companies are increasingly benchmarking their performance against best-of-class companies anywhere in the world.
- Companies are deepening their partnering arrangements with key suppliers and distributors.
- Companies are making substantial investment in information system.
- Companies are emphasising interdepartmental teamwork.

- Companies are recognising that much of their market value comes from intangible assets particularly their brands, customer base, employees, distributors and supplier relations.

Besides, today's companies are using internet, customer database and data mining and customer relationship management to improve their marketing performance. There are four major drivers of the new economy, such as digitalisation and connectivity, disintermediation and reintermediation, customisation and customerisation and industry coverage.

The changes in technology and economy are eliciting a new set of beliefs and practice on the part of business firms during 21st century. The major business belief in the old economy and how these beliefs shifted are shown below:

- From organising by products units to organising by customer segments.
- From focusing on profitable transaction to focusing on customer lifetime value.
- From focusing on shareholders to focusing on stakeholders.
- From marketing does the marketing to everyone does the marketing.
- From building brands through advertising to building brands through performance.
- From focusing on customer acquisition to focusing on customer retention.
- From customer satisfaction measurement to in-depth customer satisfaction measurement.
- From over-promise, under-deliver to under-promise, over-deliver etc.

The fact is that today's economy and most companies as a hybrid of the old economy and the new economy. Moreover, today's market-place is made up of traditional consumers (who do not by online), cyber consumers (who mostly buy online) and hybrid consumers (who do both).

The Current Marketing Practices

The following techniques are used by companies all over the world to achieve the goals of marketing in particular and the goals of business unit in general:

1. E-Business
2. Customer Relationship Management
3. Brand Management
4. Sevices Marketing.

Let us discuss the above aspects one by one briefly.

2. E-Business

E-Business describes the use of electronic means and platforms to conduct a company's business. The advent of the internet has greatly increased the ability of companies to conduct their business faster, more accurately, over a wider range of time and space to reduce cost, and with the ability to customise and personalise customer offerings.

E-Commerce is more specific than E-Business. It means that in addition to provide information to visitors about the company, its history, policies, products and job opportunities, the company or site offers to facilitate the selling of products and services online. Examples of E-commerce site are Amazon.com, e-steel, and e-plasticnet.

E-Marketing describes company's efforts to inform, communicate, promote and sell its products and services over the internet. E-Business, E-Commerce and E-Marketing take place over four major internet domains such as:

(a) B2C (Business to customer)

(b) B2B (Business to business)

(c) C2C (Consumers to consumers) and

(d) C2B (Consumers to business)

Due to globalisation and liberalisation, companies at national and international level need to move into E-Marketing and E-Purchasing by setting up their own websites. In this context, there are two companies needed in the modern business world, such as, Pure-Click Company and Brick & Brick Company. Pure Click Company is a company, which launched a website with any previous existence as a firm. Brick & Brick Company is a company, which added an online site for E-Commerce with any previous existence as a firm.

3. Customer Relationship Management (CRM)

Customer relationship management enables companies to provide excellent real-time customer service by developing relationship with each valued customer through the effective use of individual account information. Companies can improve the value of their customer base by considering the following strategies:

- ☞ Reducing the rate of customer defection
- ☞ Increasing the longevity of the customer relationship
- ☞ Focusing disproportionate effort on high value customers
- ☞ Enhancing the growth potential of each customer and so on.

Besides, for effective customer relationship management, Peppers and Martha Rogers has advocated innovative concept, i.e., "One to One Marketing" instead of Mass marketing.

CRM is a business strategy that goes beyond increasing transaction volume. It aims at producing high customer profitability, revenue and satisfaction. Besides, it aims at producing high customer equity which covers value equity, brand equity and relationship equity. The main principle of CRM is not only to treat customer individually but also to acquire and retain customer loyalty through personal relationship.

CRM approach is customer centric. The goals of CRM can be achieved with help of the following four tasks:

- ☞ Customer identification
- ☞ Customer interaction
- ☞ Customer differentiation
- ☞ Customization

There are four levels of investment in customer relationship building such as:

- ☞ Basic marketing - Salesmanship
- ☞ Reactive marketing - Attending customer call
- ☞ Proactive marketing - Contacting customers with suggestions by salesmen
- ☞ Partnership marketing - Working continuously with its large customers to help them and to improve their performance.

Merits of CRM

1. Improving organisation ability to acquire and retain customer
2. Maximising the lifetime value of each customer.
3. Improving service without increasing cost of services.

Limitations of CRM

1. A company must be organised by customer segments rather than by its products.
2. CRM requires a large centralised database with complete customer data.
3. It requires the most advanced and sophisticated analytical technique since it is a turnkey project.

4. Brand Management

A brand is a name or symbol, which gives a distinct identity to a product or service. A brand brings to the consumer a bundle of functional benefits, emotional attachment and psychological satisfaction. Brand is attached to products or services. Company may adopt separate brands for each product or product line or may adopt umbrella branding. In India, companies prefer to use their corporate identity as their brand. Today, modern companies adopt different products and position each brand in the minds of customer in order to derive maximum benefits out of brands. The following are the various elements of brand management:

- Brand positioning
- Brand identification
- Brand equity
- Brand personality
- Brand extension
- Brand image

Product position refers to brand's objective (functional) attributives in relation to other brands. It is a characteristics of the physical product and its functional features. Positiond, on the other hand, refers to a brand's subjective (perceived) attributes. Merle C. Crawford (1987) in new products management says that "once a target market has been selected, the new product marketers must differentiate their item from products already offered to that target group. This differentiating is called positioning the product and now it is in widespread use."

Tauber (1988) has defined brand equity as "the incremental value of a business above the value of its physical assets due to the market position achieved by its brand" and the extension potential of the brand. There are a number of methods of measuring brand equity such as historical cost method, replacement cost method, market value method, interbrand method, brand contribution method and so on.

When a company introduces new product or service with the existing brand name, it is called a brand extension. A brand has a distinct identity. It has the following identity, i.e., brand as a product, brand as organisation, brand as person and brand as symbol. Brand personality gives a distinct identity to a product. Brand personality is what a brand would look like if it were a person. Brand personality explains why people like some brand more than others even when there is no physical difference in between them. Further, brand image is the outcome of brand personality. Brand image is the sum total of customer's perception about brand.

Brand building is not very easy. To build a brand, a company has to first undertake marketing research, and later invest resources in advertising and image building. Companies should scientifically invest in brands since brands are assets.

5. Services Marketing

In the modern business world, service has become the "mantra". A service is any act or performance that one party can offer to another that is essentially intangible and does not result in the ownership of anything. Services are intangible, inseparable, variable and perishable. Services have four major features that greatly affect the design of marketing programmer, i.e., intangibility, inseparability, variability and perishability.

Marketing Strategies for Service Firms

Service industries like hotel, airlines, transport etc. which lagged behind manufacturing companies in their use of marketing have now changed their style of manufacturing. Today, service industries have adopted service marketing strategy not only for external marketing but now also for internal marketing to motivate employees and interactive marketing to emphasise the importance of both "High-tech" and "High-touch". This is popularly known as services marketing.

The traditional four Ps of Marketing Mix, i.e., Price, Product, Place and Promotion, work well to achieve the goals of Marketing Management. But additional elements require attention in service business. Booms and Bitner suggested three additional Ps for service marketing, such as people, physical evidence and process, which help companies to demonstrate their service quality to a greater extent.

The service organisation faces three tasks in marketing such as:

(i) Differentiating its offer, delivery or image.

(ii) Managing service quality in order to meet or exceed customer's expectations.

(iii) Managing worker productivity by getting its employees to work more skillfully.

These three tasks could be achieved by considering the following marketing practices, i.e., a strategic concept, such as top management commitment to quality, high standard, self-service technologies, system for monitoring service preformed and customer complaints and emphasis on employee satisfaction.

Even product-based companies must provide post-purchase service. To provide the best support, a manufacturer must identify the services that customers value most and their relative importance. So, the service mix by product-based companies includes both pre-sale services (facilitating and value-augmenting service) and postal services (customer service department, repair and maintenance services).

IV. Financial Management

1. Introduction

With rapid technological advancement and the growth of specialised services sector, capital market, stock market, etc., financial management and its modern techniques have gained much significance in order to achieve the goal of financial management, i.e., maximisation of wealth. The following are the various techniques of financial management and management accounting used by companies throughout the world.

Financial Management Techniques

1. Activity based costing
2. Corporate governance
3. Market Value Added Method
4. Stock market, Factoring method, Credit rating, Depository services and Derivatives etc.,

Management Accounting Techniques

1. Inflation Accounting
2. Social Accounting
3. Segment Accounting
4. Human Resources Accounting
5. Value Added Accounting
6. Environmental Accounting

Let us discuss the various techniques of Financial Management briefly.

2. Activity Based Costing (ABC)

In the modern business world, overhead cost element does contribute a very significant proportion in the total cost of production. This situation made the financial experts to develop a new method, i.e., Activity Based Costing. "It is a system that attempts to link the cost of each business activity in an organisation to the products which benefits from the activity". In other words, under activity based costing, the activities are identified, the expenses related to each activity are clubbed together to get activity-wise expenses, select a cost driver for each activity and finally workout the cost of the product.

The objective of activity based costing is to allocate overheads accurately, systematically and rationally and to identify and differentiate in transactions the value added and non-value added activities and to eliminate the latter. The following are the merits of ABC.

- Helps managers to determine selling prices more precisely.
- Leads to best allocation of scarce resources.
- Results in high inventory values.
- Helps to identify non-value added activities for easy elimination.
- Improves the performance process.

3. Corporate Governance

It is the relationship among various primary participants in determining the direction and performance of companies. The primary participants are:

(i) Shareholders

(ii) Management

(iii) The Board of Directors

The other participants include the employees, customers, suppliers, creditors and community. The emergence of corporate governance and its application to companies to safeguard the welfare of interested parties arose after the second half of 1996. To put it in a simple word, corporate governance deals with the set of system and process, which ensure that a company is managed to the best of interests of all the stakeholders.

Code of Corporate Governanace is required to guide board of directors and to ensure ethical practices. Many bodies have given the codes of Corporate Governance. They are:

- The full board should meet at intervals of two months, and atleast six times a year.
- No individual should be a director on the boards of more than 10 companies at any given time.
- Directors who have not been present for atleast 50% of board meetings should not be reappointed.
- Audit committee comprising atleast three non-executive directors should be setup and given access to all financial information.
- Data should be provided in the annual report on monthly average share prices, value added, and financial performance of divisions etc.

4. Market Value Added Method (MVA)

Market value added method is a technique used to measure the performance of company. MVA is essentially the difference between a company's current value, as determined by its stock price and its economic book value.

NVA = Capitalisation – Book Value of Net Worth.

Where, Market Capitalisation = No. of Equity shares outstanding x Market price per share

Book value of Net worth = Equity + Reserves + Surplus

A company's economic book value can be thought of as the amount of capital that shareholders and all other capital providers have committed to the firm throughout its existence, including earnings that have been retained within the business. Technically, it is called equity value added (EVA). Moreover, EVA is equal to the present value of all future EVAs. Like Net Present Value (NPV), EVA measures the degree to which a firm is successful in earning the rates of return that exceeds its cost of capital. EVA is a reasonable valuation tool for the shares of companies where prospects can be forecasted with reasonable accuracy. It is useful in spotting changes in a company's performance that are hidden in EPS numbers.

5. Stock Market, Factoring, Depository Services and Derivatives

Stock market are said to reflect the health of the country's economy. Functional factors like corporate performance, industrial growth, broad money supply, etc. always exert a certain amount of influence on the stock markets. Securities market can be classified into primary market (new issue only) and secondary market (buying and selling of second hand securities.)

Factoring

Factoring may be defined as a contract by which the factor is to provide atleast two of the services, i.e., finance, the maintenance of accounts, the collection of receivables and protection against credit risks. Factoring is a financial service.

Credit Rating

Credit Rating facilitates the company in raising funds in the Capital market and help the investor to select their risk-return trade-off. In India, the rating coverage is of a fairly recent origin, beginning 1988 when the first rating agency Credit Rating and Information Services of India, Limited (CRSIL) was established. At present, there are three rating agencies such as Investment Information and Credit Rating of India Ltd. (ICRA), Credit Analysis and Research (CARE), Duff & Phelps Credit Rating India (DCR).

The services offered are broadly classified as rating, information and consultancy.

Rating services cover ratings of debt instruments — long, medium and short term, securitised assets and builders.

Information services offer corporate research report and the CRISIL 500 index.

The infrastructure and consultancy division provides assistance on specific sectors such as power, telecom and infrastructure financing.

Depository System

Depository system is concerned with conversion of securities from physical to electronic form, settlement of traders in electronic segment, electronic transfer of ownership of shares and electronic custody of securities. The ownership and transfer of securities take place by means of electronic book entries. It facilitates restoration of faith in the capital markets and the participants with system to minimise settlement risk and the fraud.

Derivatives

Derivatives are most modern financial instrument in hedging risk. Derivatives are those assets the value of which is determined from the value of same underlying assets. The underlying assets may be equity, commodity or currency. Derivatives are a key part of the financial system. It deals with spot market, forward contract and future contract. These are several risks inherent in financial transaction. Derivatives allows companies to manage these risks more efficiently by unbundling the risks and allowing either hedging or taking only one (or more if desised) risks at a time.

V. Systems Management

1. Introduction

Organisations today face the challenges of globalisation and shortened product life cycle. This situation needs faster access to accurate information both inside the organisation and from the entire supply chain outside. Due to developments in computing and communication technology, it is possible to network organisational units through reliable communication channels, providing tighter integration among them. The following advanced techniques of system management have been used by companies all over the world.

1. Enterprise Resource Planning (ERP) and
2. Distributed Database.

2. Enterprise Resource Planning (ERP)

ERP deals with the package software solution that addresses the enterprises needs of an organisation by tightly integrating the various functions of an organisation by using a process view of the organisation. In other words, information system to support the functional units of an enterprise are referred as ERP systems. Many of the process implemented in an ERP software are core processors such as order processing, purchase order, preparation of invoice, order fulfillment, shipping, preparation of balance sheet, profit & loss accounts, etc.

ERP system in required either to solve the existing problems or to explore new opportunities. Besides it solves Y2K problem and provides an opportunity to improve productivity, operations, customer service, customer satisfaction, etc.

3. Distributed Databases

It is a collection of data which belong logically to the same system but are spread over the sites of computer network. It covers two main aspects such as distribution and logical correlation. It has become an important area of information processing.

In other words, a distributed database is a collection of data which are distributed over different computers of a computer network. Each site of the network has autonomous processing capability and can perform local applications. It can be implemented in large geographical computer networks and in small local networks. Today, many organisations are decentralised and a distributed database approach fits more naturally the structure of the organisation.

VI. Strategic Management

Strategy is the action plan for achieving organisational objectives. It is the bridge between the present and desired future. It necessarily involves allocation of resources/funds and aims at capitalising strength of the organisation keeping in perspective the environmental constraints and competitive conditions. According to Arther Sharplin, strategy means "a plan or course of action which is of vital, pervasive or continuing importance to the organisation as a whole".

There are number of approaches in which different companies formulate their strategy and take strategic decisions. Strategic decisions are those decisions that decide about company's product or customer or resource allocation for the company's future plans. There are several approaches to strategic management as given below:

- Fit approach
- Intuitive anticipatory approach
- Leverage
- Entrepreneurial opportunities approach
- Formal structured approach
- Adaptive approach
- Unplanned organic adaption
- Ad hoc management

Strategic Management Process (SMP) consists of the following steps:

1. Identification of the mission of the organisation;
2. Identification of the objectives of the organisation;
3. Scanning environmental and internal factors;
4. Analysis of environmental factors and preparation of Environmental Threat and Opportunity Profile (ETOP);
5. Comparative study of different Strategic Business Units (SBUs) and preparation of display metrics for different SBUs;
6. Thorough study of internal capabilities and preparation of Strengths, Weaknesses, Opportunities and Threats (SWOT), and Strategic Advantage Profile (SAP);
7. Formulation of strategic alternatives;
8. Deciding about the best strategy and alternative strategies;
9. Formation of strategic alternative;
10. Deciding about the best strategy and alternative strategies;
11. Preparation of budgets and resource allocation plans;
12. Communication of strategy across the organisation and formulation of minor objectives:
13. Taking feedback about the implemented strategy;
14. Periodic review of the strategy, environmental scenarios and alternative strategies;
15. Suitable modification and change in the strategy in case of major changes in the environment.

Strategic Management Process (SMP) is a continuous process. It is a cycle. The process starts with identification of objectives and strategies and ends with evaluation of implemented strategy and simultaneously a new strategy is formulated. SMP consists of environmental, organisation and financial analysis. In all the steps that are involved in SMP, environmental analysis is the most important one. It helps in formulating right strategies. There are various methods of environmental analysis, such as Delphi technique, SWOT analysis, etc. The various tools available for doing organisational analysis are Pareto analysis, Frontier curve analysis, Resource Department Matrix, Strategic advantage profile etc. Besides, there are a number of techniques that are used in financial analysis, such as Ratio analysis, Display matrices, etc. Hence, strategic management enables the modern management to carry out the activities of the organisation successfully in the global competitive conditions.

Model Questions

Section A

1. What is customer service approach?
2. What is TQM?
3. What is SWOT analysis?
4. What is ERP?

Section B

5. Explain the merits of CRM.
6. Explain the various innovative techniques of operations management.
7. Explain the nature and scope of services marketing.

Section C

8. Explain the various new techniques of financial management.
9. Explain the steps involved in implementing TQM.
10. Explain the various steps involved in strategic management process.

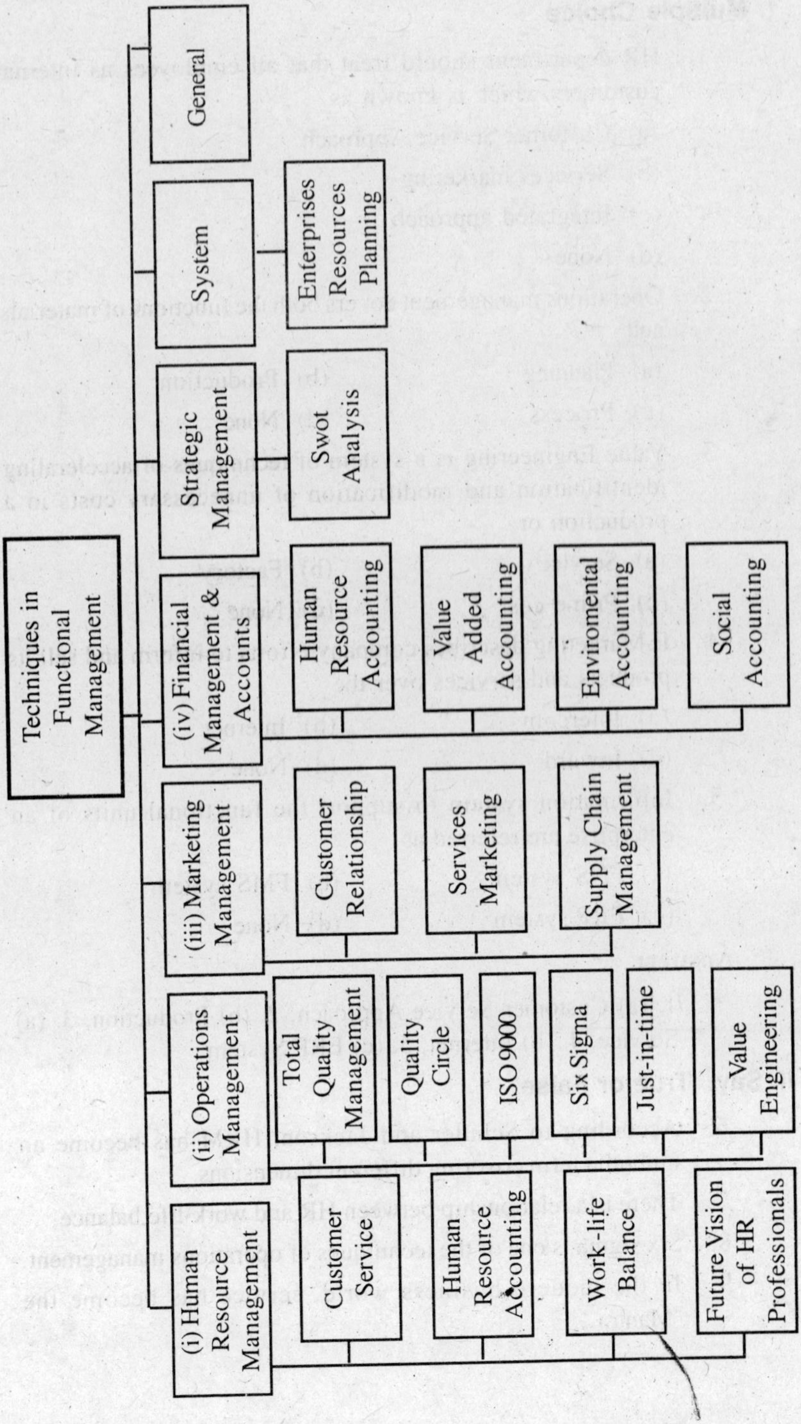
Techniques in Functional Management
General
System
Enterprises Resources Planning
Strategic Management
Swot Analysis
(iv) Financial Management & Accounts
Human Resource Accounting
Value Added Accounting
Enviromental Accounting
Social Accounting
(iii) Marketing Management
Customer Relationship
Services Marketing
Supply Chain Management
(ii) Operations Management
Total Quality Management
Quality Circle
ISO 9000
Six Sigma
Just-in-time
Value Engineering
(i) Human Resource Management
Customer Service
Human Resource Accounting
Work-life Balance
Future Vision of HR Professionals

I. Multiple Choice

1. HR department should treat that all employees as internal customers which is known as
   (a) Customer Service Approach
   (b) Services marketing
   (c) Integrated approach
   (d) None
2. Operations management covers both the functions of materials and
   (a) Planning (b) Production
   (c) Process (d) None
3. Value Engineering is a system of techniques of accelerating identification and modification of unnecessary costs in a production or
   (a) Service (b) Factory
   (c) Prime cost (d) None
4. E-Marketing describes company efforts to inform and sell its products and services over the
   (a) Intercom (b) Internet
   (c) Inward (d) None
5. Information system to support the functional units of an enterprise are referred as
   (a) FNS system (b) FMS system
   (c) ERP system (d) None

Answer:

1. (a) Customer Service Approach, 2. (b) Production, 3. (a) Service, 4. (b) Internet, 5. (c) ERP System.

II. Say, 'True or False'

6. According to Schuler and Jackson, HRM has become an umbrella term covering different dimensions.
7. There is a relationship between HR and work-life balance.
8. Six sigma is one of the techniques of operations management.
9. In the modern business world, service has become the "Mantra".

10. Value added accounting is one of the techniques of management accounting.

Answer:

6. True, 7. True, 8. True, 9. True, 10. True,

III. Fill in the blanks

11. Oregon State University at Corvallis (USA) pioneered __________.

12. CRM approach is a ____________ centric.

13. Stock markets are said to reflect the health of the country's __________.

14. According to Arhter Shaplin __________means, "a plan or course of action which is of vital, pervasive or continuing importance to the organisation as a whole".

15. ________ rating facilitates the company in raising funds in the capital market.

Answer:

11. Benchmarking, 12. Customer, 13. Economy, 14. Strategy, 15. Credit

Chapter 25

Case Studies

CASE 1: Analyse the following case and write your report.

Bharat Engineering Works Limited

Bharat Engineering Works Limited is a major manufacturer of industrial machineries besides other engineering products. It has enjoyed considerable market preferences for its machineries because of limited competition in the field. Usually, there has been more orders that what the company could supply. However, the scenario changed quickly because of of the entry of two new competitors in the field with foreign technological collaboration. For the first time, the company faced problem in marketing its products with usual profit margin. Sensing into the likely problem, the chief executive appointed Mr. Aravind Kumar as a general manager to direct the operations of industrial machinery division. Mr. Kumar had similar assignment abroad before coming back to India.

Mr. Kumar had a discussion with the chief executive about the nature of the problems being faced by the company so that he could fix up his priority. The chief executive advised him to consult various heads of department to have first-hand information. However, he emphasised that the company lacked an integrated planning system while members of the board of directors insisted on introducing this meeting both formally and informally.

After joining as General Manager, Mr. Kumar got 6 briefings from the heads to identify major problems and issues concerning them. His main concern was lack of engineers but they were spread under three separate engineering groups. Sales people had no central organisation which had responsibility to provide sales support. Therefore, some jobs were being done from outside at higher costs or with lower quality. Besides he needed a generous budget for demonstration system which could be sent on a trial basis to customers to win business.

The Production Manager complained about the old machines and equipments used in manufacturing. Therefore, cost of production was high but without corresponding quality. While competitors had equipments and machinery, Bharat Engineering neither replaced its age-old plant nor got it reconditioned. Therefore, to reduce the cost, it was essential to automate production lined by installing new equipment.

Director of research and development did not have any specific problem and, therefore, did not indicate for any change. However, a principal scientist in R & D indicated on one day that the director R & D, though very nice in his approach, did not emphasise on short-term research projects which could easily increase production efficiency to the extent of atleast 20 per cent within a very short period. Moreover, such projects did not involve any major capital outlay.

Mr. Kumar got himself convinced about the management process going on in the division and the type of problems being faced.

Questions:

(a) Discuss the nature and characteristics of management process followed in the company.

(b) What are the real problems of industrial machinery division of the company?

(c) What steps should be taken by Mr. Kumar to overcome these problems?

CASE 2: Analyse the following case and write your report.

"A point is a point", said Sharma, the foreman. "But I simply cannot hire or hold our skilled men with these rates". He referred to rates based on a straight wage line fitted to the point values and wages rate on a dozen key jobs. The new rates had been in effect only for a short time. They were established following job evaluation on a unilateral basis by the employer. The wage line raised many jobs rates in the shop but it reduced those at the top. The job evaluation programme was undertaken to provide a basis for a sound wage structure throughout the shop. It was conducted by an interdepartmental committee. Comparisons of earlier rates with wage survey data had indicated that the old structure was not in line with those of the industry. The new wage line was keyed to rates shown in the survey.

Questions

(a) What is the source of this difficulty?

(b) Prepare a memorandum to the Personnel Manager suggesting alternative methods of correcting the deficiency.

CASE 3: Analyse the following case and write your report.

Telerama Company was the pioneer in the field of TV in the country. Being the first to enter the market, the Company enjoyed all the advantages over competitors. The company's products were of excellent quality and were attractive in appearance.

However, the field of TV was relatively easy to enter into and over a period of 5 years several new brands had made a successful entry into the market. Even though they all together shared the rest 50% of the market, day by day, the share of Telerama was eroding.

Mr. Banerjee, the Sales Manager of Telerama was worried about the competition. Technically, he felt almost all the TVs in the market were equally of good quality. Telerama's TV, however, being the leader was greatly disadvantaged in one respect. The company spent its energies in developing new attractive models and promoting them. The competitors were also equally attractive. Mr. Banerjee felt that the consumers were becoming increasingly aware of the fact that quality wise almost all TVs were the same brand loyalty of the customers which had always been the backbone of marketing success of Telerama's TV. Mr. Banerjee felt that negative post-purchase feelings was crux of the problem. And with increasing competition, this would be a permanent problem which the company would have to tackle. This was especially so in the TV market which was a consumer durable. Moreover, continued appearance of improved models created serious negative post-purchase feelings in the minds of the buyers.

This, in Mr. Banerjee's opinion, was one of the most serious trends and he was really at a loss how to tackle this problem.

Questions

(a) How should Telerama tackle the problem of initiative competition?

(b) Do you feel such problem exists in case of every consumer product? If yes, what action should be taken by the manufacturers?

CASE 4: Analyse the following case and write your report.

Mr. Osama started a company in 1995 and decided to enter fruit canning industry since there was a lot of demand for good quality canned foods in Eastern India. He has selected the brand name "COOL CAFE" and started producing mango pulp and mango juice, Kesar mango, pickles, syrups, jams and canned vegetables of many varieties. It was decided to distribute the products through largest retailers and hotels, restaurants, ice-cream manufacturers etc.

Questions

(a) Analyse the case and suggest a suitable promotion mix.

CASE 5: Analyse the following case and write your report.

An employer made alteration in the wage structure as a result of which certain allowances previously paid to an employee were stopped. His hotel wages, however, were not less than before.

(a) Does stopping of these allowances amount to 'deduction' from wages?

(b) Will an application under Sec. 15(2) lie for this? Give reasons.

CASE 6: Analyse the following case and write your report.

Super Engineering is doing everything with the experts of quality management's advice. However, TQM as a way of organisational life is not as firmly rooted. It is experiencing some difficulties in holding the gains, particularly in the case of business pressure points, organisation restructuring, cost reduction and streamlining changes of personnel in key management areas.

Question

Give suitable solutions to the experts of TQM for correction.

CASE 7: Analyse the following case and write your report.

The Tamilnadu Tourism Department wishes to promote Tanjore as a pilgrimage destination for Indians and foreign tourists. The department has appointed you as a consultant to give a detailed plan to attract more people.

Question

(a) What steps would you suggest?

CASE 8: Read the following case and answer thequestions given at the end.

Raghav Foods Ltd.

Raghav Foods Ltd. is a multi-crore company engaged in manufacturing of different food products. It headquartered at Namakkal. Recently, the R & D wing of the company has come out with a new egg drink. The main strength of this drink is, it is highly nutritious and it is fat free. This can be consumed irrespective of age groups.

While the R & D wing of the company is extremely happy about its new invention, the management and marketing department of the company wants to ensure that the product is accepted by consumers. Hence, it was decided to launch test marketing so as to launch the product nationally or drop the idea altogether. The company approached you to evaluate the results of test marketing.

Questions

(a) What are the data you would collect in the test market?

(b) How would you collect and analyse the test market data?

CASE 9: Analyse the following case and write your report.

Latex Industries, a partnership concern, was in business of surgical and medical equipments, manufacturing between 25 to 30 items. It entered into the business of manufacturing surgical and post-modem hand gloves in December 1968. It invested ₹ 5 crores in plant and equipment to manufacture this item and started manufacturing 2000 pairs per day. There were about 30 other manufactures in this field. Latex faced competition mainly from Dial Rubber Works, Mumbai, Phoenix of Bhavanagar and Swastik Rubber of Pune.

When Latex first started manufacturing gloves, it tried to sell the product at the rate of ₹ 1.25 per pair. In terms of quality, its product was superior to two of its competitors but occupied a second place. Being a surgical item, the product had to satisfy the minimum specifications laid down by Government which required testing of the product in Government laboratories before permission to market them was granted.

In promoting the sale of gloves, Latex put up sign boards in important surgical and medical equipments markets. To push the sales, it also advertised its products in medical journals and put up stalls in medical and surgical conferences.

The above marketing mix does not, however, help Latex in selling its daily production. On receiving elements of marketing mix, it was found that other competitors were allowing credit for 30 days. As an improvement, Latex decided to grant 3 month's credit. But unfortunately these did not help Latex in its marketing. The firm was really at a loss to understand as to what mix and strategy it could adopt to achieve success in its sales efforts.

Questions

(a) What are the basic problems faced by the company in marketing its products?

(b) What marketing mix and strategy would you recommend to the company?

(Madurai - Kamaraj University, BBA, Nov - 2003)

CASE 10: Analyse the following case and write your report.

C.R. Smith is a window and conservatory company employing over 100 people in Scotland and now expanding in other areas of the UK. Although they have used telesales in the past, the company now operate two field sales operations, one a team of canvassers, the other and sales people to obtain orders and contracts. The canvassers distribute the company newsletter, a quarterly publication called CR Homes and follow up with a personal call to ask house owners their views on the publications and, of course, whether any of the products are interest now or in the future. The aim is to obtain appointments with genuine leads for the sales force. While this may be considered heart sell and intrusive, research has shown that most consumer prefers this to the unsoliciated telephone call and in majority of cases find the publication of interest. While the canvassers are set specific appointment targets, the work is flexible and made to suit time, matured people. The company are looking for individuals with a pleasant manner's experience and a certain maturity who can empathise with the customers on whom they call. The canvassing team is combination of males and females of different backgrounds who can range age from 25 to retirement age. The canvassers some of whom have previously been in telesales, say they prefer this approach. So far, separating sales prospecting from sales generation has proved innovative and successful.

Questions

(a) Critically appraise CR. Smith's approach.

(b) Compare the above approach with other ways of expanding their business and generating sales.

(Madurai - Kamaraj University, BBA, Nov - 2004)

CASE 11: Analyse the following case and write your report.

Ramoji Rao is incharge of a binary in Vijayawada, which employs fifteen people, five of whom work in the factory. Three of these people employees run machines, one supervises and the fifth moves the blank paper and finished print by handcar. This fifth position, which demands no skill other than driving a handcar, need to be filled, and three applicants have responded.

The first is Mr. Matti Anjaiah, who is thirty-five unmarried, and a Navy Veteran. Anjaiah has poor work record. During his five years in Vijayawada he has worked only as a seasonal labourer on occasional odd jobs. He drove a forklift in the Navy, while working at Visakapattnam. He has strong build, which could help, although the work is generally light.

Mr. Nehal Singh, age twenty-two, came to Vijayawada two years back from Punjab. He has done from labour for many years and assembly line work for one year. His command of English is poor (but can speak the regional language, Telugu, fluently). He resides with his mother and seems certain to remain in the area for some time. After having run the equipment, he should have no trouble steering a handcar.

Mr. Vandaveeti Raja is a local boy who finished high school two years ago. Subsequently, he got a diploma from a local institute and is currently employed as an assistant in Savani Transport Company, Vijayawada. His character references are excellent. Mr. Raja is small, but he seems quick and was track star in high school.

Questions

(a) How much consideration should be given to Mr. Anjaiah's poor work record? Should Mr. Ramoji's check to verify it?

(b) How important is a command of English to the job? How quickly could Mr. Nehal singh learn enough English to be effective?

(c) Should Mr. Nehal Singh be passed over because of his status as a recent migrant?

(d) Should Mr. Raja get the job? Should his excellent character references be given more weightage than his experience?

(e) Who should be hired? Why?

(Madurai - Kamaraj University, BBA, Oct - 2009)

CASE 12: Analyse the following case and write your report.

Ram Singh is a long term employee of the Pilot Corporation. He is the financial manager of the firm's manufacturing unit. He is loyal and works hard to follow the policies and procedures. He always follows the orders of managers above him. He is considered dependable and liked by the top management.

His subordinates in the financial section have the opposite view of him. They think, he is not concerned with the needs of the department. He never works hard to get bigger budget sanctioned for the department and the employees of his department feel that they are underpaid and overworked compared to other departments. He never encourages ideas from subordinates and turns them down. His subordinates feel that he is a puppet of the top management.

The performance of the department has suffered and top management seems to be unaware.

Questions

(a) How do you explain Ram Singh's leadership style?

(b) What advice would you give to Ram Singh to improve his approach?

(c) What is the nature of training Ram Singh should have?

(Madurai - Kamaraj University, BBA, Nov - 2010)

CASE 13: Analyse the following case and write your report.

The subject brand of beer has been the largest selling brand in its headquarter's market generations. The company has gradually expanded distribution into contiguous markets and now distributors in over a dozen States. Company policy was to avoid entering a new market until it is ready to go all out on advertising and distribution. During this first year in a new market, advertising expense, as a percentage of sales, runs three or four times the normal expenditure is an established market. It may take two or three years to reach the break-even point. When first entering a new market, brand awareness is low. It is necessary to match or outspend the largest selling brand in order to capture a share of the consumer's attention and gradually woo him or her to try the brand. Management believed that anyone who is not prepared to enter competitive combat, quantitatively, is wasting money trying to open new markets in this industry.

The advertising objective was to attain deep and incessant exposure, the goal was to establish an 80 per cent level of brand identity among moderate to heavy beer drinkers in the market area within six months and to maintain that level thereafter. Through a series of simple unaided and aided recall tests, consumers were asked to identify various brands of beer sold and advertised in the market introductions had shown that the brand had always succeeded in getting a firm foothold in a market in which 80 per cent brand awareness level had been established. Once the brand name was established through "investment", advertising expenditures as a percentage of the sales dollar returned to a normal level.

Questions:

(a) Where are the principles of the DAGMAR approach applied?

(b) What objectives would you establish for the upcoming period?

(Madurai - Kamaraj University, BBA, April - 2010)

University Question Paper

SOURASHTRA COLLEGE (AUTONOMOUS), MADURAI - 4
(An Institution Affiliated to Madurai Kamaraj University)
(Accredited with B++ by NAAC)
Summative Examinations – November 2011
BBA

Title: Principle of Management **Sub. Code: 11 UBN C11**

Time: 3 Hours **Max. Marks: 75**

Section A

(15 Marks)

I. Fill up the blanks (5 x 1 = 5 marks)

1. "Management is what is manager does" said by ____________.
2. Planning is ______________.
3. The term organisation is used in many ways except the following one __________.
4. Expectancy theory of motivation is given by ______________.
5. Hawthorne study was introduced by ____________.

II. Answer the following (5 x 2 = 10 marks)

6. What is administration?
7. What do you mean by the term MBO?
8. Define Organising?
9. Define Motivation.
10. Explain Work Study.

Section B

Answer all questions **(5 x 6 = 30 marks)**

11. (a) What are the managerial skills required by a manager to perform management function?

[OR]

(b) What are the different levels of management?

12. (a) Define Business forecasting. What are the various steps involved in the process of forecasting?

[OR]

(b) What do you mean by decision-making? Explain various steps involved in it.

13. (a) Differentiate Line Organisation and Functional Organization.

[OR]

(b) What are the advantages and disadvantages of Functional Departmentation?

14. (a) Define Decentralisation. What are the advantages of Decentralisation?

[OR]

(b) What are the modern control techniques commonly used at present?

15. (a) What are the conclusions of Hawthorne studies?

[OR]

(b) Explain Rensins Likert's Leadership styles in management.

Section C

Answer any three questions **(3 x 10 = 30 marks)**

16. Discuss the classification of various managerial functions.
17. Explain in detail the steps involved in the planning process. How can planning be made more effective?
18. Define organisational climate. Explain the factors influencing organisational climate.
19. Explain Maslow's Need hierarchy theory of motivation.
20. Explain Henry Fayol's fourteen general principles of management.